Get the eBook FREE!

(PDF, ePub, Kindle, and liveBook all included)

We believe that once you buy a book from us, you should be able to read it in any format we have available. To get electronic versions of this book at no additional cost to you, purchase and then register this book at the Manning website.

Go to https://www.manning.com/freebook and follow the instructions to complete your pBook registration.

That's it!
Thanks from Manning!

Kafka in Action

Kafka in Action

DYLAN SCOTT
VIKTOR GAMOV
AND DAVE KLEIN
FOREWORD BY JUN RAO

MANNING
SHELTER ISLAND

For online information and ordering of this and other Manning books, please visit
www.manning.com. The publisher offers discounts on this book when ordered in quantity.
For more information, please contact

Special Sales Department
Manning Publications Co.
20 Baldwin Road
PO Box 761
Shelter Island, NY 11964
Email: orders@manning.com

 Recognizing the importance of preserving what has been written, it is Manning's policy to have
the books we publish printed on acid-free paper, and we exert our best efforts to that end.
Recognizing also our responsibility to conserve the resources of our planet, Manning books
are printed on paper that is at least 15 percent recycled and processed without the use of
elemental chlorine.

The author and publisher have made every effort to ensure that the information in this book
was correct at press time. The author and publisher do not assume and hereby disclaim any
liability to any party for any loss, damage, or disruption caused by errors or omissions, whether
such errors or omissions result from negligence, accident, or any other cause, or from any usage
of the information herein.

Manning Publications Co.
20 Baldwin Road
PO Box 761
Shelter Island, NY 11964

Development editor:	Toni Arritola
Technical development editors:	Raphael Villela, Nickie Buckner
Review editor:	Aleksandar Dragosavljević
Production editor:	Andy Marinkovich
Copy editor:	Frances Buran
Proofreader:	Katie Tennant
Technical proofreaders:	Felipe Esteban Vildoso Castillo, Mayur Patil, Sumant Tambe, Valentin Crettaz, and William Rudenmalm
Typesetter and cover designer:	Marija Tudor

ISBN 9781617295232
Printed in the United States of America

Dylan: I dedicate this work to Harper, who makes me so proud every day, and to Noelle, who brings even more joy to our family every day. I would also like to dedicate this book to my parents, sister, and wife, who are always my biggest supporters.

Viktor: I dedicate this work to my wife, Maria, for her support during the process of writing this book. It's a time-consuming task, time that I needed to carve out here and there. Without your encouragement, nothing would have ever happened. I love you. Also, I would like to dedicate this book to (and thank) my children, Andrew and Michael, for being so naïve and straightforward. When people asked where daddy is working, they would say, "Daddy is working in Kafka."

Dave: I dedicate this work to my wife, Debbie, and our children, Zachary, Abigail, Benjamin, Sarah, Solomon, Hannah, Joanna, Rebekah, Susanna, Noah, Samuel, Gideon, Joshua, and Daniel. Ultimately, everything I do, I do for the honor of my Creator and Savior, Jesus Christ.

brief contents

vii

contents

foreword

Beginning with its first release in 2011, Apache Kafka® has helped create a new category of data-in-motion systems, and it's now the foundation of countless modern event-driven applications. This book, *Kafka in Action*, written by Dylan Scott, Viktor Gamov, and Dave Klein, equips you with the skills to design and implement event-based applications built on Apache Kafka. The authors have had many years of real-world experience using Kafka, and this book's on-the-ground feel really sets it apart.

Let's take a moment to ask the question, "Why do we need Kafka in the first place?" Historically, most applications were built on data-at-rest systems. When some interesting events happened in the world, they were stored in these systems immediately, but the utilization of those events happened later, either when the user explicitly asked for the information, or from some batch-processing jobs that would eventually kick in.

With data-in-motion systems, applications are built by predefining what they want to do when new events occur. When new events happen, they are reflected in the application automatically in near-real time. Such event-driven applications are appealing because they allow enterprises to derive new insights from their data much quicker. Switching to event-driven applications requires a change of mindset, however, which may not always be easy. This book offers a comprehensive resource for understanding event-driven thinking, along with realistic hands-on examples for you to try out.

Kafka in Action explains how Kafka works, with a focus on how a developer can build end-to-end event-driven applications with Kafka. You'll learn the components needed to build a basic Kafka application and also how to create more advanced applications using libraries such as Kafka Streams and ksqlDB. And once your application is built, this book also covers how to run it in production, including key topics such as monitoring and security.

I hope that you enjoy this book as much as I have. Happy event streaming!

—JUN RAO, CONFLUENT COFOUNDER

preface

One of the questions we often get when talking about working on a technical book is, why the written format? For Dylan, at least, reading has always been part of his preferred learning style. Another factor is the nostalgia in remembering the first practical programming book he ever really read, *Elements of Programming with Perl* by Andrew L. Johnson (Manning, 2000). The content was something that registered with him, and it was a joy to work through each page with the other authors. We hope to capture some of that practical content regarding working with and reading about Apache Kafka.

The excitement of learning something new touched each of us when we started to work with Kafka for the first time. In our opinion, Kafka was unlike any other message broker or enterprise service bus (ESB) that we had used before. The speed to get started developing producers and consumers, the ability to reprocess data, and the pace of independent consumers moving quickly without removing the data from other consumer applications were options that solved pain points we had seen in past development and impressed us most as we started looking at Kafka.

We see Kafka as changing the standard for data platforms; it can help move batch and ETL workflows near real-time data feeds. Because this foundation is likely a shift from past data architectures that many enterprise users are familiar with, we wanted to take a user with no prior knowledge of Kafka and develop their ability to work with Kafka producers and consumers, and perform basic Kafka developer and administrative tasks. By the end of this book, we hope you will feel comfortable digging into more advanced Kafka topics such as cluster monitoring, metrics, and multi-site data replication with your new core Kafka knowledge.

Always remember, this book captures a moment in time of how Kafka looks today. It will likely change and, hopefully, get even better by the time you read this work. We hope this book sets you up for an enjoyable path of learning about the foundations of Apache Kafka.

acknowledgments

DYLAN: I would like to acknowledge first, my family: thank you. The support and love shown every day is something that I can never be thankful enough for—I love you all. Dan and Debbie, I appreciate that you have always been my biggest supporters and number one fans. Sarah, Harper, and Noelle, I can't do justice in these few words to the amount of love and pride I have for you all and the support you have given me. To the DG family, thanks for always being there for me. Thank you, as well, JC.

Also, a special thanks to Viktor Gamov and Dave Klein for being coauthors of this work! I also had a team of work colleagues and technical friends that I need to mention that helped motivate me to move this project forward: Team Serenity (Becky Campbell, Adam Doman, Jason Fehr, and Dan Russell), Robert Abeyta, and Jeremy Castle. And thank you, Jabulani Simplisio Chibaya, for not only reviewing, but for your kind words.

VIKTOR: I would like to acknowledge my wife and thank her for all her support. Thanks also go to the Developer Relations and Community Team at Confluent: Ale Murray, Yeva Byzek, Robin Moffatt, and Tim Berglund. You are all doing incredible work for the greater Apache Kafka community!

DAVE: I would like to acknowledge and thank Dylan and Viktor for allowing me to tag along on this exciting journey.

The group would like to acknowledge our editor at Manning, Toni Arritola, whose experience and coaching helped make this book a reality. Thanks also go to Kristen Watterson, who was the first editor before Toni took over, and to our technical editors, Raphael Villela, Nickie Buckner, Felipe Esteban Vildoso Castillo, Mayur Patil, Valentin Crettaz, and William Rudenmalm. We also express our gratitude to Chuck Larson for the immense help with the graphics, and to Sumant Tambe for the technical proofread of the code.

The Manning team helped in so many ways, from production to promotion—a helpful team. With all the edits, revisions, and deadlines involved, typos and issues can still make their way into the content and source code (at least we haven't ever seen a book without errata!), but this team certainly helped to minimize those errors.

Thanks go also to Nathan Marz, Michael Noll, Janakiram MSV, Bill Bejeck, Gunnar Morling, Robin Moffatt, Henry Cai, Martin Fowler, Alexander Dean, Valentin Crettaz and Anyi Li. This group was so helpful in allowing us to talk about their work, and providing such great suggestions and feedback.

Jun Rao, we are honored that you were willing to take the time to write the foreword to this book. Thank you so much!

We owe a big thank you to the entire Apache Kafka community (including, of course, Jay Kreps, Neha Narkhede, and Jun Rao) and the team at Confluent that pushes Kafka forward and allowed permission for the material that helped inform this book. At the very least, we can only hope that this work encourages developers to take a look at Kafka.

Finally, to all the reviewers: Bryce Darling, Christopher Bailey, Cicero Zandona, Conor Redmond, Dan Russell, David Krief, Felipe Esteban Vildoso Castillo, Finn Newick, Florin-Gabriel Barbuceanu, Gregor Rayman, Jason Fehr, Javier Collado Cabeza, Jon Moore, Jorge Esteban Quilcate Otoya, Joshua Horwitz, Madhanmohan Savadamuthu, Michele Mauro, Peter Perlepes, Roman Levchenko, Sanket Naik, Shobha Iyer, Sumant Tambe, Viton Vitanis, and William Rudenmalm—your suggestions helped make this a better book.

It is likely we are leaving some names out and, if so, we can only ask you to forgive us for our error. We do appreciate you.

about this book

We wrote *Kafka in Action* to be a guide to getting started practically with Apache Kafka. This material walks readers through small examples that explain some knobs and configurations that you can use to alter Kafka's behavior to fulfill your specific use cases. The core of Kafka is focused on that foundation and is how it is built upon to create other products like Kafka Streams and ksqlDB. Our hope is to show you how to use Kafka to fulfill various business requirements, to be comfortable with it by the end of this book, and to know where to begin tackling your own requirements.

Who should read this book?

Kafka in Action is for any developer wanting to learn about stream processing. While no prior knowledge of Kafka is required, basic command line/terminal knowledge is helpful. Kafka has some powerful command line tools that we will use, and the user should be able to at least navigate at the command line prompt.

It might be helpful to also have some Java language skills or the ability to recognize programming concepts in any language for the reader to get the most out of this book. This will help in understanding the code examples presented, which are mainly in a Java 11 (as well as Java 8) style of coding. Also, although not required, a general knowledge of a distributed application architecture would be helpful. The more a user knows about replications and failure, the easier the on-ramp for learning about how Kafka uses replicas, for example.

How this book is organized: A roadmap

This book has three parts spread over twelve chapters. Part 1 introduces a mental model of Kafka and a discussion of why you would use Kafka in the real world:

- Chapter 1 provides an introduction to Kafka, rejects some myths, and provides some real-world use cases.
- Chapter 2 examines the high-level architecture of Kafka, as well as important terminology.

Part 2 moves to the core pieces of Kafka. This includes the clients as well as the cluster itself:

- Chapter 3 looks at when Kafka might be a good fit for your project and how to approach designing a new project. We also discuss the need for schemas as something that should be looked at when starting a Kafka project instead of later.
- Chapter 4 looks at the details of creating a producer client and the options you can use to impact the way your data enters the Kafka cluster.
- Chapter 5 flips the focus from chapter 4 and looks at how to get data from Kafka with a consumer client. We introduce the idea of offsets and reprocessing data because we can utilize the storage aspect of retained messages.
- Chapter 6 looks at the brokers' role for your cluster and how they interact with your clients. Various components are explored, such as a controller and a replica.
- Chapter 7 explores the concepts of topics and the partitions. This includes how topics can be compacted and how partitions are stored.
- Chapter 8 discusses tools and architectures that are options for handling data that you need to retain or reprocess. The need to retain data for months or years might cause you to evaluate storage options outside your cluster.
- Chapter 9 finishes part 2 by reviewing the necessary logs, metrics, and administrative duties to help keep your cluster healthy.

Part 3 moves us past looking at the core pieces of Kafka and on to options for improving a running cluster:

- Chapter 10 introduces options for strengthening a Kafka cluster by using SSL, ACLs, and features like quotas.
- Chapter 11 digs into the Schema Registry and how it is used to help data evolve, preserving compatibility with previous and future versions of datasets. Although this is seen as a feature most used with enterprise-level applications, it can be helpful with any data that evolves over time.
- Chapter 12, the final chapter, looks at introducing Kafka Streams and ksqlDB. These products are at higher levels of abstraction, built on the core you studied in part 2. Kafka Streams and ksqlDB are large enough topics that our introduction only provides enough detail to help you get started on learning more about these Kafka options on your own.

About the code

This book contains many examples of source code both in numbered listings and in line with normal text. In both cases, the source code is formatted in a fixed-width font like this to separate it from ordinary text. In many cases, the original source code has been reformatted; we've added line breaks and reworked indentation to accommodate the available page width in the book. In some cases, even this was not enough, and listings include line-continuation markers (➡). Code annotations accompany many of the listings, highlighting important concepts.

Finally, it's important to note that many of the code examples aren't meant to stand on their own; they're excerpts containing only the most relevant parts of what is currently under discussion. You'll find all the examples from the book and the accompanying source code in their complete form in GitHub at https://github.com/Kafka -In-Action-Book/Kafka-In-Action-Source-Code and the publisher's website at www .manning.com/books/kafka-in-action. You can also get executable snippets of code from the liveBook (online) version of this book at https://livebook.manning.com/ book/kafka-in-action.

liveBook discussion forum

Purchase of *Kafka in Action* includes free access to liveBook, Manning's online reading platform. Using liveBook's exclusive discussion features, you can attach comments to the book globally or to specific sections or paragraphs. To access the forum, go to https://livebook.manning.com/#!/book/kafka-in-action/discussion. You can also learn more about Manning's forums and the rules of conduct at https://livebook .manning.com/#!/discussion.

Manning's commitment to our readers is to provide a venue where a meaningful dialogue between individual readers and between readers and the author can take place. It is not a commitment to any specific amount of participation on the part of the authors, whose contribution to the forum remains voluntary (and unpaid). We suggest you try asking them some challenging questions lest their interest stray! The forum and the archives of previous discussions will be accessible from the publisher's website as long as the book is in print.

Other online resources

The following online resources will evolve as Kafka changes over time. These sites can also be used for past version documentation in most cases:

- Apache Kafka documentation—http://kafka.apache.org/documentation.html
- Confluent documentation—https://docs.confluent.io/current
- Confluent Developer portal—https://developer.confluent.io

about the authors

DYLAN SCOTT is a software developer with over ten years of experience in Java and Perl. After starting to use Kafka like a messaging system for a large data migration, Dylan started to dig further into the world of Kafka and stream processing. He has used various techniques and queues including Mule, RabbitMQ, MQSeries, and Kafka.

Dylan has various certificates that show experience in the industry: PMP, ITIL, CSM, Sun Java SE 1.6, Oracle Web EE 6, Neo4j, and Jenkins Engineer.

VIKTOR GAMOV is a Developer Advocate at Confluent, the company that makes an event-streaming platform based on Apache Kafka. Throughout his career, Viktor developed comprehensive expertise in building enterprise application architectures using open source technologies. He enjoys helping architects and developers design and develop low-latency, scalable, and highly available distributed systems.

Viktor is a professional conference speaker on distributed systems, streaming data, JVM, and DevOps topics, and is a regular at events including JavaOne, Devoxx, OSCON, QCon, and others. He is the coauthor of *Enterprise Web Development* (O'Reilly Media, Inc.).

Follow Viktor on Twitter @gamussa, where he posts there about gym life, food, open source, and, of course, Kafka!

DAVE KLEIN spent 28 years as a developer, architect, project manager (recovered), author, trainer, conference organizer, and homeschooling dad, until he recently landed his dream job as a Developer Advocate at Confluent. Dave is marveling in, and eager to help others explore, the amazing world of event streaming with Apache Kafka.

about the cover illustration

The figure on the cover of *Kafka in Action* is captioned "Femme du Madagascar" or "Madagascar Woman." The illustration is taken from a nineteenth-century edition of Sylvain Maréchal's four-volume compendium of regional dress customs, published in France. Each illustration is finely drawn and colored by hand. The rich variety of Maréchal's collection reminds us vividly of how culturally apart the world's towns and regions were just 200 years ago. Isolated from each other, people spoke different dialects and languages. Whether on city streets, in small towns, or in the countryside, it was easy to identify where they lived and what their trade or station in life was just by their dress.

Dress codes have changed since then, and the diversity by region and class, so rich at the time, has faded away. It is now hard to tell apart the inhabitants of different continents, let alone different towns or regions. Perhaps we have traded cultural diversity for a more varied personal life—certainly for a more varied and fast-paced technological life.

At a time when it is hard to tell one computer book from another, Manning celebrates the inventiveness and initiative of the computer business with book covers based on the rich diversity of regional life of two centuries ago, brought back to life by Maréchal's pictures.

Part 1

Getting started

In part 1 of this book, we'll look at introducing you to Apache Kafka and start to look at real use cases where Kafka might be a good fit to try out:

- In chapter 1, we give a detailed description of why you would want to use Kafka, and we dispel some myths you might have heard about Kafka in relation to Hadoop.
- In chapter 2, we focus on learning about the high-level architecture of Kafka as well as the various other parts that make up the Kafka ecosystem: Kafka Streams, Connect, and ksqlDB.

When you're finished with this part, you'll be ready to get started reading and writing messages to and from Kafka. Hopefully, you'll have picked up some key terminology as well.

Introduction to Kafka

1

This chapter covers
- Why you might want to use Kafka
- Common myths of big data and message systems
- Real-world use cases to help power messaging, streaming, and IoT data processing

As many developers are facing a world full of data produced from every angle, they are often presented with the fact that legacy systems might not be the best option moving forward. One of the foundational pieces of new data infrastructures that has taken over the IT landscape is Apache Kafka®.[1] Kafka is changing the standards for data platforms. It is leading the way to move from extract, transform, load (ETL) and batch workflows (in which work was often held and processed in bulk at one predefined time) to near-real-time data feeds [1]. Batch processing, which was once the standard workhorse of enterprise data processing, might not be something to turn back to after seeing the powerful feature set that Kafka provides. In

---

[1] Apache, Apache Kafka, and Kafka are trademarks of the Apache Software Foundation.

3

fact, you might not be able to handle the growing snowball of data rolling toward enterprises of all sizes unless something new is approached.

With so much data, systems can get easily overloaded. Legacy systems might be faced with nightly processing windows that run into the next day. To keep up with this ever constant stream of data or evolving data, processing this information as it happens is a way to stay up to date and current on the system's state.

Kafka touches many of the newest and the most practical trends in today's IT fields and makes its easier for daily work. For example, Kafka has already made its way into microservice designs and the Internet of Things (IoT). As a de facto technology for more and more companies, Kafka is not only for super geeks or alpha-chasers. Let's start by looking at Kafka's features, introducing Kafka itself, and understanding more about the face of modern-day streaming platforms.

1.1 *What is Kafka?*

The Apache Kafka site (http://kafka.apache.org/intro) defines Kafka as a distributed streaming platform. It has three main capabilities:

- Reading and writing records like a message queue
- Storing records with fault tolerance
- Processing streams as they occur [2]

Readers who are not as familiar with queues or message brokers in their daily work might need help when discussing the general purpose and flow of such a system. As a generalization, a core piece of Kafka can be thought of as providing the IT equivalent of a receiver that sits in a home entertainment system. Figure 1.1 shows the data flow between receivers and end users.

As figure 1.1 shows, digital satellite, cable, and Blu-ray™ players can connect to a central receiver. You can think of those individual pieces as regularly sending data in a format that they know about. That flow of data can be thought of as nearly constant while a movie or CD is playing. The receiver deals with this constant stream of data and converts it into a usable format for the external devices attached to the other end (the receiver sends the video to your television and the audio to a decoder as well as to the speakers). So what does this have to do with Kafka exactly? Let's look at the same relationship from Kafka's perspective in figure 1.2.

Kafka includes clients to interface with other systems. One such client type is called a *producer*, which sends multiple data streams to the Kafka brokers. The brokers serve a similar function as the receiver in figure 1.1. Kafka also includes *consumers*, clients that can read data from the brokers and process it. Data does not have to be limited to only a single destination. The producers and consumers are completely decoupled, allowing each client to work independently. We'll dig into the details of how this is done in later chapters.

As do other messaging platforms, Kafka acts (in reductionist terms) like a middleman for data coming into the system (from producers) and out of the system (for consumers or end users). The loose coupling can be achieved by allowing this separation

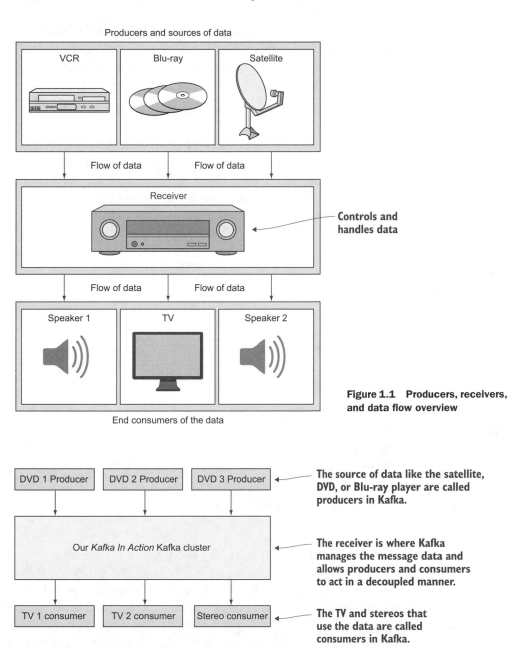

Figure 1.1 Producers, receivers, and data flow overview

Figure 1.2 Kafka's flow from producers to consumers

between the producer and the end user of the message. The producer can send what-ever message it wants and still have no clue about if anyone is subscribed. Further, Kafka has various ways that it can deliver messages to fit your business case. Kafka's message delivery can take at least the following three delivery methods [3]:

- *At-least-once semantics*—A message is sent as needed until it is acknowledged.
- *At-most-once semantics*—A message is only sent once and not resent on failure.
- *Exactly-once semantics*—A message is only seen once by the consumer of the message.

Let's dig into what those messaging options mean. Let's look at *at-least-once* semantics (figure 1.3). In this case, Kafka can be configured to allow a producer of messages to send the same message more than once and have it written to the brokers. If a message does not receive a guarantee that it was written to the broker, the producer can resend the message [3]. For those cases where you can't miss a message, say that someone has paid an invoice, this guarantee might take some filtering on the consumer end, but it is one of the safest delivery methods.

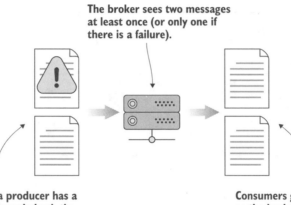

The broker sees two messages at least once (or only one if there is a failure).

If a message from a producer has a failure or is not acknowledged, the producer resends the message.

Consumers get as many messages as the broker receives. Consumers might see duplicate messages.

Figure 1.3 At-least-once message flow

At-most-once semantics (figure 1.4) is when a producer of messages might send a message once and never retry. In the event of a failure, the producer moves on and doesn't attempt to send it again [3]. Why would someone be okay with losing a message? If a popular website is tracking page views for visitors, it might be okay with missing a few page view events out of the millions it processes each day. Keeping the system performing and not waiting on acknowledgments might outweigh any cost of lost data.

Kafka added the *exactly-once* semantics, also known as EOS, to its feature set in version 0.11.0. EOS generated a lot of mixed discussion with its release [3]. On the one hand, exactly-once semantics (figure 1.5) are ideal for a lot of use cases. This seemed like a logical guarantee for removing duplicate messages, making them a thing of the past. But most developers appreciate sending one message and receiving that same message on the consuming side as well.

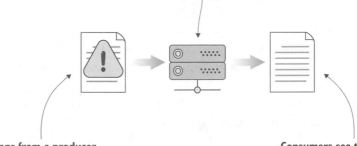

The broker sees one message at most (or zero if there is a failure).

If a message from a producer has a failure or is not acknowledged, the producer does not resend the message.

Consumers see the messages that the broker receives. If there is a failure, the consumer never sees that message.

Figure 1.4   At-most-once message flow

Another discussion that followed the release of EOS was a debate on if exactly once was even possible. Although this goes into deeper computer science theory, it is helpful to be aware of how Kafka defines their EOS feature [4]. If a producer sends a message more than once, it will still be delivered only once to the end consumer. EOS has touchpoints at all Kafka layers—producers, topics, brokers, and consumers—and will be briefly tackled later in this book as we move along in our discussion for now.

Besides various delivery options, another common message broker benefit is that if the consuming application is down due to errors or maintenance, the producer does

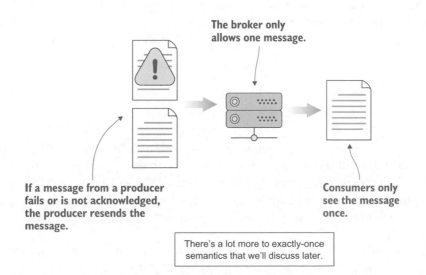

The broker only allows one message.

If a message from a producer fails or is not acknowledged, the producer resends the message.

Consumers only see the message once.

There's a lot more to exactly-once semantics that we'll discuss later.

Figure 1.5   Exactly-once message flow

not need to wait on the consumer to handle the message. When consumers start to come back online and process data, they should be able to pick up where they left off and not drop any messages.

1.2   Kafka usage

With many traditional companies facing the challenges of becoming more and more technical and software driven, one question is foremost: how will they be prepared for the future? One possible answer is Kafka. Kafka is noted for being a high-performance, message-delivery workhorse that features replication and fault tolerance as a default.

With Kafka, enormous data processing needs are handled with Kafka in production [5]. All this with a tool that was not at its 1.0 version release until 2017! However, besides these headline-grabbing facts, why would users want to start looking at Kafka? Let's look at that answer next.

1.2.1   Kafka for the developer

Why would a software developer be interested in Kafka? Kafka usage is exploding, and the developer demand isn't being met [6]. A shift in our traditional data processing way of thinking is needed. Various shared experiences or past pain points can help developers see why Kafka could be an appealing step forward in their data architectures.

One of the various on-ramps for newer developers to Kafka is to apply things they know to help them with the unknown. For example, Java® developers can use Spring® concepts, and Dependency Injection (DI) Spring for Kafka (https://projects.spring.io/spring-kafka) has already been through a couple of major release versions. Supporting projects, as well as Kafka itself, have a growing tool ecosystem all their own.

As a common developer, most programmers have likely confronted the challenges of coupling. For example, you want to make a change to one application, but you might have many other applications directly tied to it. Or, you start to unit test and see a large number of mocks you have to create. Kafka, when applied thoughtfully, can help in these situations.

Take, for example, an HR system that employees would use to submit paid vacation leaves. If you are used to a create, read, update, and delete (CRUD) system, the submission of time off would likely be processed by not only payroll but also project burndown charts for forecasting work. Do you tie the two applications together? What if the payroll system goes down? Should that impact the availability of the forecasting tooling?

With Kafka, we will see the benefits of being able to decouple some of the applications that we have tied together in older designs. (We will look more in-depth at maturing our data model in chapter 11.) Kafka, however, can be put into the middle of the workflow [7]. Your interface to data becomes Kafka instead of numerous APIs and databases.

Some say that there are better and simpler solutions. What about using ETL to at least load the data into databases for each application? That would only be one interface per application and easy, right? But what if the initial source of data is corrupted or outdated? How often do you look for updates and allow for lag or consistency? And do those copies ever get out of date or diverge so far from the source that it would be hard to run that flow again and get the same results? What is the source of truth? Kafka can help avoid these issues.

Another interesting topic that might add credibility to the use of Kafka is how much it "dogfoods" itself. For example, when we dig into consumers in chapter 5, we will see how Kafka uses topics internally to manage consumers' offsets. After the release of v0.11, exactly-once semantics for Kafka also uses internal topics. The ability to have many data consumers using the same message allows many possible outcomes.

Another developer question might be, why not learn Kafka Streams, ksqlDB, Apache Spark™ Streaming, or other platforms and skip learning about core Kafka? The number of applications that use Kafka internally is indeed impressive. Although abstraction layers are often nice to have (and sometimes close to being required with so many moving parts), we believe that Kafka itself is worth learning.

There is a difference in knowing that Kafka is a channel option for Apache Flume™ and understanding what all of the config options mean. Although Kafka Streams can simplify examples you might see in this book, it is interesting to note how successful Kafka was before Kafka Streams was even introduced. Kafka's base is fundamental and will, hopefully, help you see why it is used in some applications and what happens internally. If you want to become an expert in streaming, it is important to know the underlying distributed parts of your applications and all the knobs you can turn to fine-tune your applications. From a purely technical viewpoint, there are exciting computer science topics applied in practical ways. Perhaps the most talked about is the notion of distributed commit logs, which we will discuss in depth in chapter 2, and a personal favorite, hierarchical timing wheels [8]. These examples show you how Kafka handles an issue of scale by applying an interesting data structure to solve a practical problem.

We would also note that the fact that it's open source is a positive for digging into the source code and having documentation and examples just by searching the internet. Resources are not just limited to internal knowledge based solely on a specific workplace.

1.2.2 Explaining Kafka to your manager

As is often the case, sometimes members of the C-suite will hear the word *Kafka* and be more confused by the name than care about what it does. It might be nice to explain the value found in this product. Also, it is good to step back and look at the larger picture of what the real added value is for this tool.

One of Kafka's most important features is the ability to take volumes of data and make it available for use by various business units. Such a data backbone that makes information coming into the enterprise available to all the multiple business areas allows for flexibility and openness on a company-wide scale. Nothing is prescribed, but increased access to data is a potential outcome. Most executives also know that with more data than ever flooding in, the company wants insights as fast as possible. Rather than pay for data to get old on disk, its value can be derived as it arrives. Kafka is one way to move away from a daily batch job that limits how quickly that data can be turned into value. *Fast data* seems to be the newer term, hinting that real value focuses on something different from the promises of big data alone.

Running on a Java virtual machine JVM® should be a familiar and comfortable place for many enterprise development shops. The ability to run on premises is a crucial driver for some whose data requires on-site oversight. And the cloud and managed platforms are options as well. Kafka can scale horizontally, and not depend on vertical scaling alone, which might eventually reach an expensive peak.

Maybe one of the most important reasons to learn about Kafka is to see how startups and others in their industry can overcome the once prohibitive cost of computing power. Instead of relying on a bigger and beefier server or a mainframe that can cost millions of dollars, distributed applications and architectures put competitors quickly within reach with, hopefully, less financial outlay.

1.3   *Kafka myths*

When you start to learn any new technology, it is often natural to try to map existing knowledge to new concepts. Although that technique can be used in learning Kafka, we wanted to note some of the most common misconceptions that we have run into in our work so far. We'll cover those in the next sections.

1.3.1   *Kafka only works with Hadoop®*

As mentioned, Kafka is a powerful tool that is often used in various situations. However, it seemed to appear on radars when used in the Hadoop ecosystem and might have first appeared for users as a tool as part of a Cloudera™ or Hortonworks™ suite. It isn't uncommon to hear the myth that Kafka only works with Hadoop. What could cause this confusion? One of the causes is likely the various tools that use Kafka as part of their products. Spark Streaming and Flume are examples of tools that use Kafka (or did at one point) and could be used with Hadoop as well. The dependency (depending on the version of Kafka) on Apache ZooKeeper™ is also a tool that is often found in Hadoop clusters and might tie Kafka further to this myth.

One other fundamental myth that often appears is that Kafka requires the Hadoop Distributed Filesystem (HDFS). That is not the case. Once we start to dig into how Kafka works, we will see that Kafka's speed and techniques used to process events would likely be much slower with a NodeManager in the middle of the process. Also, the block replication, usually a part of HDFS, is not done in the same way. One such example is that in Kafka, replicas are not recovered by default. Whereas both products use replication in different ways, the durability that is marketed for Kafka might be easy to group under the Hadoop theme of expecting failure as a default (and thus planning for overcoming it) and is a similar overall goal between Hadoop and Kafka.

1.3.2 *Kafka is the same as other message brokers*

Another big myth is that Kafka is just another message broker. Direct comparisons of the features of various tools (such as Pivotal's RabbitMQ™ or IBM's MQSeries®) to Kafka often have asterisks (or fine print) attached and are not always fair to the best use cases of each. Some tools over time have gained or will gain new features just as Kafka has added the exactly-once semantics. And default configurations can be changed to mirror features closer to other tools in the same space. In general, the following lists some of the most exciting and standout features that we will dig into in a bit:

- The ability to replay messages by default
- Parallel processing of data

Kafka was designed to have multiple consumers. What that means is that one application reading a message from the message broker doesn't remove it from other applications that might want to consume it as well. One effect of this is that a consumer who has already seen the message can again choose to read it (and other messages as well). With some architecture models like lambda (discussed in chapter 8), programmer mistakes are expected just as much as hardware failures. Imagine consuming millions of messages, and you forget to use a specific field from the original message. In some queues, that message is removed or sent to a duplicate or replay location. However, Kafka provides a way for consumers to seek specific points and read messages again (with a few constraints) by just seeking an earlier position on the topic.

As touched on briefly, Kafka allows for parallel processing of data and can have multiple consumers on the same topic. Kafka also has the concept of consumers being part of a consumer group, which will be covered in depth in chapter 5. Membership in a group determines which consumers get which messages and what work has been done across that group of consumers. Consumer groups act independently of any other group and allow for multiple applications to consume messages at their own pace with as many consumers as they require working together. Processing can happen in various ways: consumption by many consumers working on one application or consumption by many applications. No matter what other message brokers support, let's now focus on the robust use cases that have made Kafka one of the options developers turn to for getting work done.

1.4 *Kafka in the real world*

Applying Kafka to practical use is the core aim of this book. One of the things to note about Kafka is that it's hard to say it does one specific function well; it excels in many specific uses. Although we have some basic ideas to grasp first, it might be helpful to discuss at a high level some of the cases that Kafka has already been noted for in real-world use cases. The Apache Kafka site lists general areas where Kafka is used in the real world that we explore in the book. [9].

1.4.1   *Early examples*

Some users' first experience with Kafka (as was mine) was using it as a messaging tool. Personally, after years of using other tools like IBM® WebSphere® MQ (formerly MQ Series), Kafka (which was around version 0.8.3 at the time) seemed simple to use to get messages from point A to point B. Kafka forgoes using popular protocols and standards—like the Extensible Messaging and Presence Protocol (XMPP), Java Message Service (JMS) API (now part of Jakarta EE), or the OASIS® Advanced Message Queuing Protocol (AMQP)—in favor of a custom TCP binary protocol. We will dig in and see some complex uses later.

For an end user developing with a Kafka client, most of the details are in the configuration, and the logic becomes relatively straightforward (for example, "I want to place a message on this topic"). Having a durable channel for sending messages is also why Kafka is used.

Oftentimes, memory storage of data in RAM will not be enough to protect your data; if that server dies, the messages are not persisted across a reboot. High availability and persistent storage are built into Kafka from the start. Apache Flume provides a Kafka channel option because the replication and availability allow Flume events to be made immediately available to other sinks if a Flume agent (or the server it is running on) crashes [10]. Kafka enables robust applications to be built and helps handle the expected failures that distributed applications are bound to run into at some point.

Log aggregation (figure 1.6) is useful in many situations, including when trying to gather application events that were written in distributed applications. In the figure,

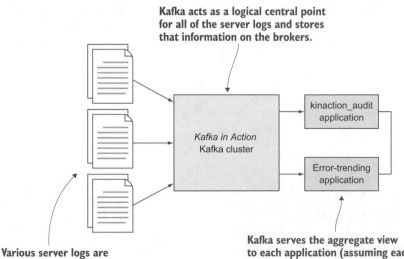

Figure 1.6   Kafka log aggregation

the log files are sent as messages into Kafka, and then different applications have a single logical topic to consume that information. With Kafka's ability to handle large amounts of data, collecting events from various servers or sources is a key feature. Depending on the contents of the log event itself, some organizations use it for auditing and failure-detection trending. Kafka is also used in various logging tools (or as an input option).

How do all of these log file entries allow Kafka to maintain performance without causing a server to run out of resources? The throughput of small messages can sometimes overwhelm a system because the processing of each method takes time and overhead. Kafka uses batching of messages for sending data as well as for writing data. Writing to the end of a log helps too, rather than random access to the filesystem. We will discuss more on the log format of messages in chapters 7.

1.4.2 Later examples

Microservices used to talk to each other with APIs like REST, but they can now leverage Kafka to communicate between asynchronous services with events [11]. Microservices can use Kafka as the interface for their interactions rather than specific API calls. Kafka has placed itself as a fundamental piece for allowing developers to get data quickly. Although Kafka Streams is now a likely default for many when starting work, Kafka had already established itself as a successful solution by the time the Streams API was released in 2016. The Streams API can be thought of as a layer that sits on top of producers and consumers. This abstraction layer is a client library that provides a higher-level view of working with your data as an unbounded stream.

In the Kafka 0.11 release, exactly-once semantics was introduced. We will cover what that means in practice later, once we get a more solid foundation. However, users running end-to-end workloads on top of Kafka with the Streams API may benefit from hardened delivery guarantees. Streams make this use case easier than it has ever been to complete a flow without the overhead of any custom application logic, ensuring that a message was only processed once from the beginning to the end of the transaction.

The number of devices for the Internet of Things (figure 1.7) will only increase with time. With all of those devices sending messages, sometimes in bursts when they get a Wi-Fi or cellular connection, something needs to be able to handle that data effectively. As you may have gathered, massive quantities of data are one of the critical areas where Kafka shines. As we discussed previously, small messages are not a problem for Kafka. Beacons, cars, phones, homes, etc.—all will be sending data, and something needs to handle the fire hose of data and make it available for action [12].

This are just a small selection of examples that are well-known uses for Kafka. As we will see in future chapters, Kafka has many practical application domains. Learning the upcoming foundational concepts is essential to see how even more practical applications are possible.

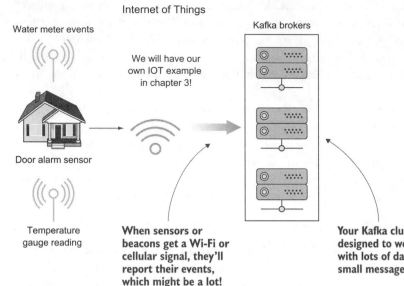

Figure 1.7   **The Internet of Things (IoT)**

1.4.3   *When Kafka might not be the right fit*

It is important to note that although Kafka has been used in some interesting use cases, it is not always the best tool for the job at hand. Let's investigate some of the uses where other tools or code might shine.

What if you only need a once-monthly or even once-yearly summary of aggregate data? Suppose you don't need an on-demand view, quick answer, or even the ability to reprocess data. In these cases, you might not need Kafka running throughout the entire year for those tasks alone (notably, if that amount of data is manageable to process at once as a batch). As always, your mileage may vary: different users have different thresholds on what is a large batch.

If your main access pattern for data is a mostly random lookup of data, Kafka might not be your best option. Linear read and writes are where Kafka shines and will keep your data moving as quickly as possible. Even if you have heard of Kafka having index files, they are not really what you would compare to a relational database having fields and primary keys from which indexes are built.

Similarly, if you need the exact ordering of messages in Kafka for the entire topic, you will have to look at how practical your workload is in that situation. To avoid any unordered messages, care should be taken to ensure that only one producer request thread is the maximum and, simultaneously, that there is only one partition in the topic. There are various workarounds, but if you have vast amounts of data that depend on strict ordering, there are potential gotchas that might come into play once you notice that your consumption is limited to one consumer per group at a time.

One of the other practical items that come to mind is that large messages are an exciting challenge. The default message size is about 1 MB [13]. With larger messages, you start to see memory pressure increase. In other words, the lower number of messages you can store in page cache could become a concern. If you are planning on sending huge archives around, you might want to see if there is a better way to manage those messages. Keep in mind that although you can probably achieve your end goal with Kafka in the previous situations (it's always possible), it might not be the first choice to reach for in your toolbox.

1.5 *Online resources to get started*

The community around Kafka has been one of the best (in our opinion) for making documentation available. Kafka has been a part of Apache (graduating from the Incubator in 2012) and keeps the current documentation at the project website at https://kafka.apache.org.

Another great resource for information is Confluent® (https://www.confluent.io/resources). Confluent was founded by the original Kafka's creators and is actively influencing the future direction of the work. They also build enterprise-specific features and support for companies to help develop their streaming platform. Their work helps support the Kafka open source nature and has extended to presentations and lectures that have discussed production challenges and successes.

As we start to dig into more APIs and configuration options in later chapters, these resources will be a useful reference if further details are needed, rather than listing them all in each chapter. In chapter 2, we will discover more details in which we can use specific terms and start to get to know Apache Kafka in a more tangible and hands-on way.

Summary

- Apache Kafka is a streaming platform that you can leverage to process large numbers of events quickly.
- Although Kafka can be used as a message bus, using it only as that ignores the capabilities that provide real-time data processing.
- Kafka may have been associated with other big data solutions in the past, but Kafka stands on its own to provide a scalable and durable system. Because it uses the same fault tolerant and distributed system techniques, Kafka fills the needs of a modern data infrastructure's core with its own clustering capabilities.
- In instances of streaming a large number of events like IoT data, Kafka handles data fast. As more information is available for your applications, Kafka provides results quickly for your data that was once processed offline in batch mode.

References

1 R. Moffatt. "The Changing Face of ETL." Confluent blog (September 17, 2018). https://www.confluent.io/blog/changing-face-etl/ (accessed May 10, 2019).

2 "Introduction." Apache Software Foundation (n.d.). https://kafka.apache.org/
   intro (accessed May 30, 2019).

3 Documentation. Apache Software Foundation (n.d.). https://kafka.apache
   .org/documentation/#semantics (accessed May 30, 2020).

4 N. Narkhede. "Exactly-once Semantics Are Possible: Here's How Apache Kafka
   Does It." Confluent blog (June 30, 2017). https://www.confluent.io/blog/
   exactly-once-semantics-are-possible-heres-how-apache-kafka-does-it   (accessed
   December 27, 2017).

5 N. Narkhede. "Apache Kafka Hits 1.1 Trillion Messages Per Day – Joins the
   4 Comma Club." Confluent blog (September 1, 2015). https://www.confluent
   .io/blog/apache-kafka-hits-1-1-trillion-messages-per-day-joins-the-4-comma-club/
   (accessed October 20, 2019).

6 L. Dauber. "The 2017 Apache Kafka Survey: Streaming Data on the Rise." Confluent blog (May 4, 2017). https://www.confluent.io/blog/2017-apache-kafka
   -survey-streaming-data-on-the-rise/ (accessed December 23, 2017).

7 K. Waehner. "How to Build and Deploy Scalable Machine Learning in Production with Apache Kafka." Confluent blog (September 29, 2017) https://
   www.confluent.io/blog/build-deploy-scalable-machine-learning-production-
   apache-kafka/ (accessed December 11, 2018).

8 Y. Matsuda. "Apache Kafka, Purgatory, and Hierarchical Timing Wheels." Confluent blog (October 28, 2015). https://www.confluent.io/blog/apache-kafka
   -purgatory-hierarchical-timing-wheels (accessed December 20, 2018).

9 "Use cases." Apache Software Foundation (n.d.). https://kafka.apache.org/
   uses (accessed May 30, 2017).

10 "Flume 1.9.0 User Guide." Apache Software Foundation (n.d.). https://
    flume.apache.org/FlumeUserGuide.html (accessed May 27, 2017).

11 B. Stopford. "Building a Microservices Ecosystem with Kafka Streams and
    KSQL." Confluent blog (November 9, 2017). https://www.confluent.io/blog/
    building-a-microservices-ecosystem-with-kafka-streams-and-ksql/ (accessed May
    1, 2020).

12 "Real-Time IoT Data Solution with Confluent." Confluent documentation.
    (n.d.). https://www.confluent.io/use-case/internet-of-things-iot/ (accessed May
    1, 2020).

13 Documentation. Apache Software Foundation (n.d.). https://kafka.apache.org/
    documentation/#brokerconfigs_message.max.bytes (accessed May 30, 2020).

Getting to know Kafka

This chapters covers

- The high-level architecture of Kafka
- Understanding client options
- How applications communicate with a broker
- Producing and consuming your first message
- Using Kafka clients with a Java application

Now that we have a high-level view of where Kafka shines and why one would use it, let's dive into the Kafka components that make up the whole system. Apache Kafka is a distributed system at heart, but it is also possible to install and run it on a single host. That gives us a starting point to dive into our sample use cases. As is often the case, the real questions start flowing once the hands hit the keyboard. By the end of this chapter, you will be able to send and retrieve your first Kafka message from the command line. Let's get started with Kafka and then spend a little more time digging into Kafka's architectural details.

> **NOTE** Visit appendix A if you do not have a Kafka cluster to use or are interested in starting one locally on your machine. Appendix A works on updating

17

the default configuration of Apache Kafka and on starting the three brokers we will use in our examples. Confirm that your instances are up and running before attempting any examples in this book! If any examples don't seem to work, please check the source code on GitHub for tips, errata, and suggestions.

2.1   *Producing and consuming a message*

A *message*, also called a *record*, is the basic piece of data flowing through Kafka. Messages are how Kafka represents your data. Each message has a timestamp, a value, and an optional key. Custom headers can be used if desired as well [1]. A simple example of a message could be something like the following: the machine with host ID "1234567" (a *message key*) failed with the message "Alert: Machine Failed" (a *message value*) at "2020-10-02T10:34:11.654Z" (a *message timestamp*). Chapter 9 shows an example of using a custom header to set a key-value pair for a tracing use case.

Figure 2.1 shows probably the most important and common parts of a message that users deal with directly. Keys and values will be the focus of most of our discussion in this chapter, which require analysis when designing our messages. Each key and value can interact in its own specific ways to serialize or deserialize its data. The details of how to use serialization will start to come into focus when covering producing messages in chapter 4.

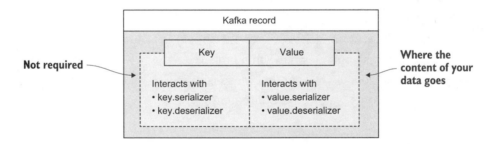

Figure 2.1   **Kafka messages are made up of a key and a value (timestamp and optional headers are not shown).**

Now that we have a record, how do we let Kafka know about it? You will deliver this message to Kafka by sending it to what are known as *brokers*.

2.2   *What are brokers?*

Brokers can be thought of as the server side of Kafka [1]. Before virtual machines and Kubernetes®, you may have seen one physical server hosting one broker. Because almost all clusters have more than one server (or node), we will have three Kafka servers running for most of our examples. This local test setup should let us see the output of commands against more than one broker, which will be similar to running with multiple brokers across different machines.

For our first example, we will create a topic and send our first message to Kafka from the command line. One thing to note is that Kafka was built with the command line in mind. There is no GUI that we will use, so we need to have a way to interact with the operating system's command line interface. The commands are entered into a text-based prompt. Whether you use vi, Emacs, Nano, or whatever, make sure that it is something you feel comfortable editing with.

NOTE Although Kafka can be used on many operating systems, it is often deployed in production on Linux, and command line skills will be helpful when using this product.

> ### Shell helper
>
> If you are a command line user and want a shortcut to autocomplete commands (and to help with the available arguments), check out a Kafka autocomplete project at http://mng.bz/K480. If you are a Zsh user, you may also want to check out and install Kafka's Zsh-completion plugin from https://github.com/Dabz/kafka-zsh-completions.

To send our first message, we will need a place to send it. To create a topic, we will run the `kafka-topics.sh` command in a shell window with the `--create` option (listing 2.1). You will find this script in the installation directory of Kafka, where the path might look like this: ~/kafka_2.13-2.7.1/bin. Note that Windows users can use the .bat files with the same name as the shell equivalent. For example, `kafka-topics.sh` has the Windows equivalent script named `kafka-topics.bat`, which should be located in the <kafka_install_directory>/bin/windows directory.

NOTE The references in this work to `kinaction` and `ka` (like used in `kaProperties`) are meant to represent different abbreviations of *Kafka in Action* and are not associated with any product or company.

Listing 2.1   Creating the `kinaction_helloworld` topic

```
bin/kafka-topics.sh --create --bootstrap-server localhost:9094
  --topic kinaction_helloworld --partitions 3 --replication-factor 3
```

You should see the output on the console where you just ran the command: `Created topic kinaction_helloworld`. In listing 2.1, the name `kinaction_helloworld` is used for our topic. We could have used any name, of course, but a popular option is to follow general Unix/Linux naming conventions, including not using spaces. We can avoid many frustrating errors and warnings by not including spaces or various special characters. These do not always play nicely with command line interfaces and autocompletion.

There are a couple of other options whose meaning may not be clear just yet, but to keep moving forward with our exploration, we will quickly define them. These topics will be covered in greater detail in chapter 6.

The `--partitions` option determines how many parts we want the topic to be split into. For example, because we have three brokers, using three partitions gives us one partition per broker. For our test workloads, we might not need this many, based on data needs alone. However, creating more than one partition at this stage lets us see how the system works in spreading data across partitions. The `--replication-factor` also is set to three in this example. In essence, this says that for each partition, we want to have three replicas. These copies are a crucial part of our design to improve reliability and fault tolerance. The `--bootstrap-server` option points to our local Kafka broker. This is why the broker should be running before invoking this script. For our work right now, the most important goal is to get a picture of the layout. We will dig into how to best estimate the numbers we need in other use cases when we get into the broker details later.

We can also look at all existing topics that have been created and make sure that our new one is on the list. The `--list` option is what we can reach for to achieve this output. Again, we run the next listing in the terminal window.

> **Listing 2.2   Verifying the topic**

```
bin/kafka-topics.sh --list --bootstrap-server localhost:9094
```

To get a feel for how our new topic looks, listing 2.3 shows another command that we can run to give us a little more insight into our cluster. Note that our topic is not like a traditional single topic in other messaging systems: we have replicas and partitions. The numbers we see next to the labels for the `Leader`, `Replicas`, and `Isr` fields are the `broker.ids` that correspond to the value for our three brokers that we set in our configuration files. Briefly looking at the output, we can see that our topic consists of three partitions: `Partition 0`, `Partition 1`, and `Partition 2`. Each partition was replicated three times as we intended on topic creation.

> **Listing 2.3   Describing the topic `kinaction_helloworld`**

```
bin/kafka-topics.sh --bootstrap-server localhost:9094 \
  --describe --topic kinaction_helloworld
```
--describe lets us look at the details of the topic we pass in.

```
Topic:kinaction_helloworld PartitionCount:3 ReplicationFactor:3  Configs:
Topic: kinaction_helloworld Partition: 0 Leader: 0 Replicas: 0,1,2  Isr: 0,1,2
Topic: kinaction_helloworld Partition: 1 Leader: 1 Replicas: 1,2,0  Isr: 1,2,0
Topic: kinaction_helloworld Partition: 2 Leader: 2 Replicas: 2,0,1  Isr: 2,0,1
```

The output from listing 2.3 shows in the first line a quick data view of the total count of partitions and replicas that this topic has. The following lines show each partition for the topic. The second line of output is specific to the partition labeled 0 and so forth. Let's zoom in on partition 0, which has its replica copy leader on broker 0. This partition also has replicas that exist on brokers 1 and 2. The last column, `Isr`, stands for *in-sync replicas*. In-sync replicas show which brokers are current and not lagging behind the leader. Having a partition replica copy that is out of date or behind the leader is an issue that we will cover later. Still, it is critical to remember that replica

Broker 0 only reads and writes for partition 0. The rest of the replicas get their copies from other brokers.

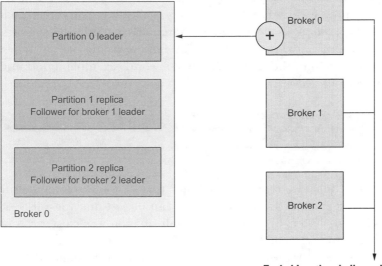

Topic kinaction_helloworld is actually made up of the leaders of each partition. In our case, that involves each broker holding a partition leader.

Figure 2.2 View of one broker

health in a distributed system is something that we will want to keep an eye on. Figure 2.2 shows a view if we look at the one broker with ID 0.

For our `kinaction_helloworld` topic, note how broker 0 holds the leader replica for partition 0. It also holds replica copies for partitions 1 and 2 for which it is not the leader replica. In the case of its copy of partition 1, the data for this replica will be copied from broker 1.

> **NOTE** When we reference a partition leader in the image, we are referring to a *replica leader*. It is important to know that a partition can consist of one or more replicas, but only one replica will be a leader. A leader's role involves being updated by external clients, whereas nonleaders take updates only from their leader.

Now once we have created our topic and verified that it exists, we can start sending real messages! Those who have worked with Kafka before might ask why we took the preceding step to create the topic before sending a message. There is a configuration to enable or disable the autocreation of topics. However, it is usually best to control the creation of topics as a specific action because we do not want new topics to randomly show up if someone mistypes a topic name once or twice or to be recreated due to producer retries.

To send a message, we will start a terminal tab or window to run a producer as a console application to take user input [2]. The command in listing 2.4 starts an interactive program that takes over the shell; you won't get your prompt back to type more commands until you press Ctrl-C to quit the running application. You can just start typing, maybe something as simple as the default programmer's first print statement with a prefix of kinaction (for *Kafka In Action*) as the following listing demonstrates. We use kinaction_helloworld in the vein of the "hello, world" example found in the book, *The C Programming Language* [3].

Listing 2.4   Kafka producer console command

```
bin/kafka-console-producer.sh --bootstrap-server localhost:9094 \
  --topic kinaction_helloworld
```

Notice in listing 2.4 that we reference the topic that we want to interact with using a bootstrap-server parameter. This parameter can be just one (or a list) of the current brokers in our cluster. By supplying this information, the cluster can obtain the metadata it needs to work with the topic.

Now, we will start a new terminal tab or window to run a consumer that also runs as a console application. The command in listing 2.5 starts a program that takes over the shell as well [2]. On this end, we should see the message we wrote in the producer console. Make sure that you use the same topic parameter for both commands; otherwise, you won't see anything.

Listing 2.5   Kafka consumer command

```
bin/kafka-console-consumer.sh --bootstrap-server localhost:9094 \
  --topic kinaction_helloworld --from-beginning
```

The following listing shows an example of the output you might see in your console window.

Listing 2.6   Example consumer output for kinaction_helloworld

```
bin/kafka-console-consumer.sh --bootstrap-server localhost:9094 \
  --topic kinaction_helloworld --from-beginning

kinaction_helloworld
...
```

As we send more messages and confirm the delivery to the consumer application, we can terminate the process and eliminate the --from-beginning option when we restart it. Notice that we didn't see all of the previously sent messages. Only those messages produced since the consumer console was started show up. The knowledge of which messages to read next and the ability to consume from a specific offset are tools we will leverage later as we discuss consumers in chapter 5. Now that we've seen a simple example in action, we have a little more background to discuss the parts we utilized.

2.3 Tour of Kafka

Table 2.1 shows the major components and their roles within the Kafka architecture. In the following sections, we'll dig into each of these items further to get a solid foundation for the following chapters.

Table 2.1 The Kafka architecture

Component	Role
Producer	Sends messages to Kafka
Consumer	Retrieves messages from Kafka
Topics	Logical name of where messages are stored in the broker
ZooKeeper ensemble	Helps maintain consensus in the cluster
Broker	Handles the commit log (how messages are stored on the disk)

2.3.1 Producers and consumers

Let's pause for a moment on the first stop on our tour: producers and consumers. Figure 2.3 highlights how producers and consumers differ in the direction of their data in relation to the cluster.

A *producer* is a tool for sending messages to Kafka topics [1]. As mentioned in our use cases in chapter 1, a good example is a log file that is produced from an application.

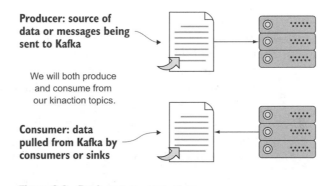

Figure 2.3 Producers vs. consumers

Those files are not a part of the Kafka system until they are collected and sent to Kafka. When you think of input (or data) going into Kafka, you are looking at a producer being involved somewhere internally.

There are no default producers, per se, but the APIs that interact with Kafka use producers in their own implementation code. Some entry paths into Kafka might include using a separate tool such as Flume or even other Kafka APIs such as Connect and Streams. WorkerSourceTask, inside the Apache Kafka Connect source code (from version 1.0), is one example where a producer is used internally of its implementation. It provides its own higher-level API. This specific version 1.0 code is available under an Apache 2 license (https://github.com/apache/kafka/blob/trunk/LICENSE) and is viewable on GitHub (see http://mng.bz/9N4r). A producer is also used to send messages inside Kafka itself. For example, if we are reading data from a specific topic and want to send it to a different topic, we would also use a producer.

To get a feel for what our own producer will look like, it might be helpful to look at code similar in concept to WorkerSourceTask, which is the Java class that we mentioned earlier. Listing 2.7 shows our example code. Not all of the source code is listed for the main method, but what is shown is the logic of sending a message with the standard KafkaProducer. It is not vital to understand each part of the following example. Just try to get familiar with the producer's usage in the listing.

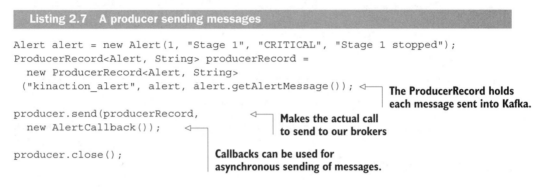

Listing 2.7   A producer sending messages

```
Alert alert = new Alert(1, "Stage 1", "CRITICAL", "Stage 1 stopped");
ProducerRecord<Alert, String> producerRecord =
  new ProducerRecord<Alert, String>
  ("kinaction_alert", alert, alert.getAlertMessage());    ◁── The ProducerRecord holds
                                                               each message sent into Kafka.

producer.send(producerRecord,    ◁── Makes the actual call
  new AlertCallback());    ◁──          to send to our brokers

producer.close();        Callbacks can be used for
                         asynchronous sending of messages.
```

To send data to Kafka, we created a ProducerRecord in listing 2.7. This object lets us define our message and specify the topic (in this case, kinaction_alert) to which we want to send the message. We used a custom Alert object as our key in the message. Next, we invoked the send method to send our ProducerRecord. While we can wait for the message, we can also use a callback to send asynchronous messages but still handle any errors. Chapter 4 provides this entire example in detail.

Figure 2.4 shows a user interaction that could start the process of sending data into a producer. A user on a web page that clicks might cause an audit event that would be produced in a Kafka cluster.

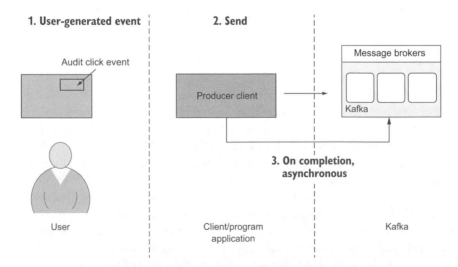

Figure 2.4   Producer example for user event

In contrast to a producer, a *consumer* is a tool for retrieving messages from Kafka [1]. In the same vein as producers, if we are talking about getting data out of Kafka, we look at consumers as being involved directly or indirectly. `WorkerSinkTask` is another class inside the Apache Kafka Connect source code from version 1.0 that shows the use of a consumer that is parallel with the producer example from Connect as well (see http://mng.bz/WrRW). Consuming applications subscribe to the topics that they are interested in and continuously poll for data. `WorkerSinkTask` provides a real example in which a consumer is used to retrieve records from topics in Kafka. The following listing shows the consumer example we will create in chapter 5. It displays concepts similar to `WorkerSinkTask.java`.

Listing 2.8 Consuming messages

```
...
consumer.subscribe(List.of("kinaction_audit"));          ◁── The consumer subscribes to
while (keepConsuming) {                                        the topics that it cares about.
  var records = consumer.
    poll(Duration.ofMillis(250));                        ◁── Messages are
    for (ConsumerRecord<String, String> record : records) {    returned from
      log.info("kinaction_info offset = {}, kinaction_value = {}",   a poll of data.
              record.offset(), record.value());

    OffsetAndMetadata offsetMeta =
      new OffsetAndMetadata(++record.offset(), "");

    Map<TopicPartition, OffsetAndMetadata> kaOffsetMap = new HashMap<>();
    kaOffsetMap.put(new TopicPartition("kinaction_audit",
      record.partition()), offsetMeta);

    consumer.commitSync(kaOffsetMap);
  }
}
...
```

Listing 2.8 shows how a consumer object calls a `subscribe` method, passing in a list of topics that it wants to gather data from (in this case, `kinaction_audit`). The consumer then polls the topic(s) (see figure 2.5) and handles any data brought back as `ConsumerRecords`.

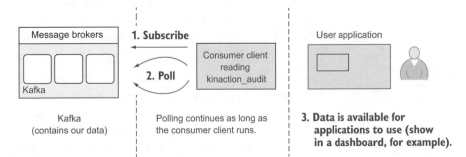

Figure 2.5 Consumer example flow

The previous code listings 2.7 and 2.8 show two parts of a concrete use case example as displayed in figures 2.4 and 2.5. Let's say that a company wants to know how many users clicked on their web page for a new factory command action. The click events generated by users would be the data going into the Kafka ecosystem. The data's consumers would be the factory itself, which would be able to use its applications to make sense of the data.

Putting data into Kafka and out of Kafka with code like the previous (or even with Kafka Connect itself) allows users to work with the data that can impact their business requirements and goals. Kafka does not focus on processing the data for applications: the consuming applications are where the data really starts to provide business value. Now that we know how to get data into and out of Kafka, the next area to focus on is where it lands in our cluster.

2.3.2   *Topics overview*

Topics are where most users start to think about the logic of what messages should go where. Topics consist of units called *partitions* [1]. In other words, one or more partitions can make up a single topic. As far as what is actually implemented on the computer's disk, partitions are what Kafka works with for the most part.

> **NOTE**   A single partition replica only exists on one broker and cannot be split between brokers.

Figure 2.6 shows how each partition replica leader exists on a single Kafka broker and cannot be divided smaller than that unit. Think back to our first example, the kinaction_helloworld topic. If you're looking for reliability and want three copies of the data, the topic itself is not one entity (or a single file) that is copied; instead, it is the various partitions that are replicated three times each.

> **NOTE**   The partition is even further broken up into segment files written on the disk drive. We will cover these files' details and their location when we talk about brokers in later chapters. Although segment files make up partitions, you will likely not interact directly with them, and this should be considered an internal implementation detail.

One of the most important concepts to understand at this point is the idea that one of the partition copies (replicas) will be what is referred to as a *leader*. For example, if you have a topic made up of three partitions and a total of three copies of each partition, every partition will have an

The topic kinaction_helloworld is made up of three partitions that will likely be spread out among different brokers.

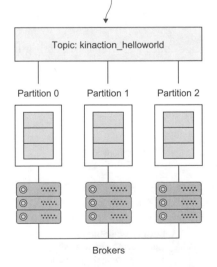

Partition 0   Partition 1   Partition 2

Brokers

Figure 2.6   Partitions make up topics.

elected leader replica. That leader will be one of the copies of the partition, and the other two (in this case, not shown in figure 2.6) will be *followers*, which update their information from their partition replica leader [1]. Producers and consumers only read or write from the leader replica of each partition it is assigned to during scenarios where there are no exceptions or failures (also known as a "happy path" scenario). But how does your producer or consumer know which partition replica is the leader? In the event of distributed computing and random failures, that answer is often influenced with help from ZooKeeper, the next stop on our tour.

2.3.3 *ZooKeeper usage*

One of the oldest sources of feared added complexity in the Kafka ecosystem might be that it uses ZooKeeper. Apache ZooKeeper (http://zookeeper.apache.org/) is a distributed store that provides discovery, configuration, and synchronization services in a highly available way. In versions of Kafka since 0.9, changes were made in ZooKeeper that allowed for a consumer to have the option not to store information about how far it had consumed messages (called *offsets*). We will cover the importance of offsets in later chapters. This reduced usage did not get rid of the need for consensus and coordination in distributed systems, however.

> **ZooKeeper removal**
>
> To simplify the requirements of running Kafka, there was a proposal for the replacement of ZooKeeper with its own managed quorum [4]. Because this work was not yet complete at the time of publication, with an early access release version 2.8.0, ZooKeeper is still discussed in this work. Why is ZooKeeper still important?
>
> This book covers version 2.7.1, and you are likely to see older versions in production that will use ZooKeeper for a while, until the changes are fully implemented. Also, although ZooKeeper will be replaced by the Kafka Raft Metadata mode (KRaft), the concepts of needing coordination in a distributed system are still valid, and understanding the role that ZooKeeper plays currently will, hopefully, lay the foundation of that understanding. Although Kafka provides fault tolerance and resilience, something has to provide coordination, and ZooKeeper enables that piece of the overall system. We will not cover the internals of ZooKeeper in detail but will touch on how Kafka uses it throughout the following chapters.

As you already saw, our cluster for Kafka includes more than one broker (server). To act as one correct application, these brokers need to not only communicate with each other, they also need to reach an *agreement*. Agreeing on which one is the replica leader of a partition is one example of the practical application of ZooKeeper within the Kafka ecosystem. For a real-world comparison, most of us have seen examples of clocks getting out of sync and how it becomes impossible to tell the correct time if multiple clocks are showing different times. The agreement can be challenging across separate brokers. Something is needed to keep Kafka coordinated and working in both success and failure scenarios.

One thing to note for any production use case is that ZooKeeper will be an ensemble, but we will run just one server in our local setup [5]. Figure 2.7 shows the ZooKeeper cluster and how Kafka's interaction is with the brokers and not the clients. KIP-500 refers to this usage as the "current" cluster design [4].

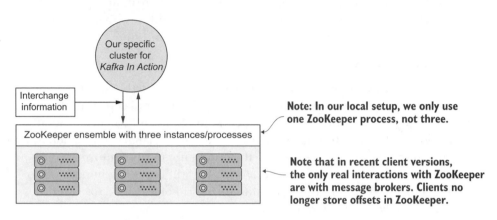

Figure 2.7   ZooKeeper interaction

TIP If you are familiar with `znodes` or have experience with ZooKeeper already, one good place to start looking at the interactions inside Kafka's source code is `ZkUtils.scala`.

Knowing the fundamentals of the preceding concepts increases our ability to make a practical application with Kafka. Also, we will start to see how existing systems that use Kafka are likely to interact to complete real use cases.

2.3.4   *Kafka's high-level architecture*

In general, core Kafka can be thought of as Scala application processes that run on a Java virtual machine (JVM). Although noted for being able to handle millions of messages quickly, what is it about Kafka's design that makes this possible? One of Kafka's keys is its usage of the operating system's *page cache* (as shown in figure 2.8). By avoiding caching in the JVM heap, the brokers can help prevent some of the issues that large heaps may have (for example, long or frequent garbage collection pauses) [6].

Another design consideration is the access pattern of data. When new messages flood in, it is likely that the latest messages are of more interest to many consumers, which can then be served from this cache. Serving from a page cache instead of a disk is likely faster in most cases. Where there are exceptions, adding more RAM helps more of your workload to fall into the page cache.

As mentioned earlier, Kafka uses its own protocol [7]. Using an existing protocol like AMQP (Advanced Message Queuing Protocol) was noted by Kafka's creators as

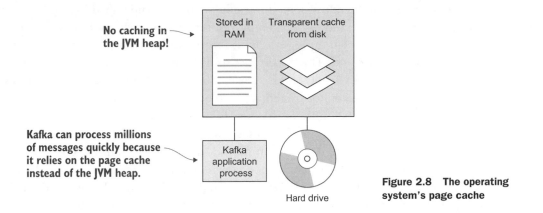

No caching in the JVM heap!

Stored in RAM

Transparent cache from disk

Kafka can process millions of messages quickly because it relies on the page cache instead of the JVM heap.

Kafka application process

Hard drive

Figure 2.8 The operating system's page cache

having too large a part in the impacts on the actual implementation. For example, new fields were added to the message header to implement the exactly-once semantics of the 0.11 release. Also, that same release reworked the message format to compress messages more effectively. The protocol could change and be specific to the needs of the creators of Kafka.

We are almost at the end of our tour. There's just one more stop—brokers and the commit log.

2.3.5 *The commit log*

One of the core concepts to help you master Kafka's foundation is to understand the commit log. The concept is simple but powerful. This becomes clearer as you understand the significance of this design choice. To clarify, the log we are talking about is not the same as the log use case that involved aggregating the output from loggers from an application process such as the LOGGER.error messages in Java.

Figure 2.9 shows how simple the concept of a commit log can be as messages are added over time [8]. Although there are more mechanics that take place, such as what happens when a log file needs to come back from a broker failure, this basic concept is a crucial part of understanding Kafka. The log used in Kafka is not just a detail that is hidden in

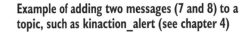

Example of adding two messages (7 and 8) to a topic, such as kinaction_alert (see chapter 4)

Here you see messages being received and added.

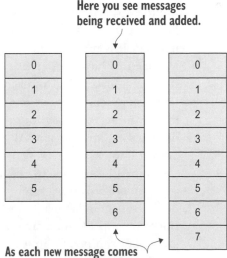

As each new message comes in, it's added to the end of the log.

Figure 2.9 Commit log

other systems that might use something similar (like a write-ahead log for a database). It is front and center, and its users employ offsets to know where they are in that log.

What makes the commit log special is its append-only nature in which events are always added to the end. The persistence as a log itself for storage is a major part of what separates Kafka from other message brokers. Reading a message does not remove it from the system or exclude it from other consumers.

One common question then becomes, how long can I retain data in Kafka? In various companies today, it is not rare to see that after the data in Kafka commit logs hits a configurable size or time retention period, the data is often moved into a permanent store. However, this is a matter of how much disk space you need and your processing workflow. The *New York Times* has a single partition that holds less than 100 GB [9]. Kafka is made to keep its performance fast even while keeping its messages. Retention details will be covered when we talk about brokers in chapter 6. For now, just understand that log data retention can be controlled by age or size using configuration properties.

2.4 Various source code packages and what they do

Kafka is often mentioned in the titles of various APIs. There are also certain components that are described as standalone products. We are going to look at some of these to see what options we have. The packages in the following sections are APIs found in the same source code repository as Kafka core, except for ksqlDB [10].

2.4.1 Kafka Streams

Kafka Streams has grabbed a lot of attention compared to core Kafka itself. This API is found in the Kafka source code project's streams directory and is mostly written in Java. One of the sweet spots for Kafka Streams is that no separate processing cluster is needed. It is meant to be a lightweight library to use in your application. You aren't required to have cluster or resource management software like Apache Hadoop to run your workloads. However, it still has powerful features, including local state with fault tolerance, one-at-a-time message processing, and exactly-once support [10]. The more you move throughout this book, the more you will understand the foundations of how the Kafka Streams API uses the existing core of Kafka to do some exciting and powerful work.

This API was made to ensure that creating streaming applications is as easy as possible, and it provides a fluent API, similar to Java 8's Stream API (also referred to as a domain-specific language, or DSL). Kafka Streams takes the core parts of Kafka and works on top of those smaller pieces by adding stateful processing and distributed joins, for example, without much more complexity or overhead [10].

Microservice designs are also being influenced by this API. Instead of data being isolated in various applications, it is pulled into applications that can use data independently. Figure 2.10 shows a before and after view of using Kafka to implement a microservice system (see the YouTube video, "Microservices Explained by Confluent" [11]).

Although the top part of figure 2.10 (without Kafka) relies on each application talking directly to other applications at multiple interfaces, the bottom shows an approach that uses Kafka. Using Kafka not only exposes the data to all applications without some service munging it first, but it provides a single interface for all applications to consume. The benefit of not being tied to each application directly shows how Kafka can help loosen dependencies between specific applications.

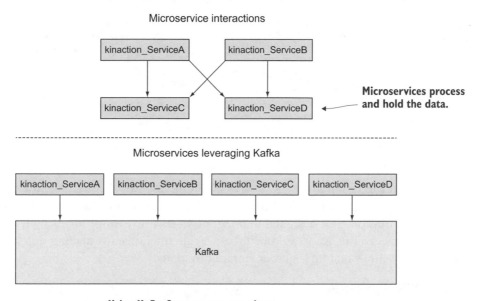

Figure 2.10   Microservice design

2.4.2   *Kafka Connect*

Kafka Connect is found in the core Kafka Connect folder and is also mostly written in Java. This framework was created to make integrations with other systems easier [10]. In many ways, it can be thought to help replace other tools such as the Apache project Gobblin™ and Apache Flume. If you are familiar with Flume, some of the terms used will likely seem familiar.

Source connectors are used to import data from a source into Kafka. For example, if we want to move data from MySQL® tables to Kafka's topics, we would use a Connect source to produce those messages into Kafka. On the other hand, sink connectors are used to export data from Kafka into different systems. For example, if we want messages in some topic to be maintained long term, we would use a sink connector to consume those messages from the topic and place them somewhere like cloud storage. Figure 2.11 shows this data flow from the database to Connect and then finally to a storage location in the cloud similar to a use case talked about in the article "The Simplest Useful Kafka Connect Data Pipeline in the World…or Thereabouts – Part 1" [12].

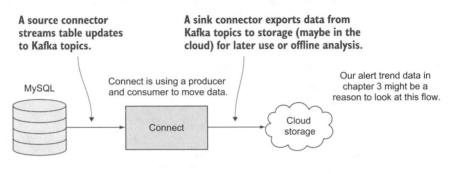

Figure 2.11   Connect use case

As a note, a direct replacement of Apache Flume features is probably not the intention or primary goal of Kafka Connect. Kafka Connect does not have an agent per Kafka node setup and is designed to integrate well with stream-processing frameworks to copy data. Overall, Kafka Connect is an excellent choice for making quick and simple data pipelines that tie together common systems.

2.4.3   *AdminClient package*

Kafka introduced the AdminClient API recently. Before this API, scripts and other programs that wanted to perform specific administrative actions would either have to run shell scripts (which Kafka provides) or invoke internal classes often used by those shell scripts. This API is part of the kafka-clients.jar file, which is a different JAR than the other APIs discussed previously. This interface is a great tool that will come in handy the more involved we become with Kafka's administration [10]. This tool also uses a similar configuration that producers and consumers use. The source code can be found in the org/apache/kafka/clients/admin package.

2.4.4   *ksqlDB*

In late 2017, Confluent released a developer preview of a new SQL engine for Kafka that was called KSQL before being renamed to ksqlDB. This allowed developers and data analysts who used mostly SQL for data analysis to leverage streams by using the interface they have known for years. Although the syntax might be somewhat familiar, there are still significant differences.

Most queries that relational database users are familiar with involve on-demand or one-time queries that include lookups. The mindset shift to a continuous query over a data stream is a significant shift and a new viewpoint for developers. As with the Kafka Streams API, ksqlDB is making it easier to use the power of continuous data flows. Although the interface for data engineers will be a familiar SQL-like grammar, the idea that queries are continuously running and updating is where use cases like dashboards on service outages would likely replace applications that once used point-in-time SELECT statements.

2.5 *Confluent clients*

Due to Kafka's popularity, the choice of which language to interact with Kafka usually isn't a problem. For our exercises and examples, we will use the Java clients created by the core Kafka project itself. There are many other clients supported by Confluent as well [13].

Since all clients are not the same feature-wise, Confluent provides a matrix of supported features by programming language at the following site to help you out: https://docs.confluent.io/ current/clients/index.html. As a side note, taking a look at other open source clients can help you develop your own client or even help you learn a new language.

Because using a client is the most likely way you will interact with Kafka in your applications, let's look at using the Java client (listing 2.9). We will do the same produce-and-consume process that we did when using the command line earlier. With a bit of additional boilerplate code (not listed here to focus on the Kafka-specific parts only), you can run this code in a Java main method to produce a message.

Listing 2.9 Java client producer

```java
public class HelloWorldProducer {
  public static void main(String[] args) {

    Properties kaProperties =
      new Properties();
    kaProperties.put("bootstrap.servers",
      "localhost:9092,localhost:9093,localhost:9094");

    kaProperties.put("key.serializer",
      "org.apache.kafka.common.serialization.StringSerializer");
    kaProperties.put("value.serializer",
      "org.apache.kafka.common.serialization.StringSerializer");

    try (Producer<String, String> producer =
      new KafkaProducer<>(kaProperties))

      ProducerRecord<String, String> producerRecord =
        new ProducerRecord<>("kinaction_helloworld",
```

The producer takes a map of name-value items to configure its various options.

This property can take a list of Kafka brokers.

Tells the message's key and value what format to serialize

Creates a producer instance. Producers implement the closable interface that's closed automatically by the Java runtime.

```
        null, "hello world again!");                    ◁──┐  Represents
                                                            │  our message
      producer.send(producerRecord);  ◁──┐  Sends the record
                                          │  to the Kafka broker
    }
  }
}
```

The code in listing 2.9 is a simple producer. The first step to create a producer involves setting up configuration properties. The properties are set in a way that anyone who has used a map will be comfortable using.

The `bootstrap.servers` parameter is one essential configuration item, and its purpose may not be apparent at first glance. This is a list of your Kafka brokers. The list does not have to be every server you have, though, because after the client connects, it will find the information about the rest of the cluster's brokers and not depend on that list.

The `key.serializer` and `value.serializer` parameters are also something to take note of in development. We need to provide a class that will serialize the data as it moves into Kafka. Keys and values do not have to use the same serializer.

Figure 2.12 displays the flow that happens when a producer sends a message. The producer we created takes in the configuration properties as an argument in the constructor we used. With this producer, we can now send messages. The `ProducerRecord` contains the actual input that we want to send. In our examples, `kinaction_helloworld` is the name of the topic that we sent. The next fields are the message key followed by the message value. We will discuss keys more in chapter 4, but it is enough to know that these can, indeed, be a null value, which makes our current example less complicated.

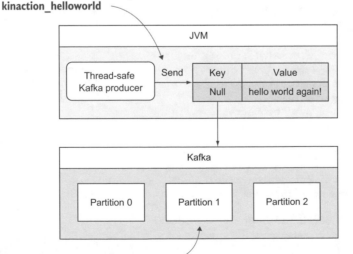

Figure 2.12
Producer flow

The message we send as the last argument is something different from the first message we sent with our console producer. Do you know why we want to make sure the message is different? We are working with the same topic with both producers, and because we have a new consumer, we should be retrieving the old message we produced before in our Java client-initiated message. Once our message is ready, we asynchronously send it using the producer. In this case, because we are only sending one message, we close the producer, which waits until previously sent requests complete and then shuts down gracefully.

Before running these Java client examples, we'll need to make sure we have the entry in the following listing in our pom.xml file [14]. We will use Apache Maven™ in all of the examples in this book.

Listing 2.10 Java client POM entry

```
<dependency>
  <groupId>org.apache.kafka</groupId>
  <artifactId>kafka-clients</artifactId>
  <version>2.7.1</version>
</dependency>
```

Now that we have created a new message, let's use our Java client as in the following listing to create a consumer that can see the message. We can run the code inside a Java `main` method and terminate the program after we are done reading messages.

Listing 2.11 Java client consumer

```
public class HelloWorldConsumer {

  final static Logger log =
    LoggerFactory.getLogger(HelloWorldConsumer.class);

  private volatile boolean keepConsuming = true;

  public static void main(String[] args) {                    Properties are set the
    Properties kaProperties = new Properties();          ◁──  same way as producers.
    kaProperties.put("bootstrap.servers",
      "localhost:9092,localhost:9093,localhost:9094");
    kaProperties.put("group.id", "kinaction_helloconsumer");
    kaProperties.put("enable.auto.commit", "true");
    kaProperties.put("auto.commit.interval.ms", "1000");
    kaProperties.put("key.deserializer",
      "org.apache.kafka.common.serialization.StringDeserializer");
    kaProperties.put("value.deserializer",
      "org.apache.kafka.common.serialization.StringDeserializer");

    HelloWorldConsumer helloWorldConsumer = new HelloWorldConsumer();
    helloWorldConsumer.consume(kaProperties);
    Runtime.getRuntime().
      addShutdownHook(new Thread(helloWorldConsumer::shutdown));
  }
```

```
private void consume(Properties kaProperties) {
  try (KafkaConsumer<String, String> consumer =
    new KafkaConsumer<>(kaProperties)) {
    consumer.subscribe(
      List.of(
        "kinaction_helloworld"          ◁──┐  The consumer tells Kafka what
      )                                     │  topics it's interested in.
    );

    while (keepConsuming) {
      ConsumerRecords<String, String> records =           ┐  Polls for new messages
        consumer.poll(Duration.ofMillis(250));   ◁──┘     as they come in
      for (ConsumerRecord<String, String> record :
        records) {                                                          ◁──────┐
        log.info("kinaction_info offset = {}, kinaction_value = {}",               │
          record.offset(), record.value());                                        │
      }                                                                            │
    }                                             To see the result, prints        │
  }                                                   each record that we          │
}                                                   consume to the console ────────┘

private void shutdown() {
  keepConsuming = false;
}
}
```

One thing that jumps out is that we have an infinite loop in listing 2.11. It seems weird to do that on purpose, but we want to handle an infinite stream of data. The consumer is similar to the producer in taking a map of properties to create a consumer. However, unlike the producer, the Java consumer client is not thread safe [15]. We will need to take that into account as we scale past one consumer in later sections. Our code is responsible for ensuring that any access is synchronized: one simple option is having only one consumer per Java thread. Also, whereas we told the producer where to send the message, we now have the consumer subscribe to the topics it wants. A subscribe command can subscribe to more than one topic at a time.

One of the most important sections to note in listing 2.11 is the poll call on the consumer. This is what is actively trying to bring messages to our application. No messages, one message, or many messages can all come back with a single poll, so it is important to note that our logic should account for more than one result with each poll call.

Finally, we can Ctrl-C the consumer program when we retrieve the test messages and be done for now. As a note, these examples rely on many configuration properties that are enabled by default. We will have a chance to dig into them more in later chapters.

2.6   *Stream processing and terminology*

We are not going to challenge distributed systems theories or certain definitions that could have various meanings, but rather look at how Kafka works. As you start to think of applying Kafka to your work, you will be presented with the following terms and can, hopefully, use the following descriptions as a lens through which to view your processing mindset.

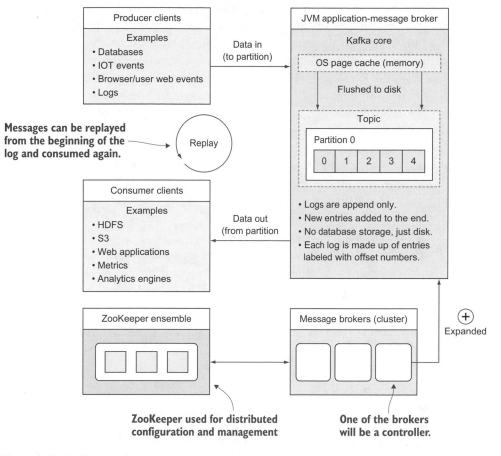

Figure 2.13   Kafka overview

Figure 2.13 provides a high-level view of what Kafka does. Kafka has many moving parts that depend on data coming into and out of its core to provide value to its users. Producers send data into Kafka, which works as a distributed system for reliability and scale, with logs, which are the basis for storage. Once data is inside the Kafka ecosystem, consumers can help users utilize that data in their other applications and use cases. Our brokers make up the cluster and coordinate with a ZooKeeper cluster to maintain metadata. Because Kafka stores data on disk, the ability to replay data in case of an application failure is also part of Kafka's feature set. These attributes allow Kafka to become the foundation of powerful stream-processing applications.

2.6.1   *Stream processing*

Stream processing seems to have various definitions throughout various projects. The core principle of streaming data is that data will keep arriving and will not end [16]. Also, your code should be processing this data all the time and not wait for a request or time frame with which to run. As we saw earlier, an infinite loop in our code hinted at this constant flow of data that does not have a defined endpoint.

This approach does not batch data and then process it in groups. The idea of a nightly or monthly run is also not a part of this workflow. If you think of a never-ending waterfall, the same principles apply. Sometimes there is a massive amount of data to transit and sometimes not that much, but it continuously flows between destinations.

Figure 2.14 shows that the Kafka Streams API depends on core Kafka. While event messages continue to come into the cluster, a consumer application can provide the end user with updated information continuously rather than wait for a query to pull a static snapshot of the events. No more refreshing the web page after 5 minutes for users to see the latest events!

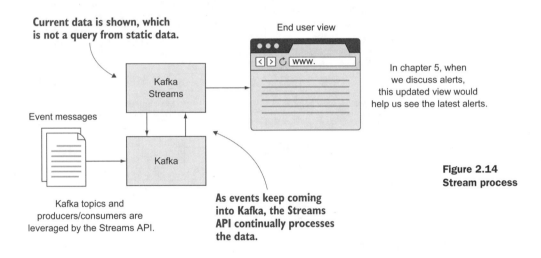

**Figure 2.14
Stream process**

2.6.2   *What exactly-once means*

One of the most exciting and maybe most discussed features in Kafka is its exactly-once semantics. This book will not discuss the theory behind those views; however, we will touch on what these semantics mean for Kafka's everyday usage.

One important thing to note is that the easiest way to maintain exactly-once is to stay within Kafka's walls (and topics). Having a closed system that can be completed as a transaction is why using the Streams API is one of the easiest paths to exactly-once. Various Kafka Connect connectors also support exactly-once and are great examples of bringing data out of Kafka because it won't always be the final endpoint for all data in every scenario.

Summary

- Messages represent your data in Kafka. Kafka's cluster of brokers handles this data and interacts with outside systems and clients.

- Kafka's use of a commit log helps in understanding the system overall.
- Messages appended to the end of a log frame how data is stored and how it can be used again. By being able to start at the beginning of the log, applications can reprocess data in a specific order to fulfill different use cases.
- Producers are clients that help move data into the Kafka ecosystem. Populating existing information from other data sources like databases into Kafka can help expose data that was once siloed in systems that provided a data interface for other applications.
- Consumer clients retrieve messages from Kafka. Many consumers can read the same data at the same time. The ability for separate consumers to start reading at various positions also shows the flexibility of consumption possible from Kafka topics.
- Continuously flowing data between destinations with Kafka can help us redesign systems that used to be limited to batch or time-delayed workflows.

References

1 "Main Concepts and Terminology." Apache Software Foundation (n.d.). https:// kafka.apache.org/documentation.html#intro_concepts_and_terms (accessed May 22, 2019).

2 "Apache Kafka Quickstart." Apache Software Foundation (2017). https://kafka .apache.org/quickstart (accessed July 15, 2020).

3 B. Kernighan and D. Ritchie. *The C Programming Language,* 1st ed. Englewood Cliffs, NJ, USA: Prentice Hall, 1978.

4 KIP-500: "Replace ZooKeeper with a Self-Managed Metadata Quorum." Wiki for Apache Kafka. Apache Software Foundation (July 09, 2020). https://cwiki .apache.org/confluence/display/KAFKA/KIP-500%3A+Replace+ZooKeeper+ with+a+Self-Managed+Metadata+Quorum (accessed August 22, 2020).

5 "ZooKeeper Administrator's Guide." Apache Software Foundation. (n.d.). https://zookeeper.apache.org/doc/r3.4.5/zookeeperAdmin.html (accessed June 10, 2020).

6 "Kafka Design: Persistence." Confluent documentation (n.d.). https://docs.con-fluent.io/platform/current/kafka/design.html#persistence (accessed November 19, 2020).

7 "A Guide To The Kafka Protocol: Some Common Philosophical Questions." Wiki for Apache Kafka. Apache Software Foundation (n.d.). https://cwiki.apache.org/ confluence/display/KAFKA/A+Guide+To+The+Kafka+Protocol#AGuideToThe KafkaProtocol-SomeCommonPhilosophicalQuestions (accessed August 21, 2019).

8 "Documentation: Topics and Logs." Apache Software Foundation (n.d.). https:// kafka.apache.org/23/documentation.html#intro_topics (accessed May 25, 2020).

9   B. Svingen. "Publishing with Apache Kafka at The New York Times." Confluent blog (September 6, 2017). https://www.confluent.io/blog/publishing-apache -kafka-new-york-times/ (accessed September 25, 2018).

10 "Documentation: Kafka APIs." Apache Software Foundation (n.d.). https:// kafka.apache.org/documentation.html#intro_apis (accessed June 15, 2021).

11 "Microservices Explained by Confluent." Confluent. Web presentation (August 23, 2017). https://youtu.be/aWI7iU36qv0 (accessed August 9, 2021).

12 R. Moffatt. "The Simplest Useful Kafka Connect Data Pipeline in the World…or Thereabouts – Part 1." Confluent blog (August 11, 2017). https://www.confluent .io/blog/simplest-useful-kafka-connect-data-pipeline-world-thereabouts-part-1/ (accessed December 17, 2017).

13 "Kafka Clients." Confluent documentation (n.d.). https://docs.confluent.io/ current/clients/index.html (accessed June 15, 2020).

14 "Kafka Java Client." Confluent documentation (n.d.). https://docs.confluent .io/clients-kafka-java/current/overview.html (accessed June 21, 2021).

15 "Class KafkaConsumer<K,V>." Apache Software Foundation (November 09, 2019). https://kafka.apache.org/24/javadoc/org/apache/kafka/clients/con sumer/KafkaConsumer.html (accessed November 20, 2019).

16 "Streams Concepts." Confluent documentation (n.d.). https://docs.confluent .io/platform/current/streams/concepts.html (accessed June 17, 2020).

Part 2

Applying Kafka

In part 2, we will build on our mental model of Kafka that we developed in part 1 by putting our knowledge into action. We will look at the foundations of Kafka and start with the fundamental subjects of producer and consumer clients. Even if you only plan to develop Kafka Streams or ksqlDB applications, part 2 is still worth your time. The core pieces discussed in this part will underlay most higher-level libraries and abstractions in the Kafka ecosystem:

- In chapter 3, we begin designing a sample project and learn how to apply Kafka to it. While schemas are covered in more detail in chapter 11, our project requirements show this need early on in our data project designs.
- In chapter 4, we go into detail about how we can use producers to move data into Kafka. We discuss important configuration options and their impact on our data sources.
- In chapter 5, we dig into the consumption of data from Kafka by using consumers. Parallels and differences are drawn between consumer clients and the producers from chapter 4.
- In chapter 6, we start to look at the brokers' role in our clusters. This chapter covers roles for both leaders and controllers as well as their relationship to our clients.
- In chapter 7, we look at how topics and partitions fit together to provide the data we depend on. Compacted topics are also introduced.
- In chapter 8, we explore tools and architectures that are options for handling data that we need to retain or reprocess.
- In chapter 9, which finishes part 2, we review essential logs and metrics to help with administrative duties to keep our clusters healthy.

Following part 2, you should have a solid understanding of the core pieces of Kafka and how to use these pieces in your use cases. Let's get started!

Designing a Kafka project

This chapters covers

- Designing a real-world Kafka project
- Determining which data format to use
- Existing issues impacting data usage
- Deciding when data transformation takes place
- How Kafka Connect helps us start a data-streaming path

In our previous chapter, we saw how we can work with Kafka from the command line and how to use a Java client. Now, we will expand on those first concepts and look at designing various solutions with Kafka. We will discuss some questions to consider as we lay out a strategy for the example project we'll start in this chapter. As we begin to develop our solutions, keep in mind that, like most projects, we might make minor changes along the way and are just looking for a place to jump in and start developing. After reading this chapter, you will be well on your way to solving real-world use cases while producing a design to facilitate your further exploration of Kafka in the rest of this book. Let's start on this exciting learning path!

3.1   Designing a Kafka project

Although new companies and projects can use Kafka as they get started, that is not the case for all Kafka adopters. For those of us who have been in enterprise environments or worked with legacy systems (and anything over five years old is probably considered legacy these days), in reality, starting from scratch is not a luxury we always have. However, one benefit of dealing with existing architectures is that it gives us a list of pain points, that we can address. The contrast also helps us to highlight the shift in thinking about the data in our work. In this chapter, we will work on a project for a company that is ready to shift from their current way of handling data and apply this new hammer named Kafka.

3.1.1   Taking over an existing data architecture

Let's look at some background to give us our fictional example inspired by Kafka's ever-growing usage. One topic by Confluent mentioned in chapter 1 (https://www.confluent.io/use-case/internet-of-things-iot/) and also an excellent article by Janakiram MSV, titled "Apache Kafka: The Cornerstone of an Internet-of-Things Data Platform," includes Kafka's use of sensors [1]. Using the topic of sensors as a use case, we will dig into a fictional example project.

Our new fictional consulting company has just won a contract to help re-architect a plant that works on e-bikes and manages them remotely. Sensors are placed throughout the bike that continuously provide events about the condition and status of the internal equipment they are monitoring. However, so many events are generated that the current system ignores most of the messages. We have been asked to help the site owners unlock the potential in that data for their various applications to utilize. Besides this, our current data includes traditional relational database systems that are large and clustered. With so many sensors and an existing database, how might we create our new Kafka-based architecture without impacting manufacturing?

3.1.2   A first change

One of the best ways to start our task is probably not with a big-bang approach—all our data does not have to move into Kafka at once. If we use a database today and want to kick the tires on the streaming data tomorrow, one of the easiest on-ramps starts with Kafka Connect. Although it can handle production loads, it does not have to out of the gate. We will take one database table and start our new architecture while letting the existing applications run for the time being. But first, let's get into some examples to gain familiarity with Kafka Connect.

3.1.3   Built-in features

The purpose of Kafka Connect is to help move data into or out of Kafka without writing our own producers and consumers. Connect is a framework that is already part of Kafka, which makes it simple to use previously built pieces to start your streaming work. These pieces are called *connectors*, and they were developed to work reliably with other data sources [2].

If you recall from chapter 2, some of the producer and consumer Java client real-world code that we used as examples showed how Connect abstracts those concepts away by using them internally with Connect. One of the easiest ways to start is by looking at how Connect can take a typical application log file and move it into a Kafka topic. The easiest option to run and test Connect on your local machine is standalone mode. Scaling can come later if we like what we can do in standalone mode! In the folder where you installed Kafka, locate the following files under the config directory:

- connect-standalone.properties
- connect-file-source.properties

Peeking inside the connect-standalone.properties file, you should see some configuration keys and values that should look familiar from some of the properties we used to make our own Java clients in chapter 2. Knowing the underlying producers and consumer clients can help us understand how Connect uses that same configuration to complete its work by listing items such as bootstrap.servers.

In our example, we'll take data from one data source and put that into Kafka so that we can treat data as being sourced from a Kafka file. Using the file connect-file-source.properties, included with your Kafka installation as an example template, let's create a file called alert-source.properties and place the text from listing 3.1 inside as the contents of our file. This file defines the configurations that we need to set up the file alert.txt and to specify the data be sent to the specific topic kinaction_alert_connect. Note that this example is following steps similar to the excellent Connect Quickstart guide at https://docs.confluent.io/3.1.2/connect/quickstart.html if you need more reference material. To learn even more detailed information, we recommend watching the excellent presentation of Randall Hauch (Apache Kafka committer and PMC) from the Kafka Summit (San Francisco, 2018) located at http://mng.bz/8WeD.

With configurations (and not code), we can get data into Kafka from any file. Because reading from a file is a common task, we can use Connect's prebuilt classes. In this case, the class is FileStreamSource [2]. For the following listing, let's pretend that we have an application that sends alerts to a text file.

Listing 3.1 Configuring Connect for a file source

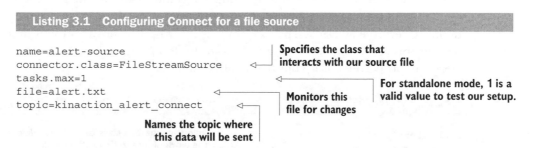

```
name=alert-source
connector.class=FileStreamSource        ← Specifies the class that
tasks.max=1                                interacts with our source file
file=alert.txt                          ←
topic=kinaction_alert_connect           ←        For standalone mode, 1 is a
                              Monitors this       valid value to test our setup.
                              file for changes
              Names the topic where
              this data will be sent
```

The value of the topic property is significant. We will use it later to verify that messages are pulled from a file into the specific kinaction_alert_connect topic. The file alert.txt is monitored for changes as new messages flow in. And finally, we chose 1 for the value of tasks.max because we only really need one task for our connector and, in this example, we are not worried about parallelism.

NOTE If you are running ZooKeeper and Kafka locally, make sure that you have your own Kafka brokers still running as part of this exercise (in case you shut them down after the previous chapter).

Now that we have done the needed configuration, we need to start Connect and send in our configurations. We can start the Connect process by invoking the shell script `connect-standalone.sh`, including our custom configuration file as a parameter to that script. To start Connect in a terminal, run the command in the following listing and leave it running [2].

Listing 3.2 Starting Connect for a file source

```
bin/connect-standalone.sh config/connect-standalone.properties \
  alert-source.properties
```

Moving to another terminal window, create a text file named alert.txt in the directory in which we started the Connect service and add a couple of lines of text to this file using your text editor; the text can be anything you want. Now let's use the `console-consumer` command to verify that Connect is doing its job. For that, we'll open another terminal window and consume from the `kinaction_alert_connect` topic, using the following listing as an example. Connect should ingest this file's contents and produce the data into Kafka [2].

Listing 3.3 Confirming file messages made it into Kafka

```
bin/kafka-console-consumer.sh \
  --bootstrap-server localhost:9094 \
  --topic kinaction_alert_connect --from-beginning
```

Before moving to another connector type, let's quickly talk about the sink connector and how it carries Kafka's messages back out to another file. Because the destination (or sink) for this data is another file, we want to look at the connect-file-sink.properties file. A small change is shown in listing 3.4 as the new outcome is written to a file rather than read from a file as we did previously. We'll declare `FileStreamSink` to define a new role as a sink. The topic `kinaction_alert_connect` is the source of our data in this scenario. Placing the text from the following listing in a new file called alert-sink.properties sets up our new configuration [2].

Listing 3.4 Configuring Connect for a file source and a sink

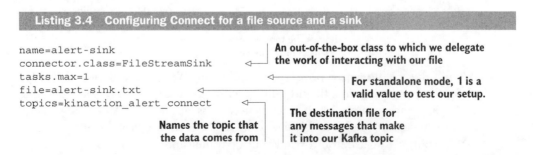

If the Connect instance is still running in a terminal, we'll need to close that terminal window or stop the process by pressing Ctrl-C. Then we'll restart it with the file-source and file-sink property files. Listing 3.5 shows how to restart Connect with both our custom alert source and sink properties [2]. The end result should be data flowing from a file into Kafka and back out to a separate destination.

Listing 3.5   Starting Connect for a file source and a sink

```
bin/connect-standalone.sh config/connect-standalone.properties \
  alert-source.properties alert-sink.properties
```

To confirm that Connect is using our new sink, open the sink file we used in our configuration, alert-sink.txt, and verify that you can see the messages that were in the source file and that these were sent to the Kafka topic.

3.1.4   *Data for our invoices*

Let's look at another requirement, dealing with our invoices for bike orders. Connect easily lets those with in-depth knowledge of creating custom connectors share them with others (to help those of us who may not be experts in these systems). Now that we have used a connector (listings 3.4 and 3.5), it should be relatively simple to integrate a different connector because Connect standardizes interaction with other systems.

To use Connect in our manufacturing example, let's look at applying an existing source connector that streams table updates from a local database to a Kafka topic. Again, our goal is not to change the entire data processing architecture at once. Instead, we'll show how we can bring in updates from a table-based database application and develop our new application in parallel while letting the other system exist as is. Note that this example is following steps similar to the guide at https://docs.confluent.io/kafka-connect-jdbc/current/source-connector/index.html, if you need more reference material.

Our first step is to set up a database for our local examples. For ease of use and to get started quickly, we'll use connectors from Confluent for SQLite. If you can run `sqlite3` in your terminal and get a prompt, then you are already set. Otherwise, use your favorite package manager or installer to get a version of SQLite that works on your operating system.

> **TIP**   Check out the Commands.md file in the source code for this chapter to find installation instructions for the Confluent command line interface (CLI) as well as the JDBC connector using `confluent-hub`. The rest of the examples reference commands in the Confluent-installed directory *only* and not in the Kafka-installed directory.

To create a database, we will run `sqlite3 kafkatest.db` from the command line. In this database, we will then run the code in listing 3.6 to create the invoices table and to insert some test data in the table. As we design our table, it is helpful to think of how we will capture changes into Kafka. Most use cases will not require us to capture the entire database but only changes after the initial load. A timestamp, sequence number, or ID can help us determine which data has changed and needs to be sent to Kafka. In the following listing, the ID or modified columns could be our guide for Connect to let Kafka know which data was modified in the table [3].

Listing 3.6   Creating the invoices table

```
CREATE TABLE invoices(                          ⟵      Creates an invoices table
    id INT PRIMARY KEY      NOT NULL,       ⟵
    title               TEXT    NOT NULL,        Sets an incremental ID so Connect
    details             CHAR(50),                knows which entries to capture
    billedamt           REAL,
    modified        TIMESTAMP DEFAULT (STRFTIME('%s', 'now')) NOT NULL
);

INSERT INTO invoices (id,title,details,billedamt)   \    Inserts test data
    VALUES (1, 'book', 'Franz Kafka', 500.00 );     ⟵    into our table
```

By creating a file in the location etc/kafka-connect-jdbc/kafkatest-sqlite.properties, and after making slight changes to our database table name, we can see how additional inserts and updates to the rows cause messages to be sent into Kafka. Refer to the source code for chapter 3 in the Git repository to find more detailed setup instructions for finding and creating the JDBC connector files in the Confluent installation directory. It is not part of the Apache Kafka distribution like the file connector. Also, if the modified timestamp format gives an error, make sure to check out other options in the source code with this chapter.

Now that we have a new configuration, we need to start Connect to pass it kafka-test-sqlite.properties.

Listing 3.7   Starting Connect for a database table source

```
confluent-hub install confluentinc/kafka-connect-jdbc:10.2.0
confluent local services connect start
...
# See Commands.md for other steps
confluent local services connect connector config jdbc-source
--config etc/kafka-connect-jdbc/kafkatest-sqlite.properties   ⟵
                                    We are using our new
                                    database properties file.
```

Listing 3.7 shows how you can launch Connect with the Confluent CLI tool. The standalone connnect script, `connect-standalone.sh`, could have also been used [3]. Although the power of Kafka Connect is great for moving existing database tables to Kafka, our sensors (which are not database backed) are going to require a different technique.

3.2 Sensor event design

Because there are no existing connectors for our state-of-the-art sensors, we can directly interact with their event system through custom producers. The ability to hook into and write our producers to send data into Kafka is where we will look at the requirements in the following sections.

Figure 3.1 shows that there is a critical path of stages that need to work together. One of the steps is an additional quality check sensor. This sensor can be skipped to avoid processing delays if it goes down for maintenance or failure. Sensors are attached to all of the bikes' internal steps (represented by gears in figure 3.1), and they send messages to the clustered database machines that exist in the current system. There is also an administration console used remotely to update and run commands against the sensors already built into the system.

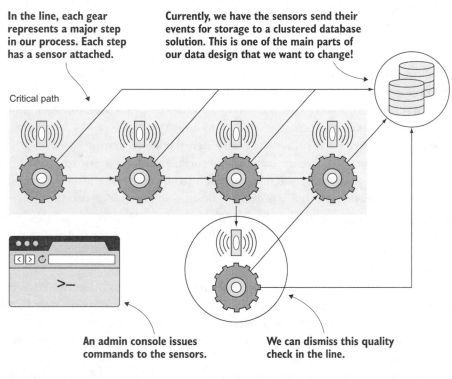

In the line, each gear represents a major step in our process. Each step has a sensor attached.

Currently, we have the sensors send their events for storage to a clustered database solution. This is one of the main parts of our data design that we want to change!

Critical path

An admin console issues commands to the sensors.

We can dismiss this quality check in the line.

Figure 3.1 Factory setup

3.2.1 Existing issues

Let's start by discussing some of the issues that have come up in most of our previous use cases. The need for data to exist and to be available to users is a deep and challenging problem. Let's look at how we can deal with two of those challenges: data silos and recoverability.

DEALING WITH DATA SILOS

In our factory, the data and the processing are owned by an application. If others want to use that data, they would need to talk to the application owner. And what are the chances that the data is provided in a format that can be easily processed? Or what if it does not provide the data at all?

The shift from traditional "data thinking" makes the data available to everyone in its raw source. If you have access to the data as it comes in, you do not have to worry about the application API exposing it to specific formats or after custom transformations. And what if the application providing the API parses the original data incorrectly? To untangle that mess might take a while if we have to recreate the data from changes to the original data source.

RECOVERABILITY

One of the excellent perks of a distributed system like Kafka is that failure is an expected condition: it's planned for and handled! However, along with system blips, we also have the human element in developing applications. If an application has a defect or a logic issue that destroys our data, what would be our path to correct it? With Kafka, that can be as simple as starting to consume from the beginning topic as we did with the console consumer flag `--from-beginning` in chapter 2. Additionally, data retention makes it available for use again and again. The ability to reprocess data for corrections is powerful. But if the original event is not available, it might be hard to retrofit the existing data.

Because events are only produced once from the sensor source for a specific instance, the message broker can play a crucial part in our consumption pattern. If the message in a queuing system is removed from the broker after a subscriber reads the message, as in version 1.0 of the application in figure 3.2, it is gone from the system. If a defect in an application's logic is found after the fact, analysis would be needed to see if data can be corrected using what was left over from the processing of that original event because it will not be fired again. Fortunately, Kafka brokers allow for a different option.

Beginning with version 1.1, the application can replay those messages already consumed with the new application logic. Our new application code that fixed a logic mistake from version 1.0 can process all the events again. The chance to process our events again makes it easier to enhance our applications without data loss or corruption.

The replay of data can also show us how a value changes over time. It might be beneficial to draw a parallel between replaying the Kafka topic and the idea of a write-ahead log (WAL). With a WAL, we can tell what a value used to be and the changes that happened over time because modifications to values are written in the log before they are applied. WALs are commonly found in database systems and help a system recover if an action fails during a transaction. If you follow the events from the beginning to the end, you would see how data moves from its initial value to its current value.

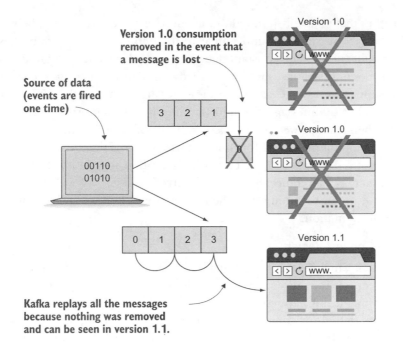

Version 1.0 consumption removed in the event that a message is lost

Source of data (events are fired one time)

Version 1.0

Version 1.0

Version 1.1

Kafka replays all the messages because nothing was removed and can be seen in version 1.1.

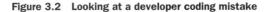

Figure 3.2 Looking at a developer coding mistake

WHEN SHOULD DATA BE CHANGED?

Whether data is coming from a database or a log event, our preference is to get the data into Kafka first; then the data will be available in its purest form. But each step before it is stored in Kafka is an opportunity for the data to be altered or injected with various formatting or programming logic errors. Keep in mind that hardware, software, and logic can and will fail in distributed computing, so it's always great to get data into Kafka first, which gives you the ability to replay data if any of those failures occur.

3.2.2 *Why Kafka is the right fit*

Does Kafka even make sense in our fictional sensor use case? Of course, this is a book about Kafka, right? However, let's quickly try to pinpoint a couple of compelling reasons to give Kafka a try.

One thing that has been made clear by our clients is that their current database is getting expensive to scale vertically. By vertical scaling, we mean increasing things like CPU, RAM, and disk drives in an existing machine. (To scale dynamically, we would look at adding more servers to our environment.) With the ability to horizontally scale our cluster, we can hope to get more overall benefits for our buck. Although the servers that we run our brokers on might not be the cheapest machines money can buy, 32 GB or 64 GB of RAM on these servers can handle production loads [4].

The other item that probably jumped out at you is that we have events being produced continuously. This should sound similar to the definition of stream processing that we talked about earlier. The constant data feed won't have a defined end time or stopping point, so our systems should be ready to handle messages constantly. Another interesting point to note is that our messages are usually under 10 KB for our example. The smaller the message size and the amount of memory we can offer to page caches, the better shape we are in to keep our performance healthy.

During this requirements review for our scenario, some security-minded developers might have noticed there's no built-in disk encryption for the brokers (data at rest). However, that isn't a requirement for the current system. We will first focus on getting our system up and running and then worry about adding security at a later point in our implementation.

3.2.3   *Thought starters on our design*

One thing to note is which features are available for specific Kafka versions. Although we use a recent version for our examples (at the time of this writing, version 2.7.1), some developers might not have control over the current broker and client versions they are using due to their existing infrastructures. For this reason, it is good to keep in mind when some of the features and APIs we might use made their debut. Table 3.1 highlights some of the past major features but is not inclusive of all versions [5].

Table 3.1   Past Kafka version milestones

Kafka version	Feature
2.0.0	ACLS with prefix support and hostname verification (default for SSL)
1.0.0	Java 9 support and JBOD disk failure improvements
0.11.0.0	Admin API
0.10.2.0	Improved client compatibility
0.10.1.0	Time-based search
0.10.0.0	Kafka streams, timestamps, and rack awareness
0.9.0.0	Various security features (ACLS, SSL), Kafka Connect, and a new consumer client

Another thing to note as we focus on clients in the next few chapters is the feature-improved client compatibility. Broker versions since 0.10.0 can work with newer client versions. This is important because we can now try new versions of clients by upgrading them first, and the brokers can remain at their version until we decide that we want to upgrade them. This comes in handy as you work through this material if you are running against a cluster that already exists.

Now that we have decided to give Kafka a try, this might be a good time to decide how we want our data to exist. The following questions are intended to make us think about how we want to process our data. These preferences impact various parts of our design, but our main focus here is on figuring out the data structure; we will cover the implementation in later chapters. This list is not meant to be complete, but it is a good starting point in planning our design:

- *Is it okay to lose any messages in the system?* For example, is one missed event about a mortgage payment going to ruin your customer's day and their trust in your business? Or is it a minor issue such as your social media account RSS feed missing a post? Although the latter is unfortunate, would it be the end of your customer's world?

- *Does your data need to be grouped in any way?* Are the events correlated with other events that are coming in? For example, are we going to be taking in account changes? In that case, we'd want to associate the various account changes with the customer whose account is changing. Grouping events up front might also prevent the need for applications to coordinate messages from multiple consumers while reading from the topic.

- *Do you need data delivered in a specific order?* What if a message gets delivered in an order other than when it occurred? For example, you get an order-canceled notice before the actual order. Because product ends up shipping due to order alone, the customer service impact is probably good enough reason to say that the ordering is indeed essential. Or course, not everything will need exact ordering. For example, if you are looking at SEO data for your business, the order is not as important as making sure that you can get a total at the end.

- *Do you only want the last value of a specific item, or is the history of that item important?* Do you care about how your data has evolved? One way to think about this looks at how data is updated in a traditional relational database table. It is mutated in place (the older value is gone and the newer value replaces it). The history of what that value looked like a day ago (or even a month ago) is lost.

- *How many consumers are you going to have?* Will they all be independent of each other, or will they need to maintain some sort of order when reading the messages? If you are going to have a lot of data that you want to consume as quickly as possible, that will inform and help shape how you break up your messages on the tail end of your processing.

Now that we have a couple of questions to ask for our factory, let's try to apply these to our actual requirements. We will use a chart to answer each scenario. We will learn how to do this in the following section.

3.2.4 *User data requirements*

Our new architecture needs to provide a couple of specific key features. In general, we want the ability to capture messages even if the consuming service is down. For example, if one of the consumer applications is down in our remote plant, we want to make sure that it can later process the events without dropping messages entirely. Additionally, when the application is out of maintenance or comes back up after a failure, we want it to still have the data it needs. For our example use case, we also want the status from our sensors as either working or broken (a sort of alert), and we want to make sure we can see if any part of our bike process could lead to total failure.

Along with the preceding information, we also want to maintain a history of the sensors' alert status. This data could be used in determining trends and in predicting failures from sensor data before actual events lead to broken equipment. We also want to keep an audit log of any users that push updates or queries directly against the sensors. Finally, for compliance reasons, we want to know who did what administration actions on the sensors themselves.

3.2.5   *High-level plan for applying our questions*

Let's focus closer on our requirements to create an audit log. Overall, it seems like everything that comes in from the management API will need to be captured. We want to make sure that only users with access permissions are able to perform actions against the sensors, and we should not lose messages, as our audit would not be complete without all the events. In this case, we do not need any grouping key because each event can be treated as independent.

The order does not matter inside our audit topic because each message will have a timestamp in the data itself. Our primary concern is that all the data is there to process. As a side note, Kafka itself does allow messages to be sorted by time, but the message payload can include time. However, this specific use case does not warrant this usage.

Figure 3.3 shows how a user would generate two audit events from a web administration console by sending a command to sensor 1 and another to sensor 3. Both commands should end up as separate events in Kafka. To make this a little clearer, table 3.2 presents a rough checklist of things we should consider regarding data for each

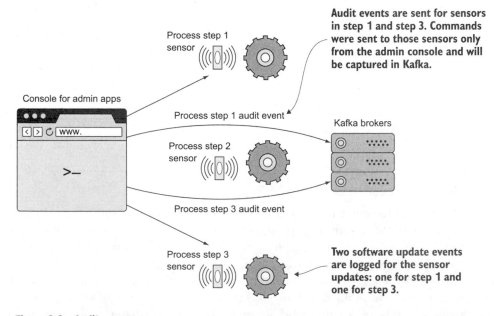

Figure 3.3   Audit use case

requirement. This at-a-glance view will help us when determining the configuration options we want to use for our producer clients.

In this audit producer, we are concerned with making sure that no data is lost and that consuming applications do not have any worries about data being ordered or coordinated. Furthermore, the alert trend of our status requirements deals with

Table 3.2 Audit checklist

Kafka feature	Concern?
Message loss	Yes
Grouping	No
Ordering	No
Last value only	No
Independent consumer	Yes

each process in the bike's system with a goal of spotting trends. It might be helpful to group this data using a key. We have not addressed the term *key* in depth, but it can be thought of as a way to group related events.

We will likely use the bikes' part ID names at each stage of the internal system where the sensor is installed because they will be unique from any other name. We want to be able to look across the key at all of the events for a given stage to spot these trends over time. By using the same key for each sensor, we should be able to consume these events easily. Because alert statuses are sent every 5 seconds, we are not concerned about missing a message, as the next one should arrive shortly. If a sensor sends a "Needs Maintenance" message every couple of days, that is the type of information we want to have to spot trends in equipment failure.

Figure 3.4 shows a sensor watching each stage of the process. Those equipment alert events go into Kafka. Although not an immediate concern for our system, Kafka does enable us to pull that data into other data storage or processing system like Hadoop.

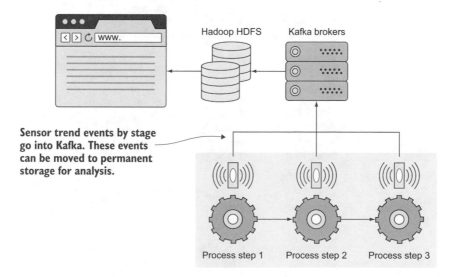

Figure 3.4 Alert trend use case

Table 3.3   Audit checklist

Kafka feature	Concern?
Message loss	No
Grouping	Yes
Ordering	No
Last value only	No
Independent consumer	Yes

Table 3.3 highlights that our goal is to group the alert results by stage and that we are not concerned about losing a message from time to time.

As for alerting on statuses, we also want to group by a key, which is the process stage. However, we do not care about past states of the sensor but rather the current status. In other words, the current status is all we care about and need for our requirements.

The new status replaces the old, and we do not need to maintain a history. The word *replace* here is not entirely correct (or not what we are used to thinking). Internally, Kafka adds the new event that it receives to the end of its log file like any other message it receives. After all, the log is immutable and can only be appended to at the end of the file. How does Kafka make what appears to be an update happen? It uses a process called *log compaction*, which we will dig into in chapter 7.

Another difference we have with this requirement is the consumer usage assigned to specific alert partitions. Critical alerts are processed first due to an uptime requirement in which those events need to be handled quickly. Figure 3.5 shows an example of how critical alerts could be sent to Kafka and then consumed to

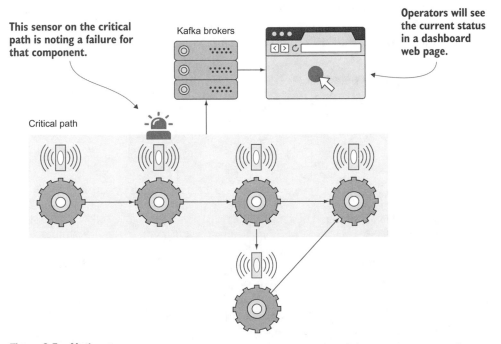

Figure 3.5   Alert use case

populate an operator's display to get attention quickly. Table 3.4 reinforces the idea that we want to group an alert to the stage it was created in and that we want to know the latest status only.

Taking the time to plan out our data requirements will not only help us clarify our application requirements but, hopefully, validate the use of Kafka in our design.

Table 3.4   Audit checklist

Kafka feature	Concern?
Message loss	No
Grouping	Yes
Ordering	No
Last value only	Yes
Independent consumer	No

3.2.6   *Reviewing our blueprint*

One of the last things to think about is how we want to keep these groups of data organized. Logically, the groups of data can be thought of in the following manner:

- Audit data
- Alert trend data
- Alert data

For those of you already jumping ahead, keep in mind that we might use our alert trend data as a starting point for our alerts topic; you can use one topic as the starting point to populate another topic. However, to start our design, we will write each event type from the sensors to their logical topic to make our first attempt uncomplicated and easy to follow. In other words, all audit events end up on an audit topic, all alert trend events end up on a alert trend topic, and our alert events on an alert topic. This one-to-one mapping makes it easier to focus on the requirements at hand for the time being.

3.3   *Format of your data*

One of the easiest things to skip, but critical to cover in our design, is the format of our data. XML and JSON are pretty standard formats that help define some sort of structure to our data. However, even with a clear syntax format, there can be information missing in our data. What is the meaning of the first column or the third one? What is the data type of the field in the second column of a file? The knowledge of how to parse or analyze our data can be hidden in applications that repeatedly pull the data from its storage location. Schemas are a means of providing some of this needed information in a way that can be used by our code or by other applications that may need the same data.

If you look at the Kafka documentation, you may have noticed references to another serialization system called Apache Avro. Avro provides schema definition support as well as schema storage in Avro files [6]. In our opinion, Avro is likely what you will see in Kafka code that you might encounter in the real world and why we will focus on this choice out of all the available options. Let's take a closer look at why this format is commonly used in Kafka.

3.3.1   *Plan for data*

One of the significant gains of using Kafka is that the producers and consumers are not tied directly to each other. Further, Kafka does not do any data validation by default. However, there is likely a need for each process or application to understand what that data means and what format is in use. By using a schema, we provide a way for our application's developers to understand the structure and intent of the data. The definition doesn't have to be posted in a README file for others in the organization to determine data types or to try to reverse-engineer from data dumps.

Listing 3.8 shows an example of an Avro schema defined as JSON. Fields can be created with details such as name, type, and any default values. For example, looking at the field `daysOverDue`, the schema tells us that the days a book is overdue is an `int` with a default value of `0`. Knowing that this value is numeric and not text (such as one week) helps to create a clear contract for the data producers and consumers.

Listing 3.8   Avro schema example

```
{
    "type" : "record",                          ←    JSON-defined
    "name" : "kinaction_libraryCheckout",            Avro schema
    ...
    "fields" : [{"name" : "materialName",
                 "type" : "string",
                 "default" : ""},
                                                      Maps directly
                                                      to a field name
           {"name" : "daysOverDue",            ←
Defines a field     "type" : "int",
with a name, type,   "default" : 0},           ←    Provides the
and default value                                    default value
              {"name" : "checkoutDate",
               "type" : "int",
               "logicalType": "date",
               "default" : "-1"},

              {"name" : "borrower",
               "type" : {
                   "type" : "record",
                   "name" : "borrowerDetails",
                   "fields" : [
                      {"name" : "cardNumber",
                       "type" : "string",
                       "default" : "NONE"}
                   ]},
                   "default" : {}
              }
        ]
}
```

By looking at the example of the Avro schema in listing 3.8, we can see that questions such as "Do we parse the `cardNumber` as a number or a string (in this case, `string`)" are easily answered by a developer looking at the schema. Applications could automatically use this information to generate data objects for this data, which helps to avoid parsing data type errors.

Schemas can be used by tools like Apache Avro to handle data that evolves. Most of us have dealt with altered statements or tools like Liquibase to work around these changes in relational databases. With schemas, we start with the knowledge that our data will probably change.

Do we need a schema when we are first starting with our data designs? One of the main concerns is that if our system's scale keeps getting larger, will we be able to control the correctness of data? The more consumers we have could lead to a burden on the testing that we would need to do. Besides the growth in numbers alone, we might not even know all of the consumers of that data.

3.3.2 *Dependency setup*

Now that we have discussed some of the advantages of using a schema, why would we look at Avro? First of all, Avro always is serialized with its schema [7]. Although not a schema itself, Avro supports schemas when reading and writing data and can apply rules to handle schemas that change over time. Also, if you have ever seen JSON, it is pretty easy to understand Avro. Besides the data, the schema language itself is defined in JSON as well. If the schema changes, you can still process data [7]. The old data uses the schema that existed as part of its data. On the other hand, any new formats will use the schema present in their data. Clients are the ones who gain the benefit of using Avro.

Another benefit of looking at Avro is the popularity of its usage. We first saw it used on various Hadoop efforts, but it can be used in many other applications. Confluent also has built-in support for most parts of their tooling [6]. Bindings exist for many programming languages and should not be hard to find, in general. Those who have past "bad" experiences and prefer to avoid generated code can use Avro dynamically without code generation.

Let's get started with using Avro by adding it to our pom.xml file as the following listing shows [8]. If you are not used to pom.xml or Maven, you can find this file in our project's root directory.

> **Listing 3.9 Adding Avro to pom.xml**

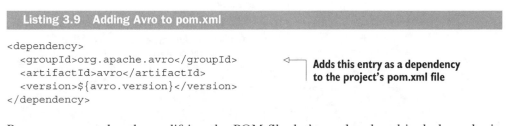

```
<dependency>
  <groupId>org.apache.avro</groupId>         Adds this entry as a dependency
  <artifactId>avro</artifactId>              to the project's pom.xml file
  <version>${avro.version}</version>
</dependency>
```

Because we are already modifying the POM file, let's go ahead and include a plugin that generates the Java source code for our schema definitions. As a side note, you can also generate the sources from a standalone Java JAR, avro-tools, if you do not want to use a Maven plugin. For those who do not prefer code generation in their source code projects, this is not a hard requirement [9].

Listing 3.10 shows how to add the avro-maven-plugin to our pom.xml as suggested by the Apache Avro Getting Started with Java documentation site [8]. The code in this listing omits the configuration XML block. Adding the needed configuration also lets Maven know that we want to generate source code for the Avro files found in the source directory we list and to output the generated code to the specified output directory. If you like, you can change the source and output locations to match your specific project structure.

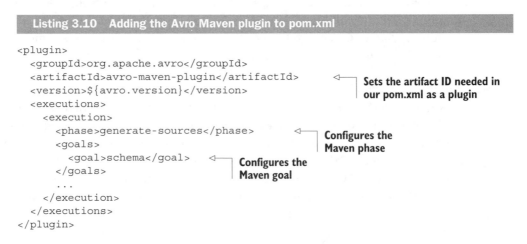

Listing 3.10 Adding the Avro Maven plugin to pom.xml

```
<plugin>
  <groupId>org.apache.avro</groupId>
  <artifactId>avro-maven-plugin</artifactId>        Sets the artifact ID needed in
  <version>${avro.version}</version>                 our pom.xml as a plugin
  <executions>
    <execution>
      <phase>generate-sources</phase>      Configures the
      <goals>                              Maven phase
        <goal>schema</goal>      Configures the
      </goals>                   Maven goal
      ...
    </execution>
  </executions>
</plugin>
```

Let's start defining our schema by thinking about the data types we want to use, beginning with our alert status scenario. To start, we'll create a new file named kinaction _alert.avsc with a text editor. The following listing shows the schema definition. We will name our Java class `Alert` as we will interact with it after the generation of source code from this file.

Listing 3.11 Alert schema: kinaction_alert.avsc

```
{
  ...
  "type": "record",           Names the
  "name": "Alert",            created Java class
  "fields": [                   Defines the data types and
    {                           documentation notes
      "name": "sensor_id",
      "type": "long",
      "doc": "The unique id that identifies the sensor"
    },
    {
      "name": "time",
      "type": "long",
      "doc":
        "Time alert generated as UTC milliseconds from epoch"
    },
    {
```

```
      "name": "status",
      "type": {
        "type": "enum",
        "name": "AlertStatus",
        "symbols": [
          "Critical",
          "Major",
          "Minor",
          "Warning"
        ]
      },
      "doc":
        "Allowed values sensors use for current status"
    }
  ]
}
```

In listing 3.11, which shows a definition of alerts, one thing to note is that `"doc"` is not a required part of the definition. However, there is certainly value in adding details that will help future producer or consumer developers understand what the data means. The hope is to stop others from inferring our data's meaning and to be more explicit about the content. For example, the field `"time"` always seems to invoke developer anxiety when seen. Is it stored in a string format? Is time zone information included? Does it include leap seconds? The `"doc"` field can provide that information. A namespace field, not shown in listing 3.11, turns into the Java package for the generated Java class. You can view the full example in the source code for the book. The various field definitions include the name as well as a type.

Now that we have the schema defined, let's run the Maven build to see what we are working with. The commands `mvn generate-sources` or `mvn install` can generate the sources in our project. This should give us a couple of classes, `Alert.java` and `AlertStatus.java`, that we can now use in our examples.

Although we have focused on Avro itself, the remaining part of the setup is related to the changes we need to make in our producer and consumer clients to use the schema that we created. We can always define our own serializer for Avro, but we already have an excellent example provided by Confluent. Access to the existing classes is accomplished by adding the `kafka-avro-serializer` dependency to our build [10]. The following listing shows the pom.xml entry that we'll add. This is needed to avoid having to create our own Avro serializer and deserializer for the keys and values of our events.

Listing 3.12   Adding the Kafka serializer to pom.xml

```
<dependency>
    <groupId>io.confluent</groupId>
    <artifactId>kafka-avro-serializer</artifactId>      ◁─┐  Adds this entry as a dependency
    <version>${confluent.version}</version>                │  in the project's pom.xml file
</dependency>
```

If you are using Maven to follow along, make sure that you place the Confluent repository in your pom file. This information is needed to let Maven know where to get specific dependencies [11].

```
<repository>
    <id>confluent</id>
    <url>https://packages.confluent.io/maven/</url>
</repository>
```

With the build set up and our Avro object ready to use, let's take our example producer, `HelloWorldProducer`, from the last chapter and slightly modify the class to use Avro. Listing 3.13 shows the pertinent changes to the producer class (not including imports). Notice the use of `io.confluent.kafka.serializers.KafkaAvroSerializer` as the value of the property `value.serializer`. This handles the `Alert` object that we created and sent to our new `kinaction_schematest` topic.

Before, we could use a string serializer, but with Avro, we need to define a specific value serializer to tell the client how to deal with our data. The use of an `Alert` object rather than a string shows how we can utilize types in our applications as long as we can serialize them. This example also makes use of the Schema Registry. We will cover more details about the Schema Registry in chapter 11. This registry can have a versioned history of schemas to help us manage schema evolution.

Listing 3.13   Producer using Avro serialization

```
public class HelloWorldProducer {

  static final Logger log =
    LoggerFactory.getLogger(HelloWorldProducer.class);

  public static void main(String[] args) {
    Properties kaProperties = new Properties();
    kaProperties.put("bootstrap.servers",
      "localhost:9092,localhost:9093,localhost:9094");
    kaProperties.put("key.serializer",
      "org.apache.kafka.common.serialization.LongSerializer");
    kaProperties.put("value.serializer",                         ◁──  Sets value.serializer to
      "io.confluent.kafka.serializers.KafkaAvroSerializer");         the KafkaAvroSerializer
    kaProperties.put("schema.registry.url",                          class for our custom
      "http://localhost:8081");                                      Alert value

    try (Producer<Long, Alert> producer =
      new KafkaProducer<>(kaProperties)) {
      Alert alert =
        new Alert(12345L,
          Instant.now().toEpochMilli(),        Creates a
          Critical);                     ◁──   critical alert

      log.info("kinaction_info Alert -> {}", alert);
```

```
    ProducerRecord<Long, Alert> producerRecord =
        new ProducerRecord<>("kinaction_schematest",
                              alert.getSensorId(),
                              alert);

    producer.send(producerRecord);
    }
  }
}
```

The differences are pretty minor. The type changes for our `Producer` and `Producer-Record` definitions, as do the configuration settings for the `value.serializer`.

Now that we have produced messages using `Alert`, the other changes would be on the consumption side of the messages. For a consumer to get the values produced to our new topic, it will have to use a value deserializer; in this case, `KafkaAvroDeserializer` [10]. This deserializer works to get back the value that was serialized by the producer. This code can also reference the same `Alert` class generated in the project. The following listing shows the significant changes for the consumer class `HelloWorldConsumer`.

Listing 3.14 Consumer using Avro serialization

```
public class HelloWorldConsumer {

  final static Logger log =
    LoggerFactory.getLogger(HelloWorldConsumer.class);

  private volatile boolean keepConsuming = true;

  public static void main(String[] args) {
    Properties kaProperties = new Properties();
    kaProperties.put("bootstrap.servers", "localhost:9094");
    ...
    kaProperties.put("key.deserializer",
      "org.apache.kafka.common.serialization.LongDeserializer");
    kaProperties.put("value.deserializer",
      "io.confluent.kafka.serializers.KafkaAvroDeserializer");    ◁——
    kaProperties.put("schema.registry.url", "http://localhost:8081");

    HelloWorldConsumer helloWorldConsumer = new HelloWorldConsumer();
    helloWorldConsumer.consume(kaProperties);

    Runtime.getRuntime()
      .addShutdownHook(
        new Thread(helloWorldConsumer::shutdown)
      );
  }

  private void consume(Properties kaProperties) {

    try (KafkaConsumer<Long, Alert> consumer =    ◁——
      new KafkaConsumer<>(kaProperties)) {
      consumer.subscribe(
```

Sets value.serializer to the KafkaAvroSerializer class due to the Alert usage

KafkaConsumer typed to handle Alert values

```
      List.of("kinaction_schematest")
    );

    while (keepConsuming) {
      ConsumerRecords<Long, Alert> records =
        consumer.poll(Duration.ofMillis(250));        ⟵┐ Updates ConsumerRecord
      for (ConsumerRecord<Long, Alert> record :        ⟵┘ to handle Alert values
        records) {
          log.info("kinaction_info offset = {}, kinaction_value = {}",
            record.offset(),
            record.value());
      }
    }
  }
}

  private void shutdown() {
    keepConsuming = false;
  }
}
```

As with the producer, the consumer client does not require many changes due to the power of updating the configuration deserializer and Avro! Now that we have some ideas about the *what* we want to accomplish and our data format, we are well equipped to tackle the *how* in our next chapter. We will cover more schema-related topics in chapter 11 and move on to a different way to handle our object types in the example project in chapters 4 and 5. Although the task of sending data to Kafka is straightforward, there are various configuration-driven behaviors that we can use to help us satisfy our specific requirements.

Summary

- Designing a Kafka solution involves understanding our data first. These details include how we need to handle data loss, ordering of messages, and grouping in our use cases.

- The need to group data determines whether we will key the messages in Kafka.

- Leveraging schema definitions not only helps us generate code, but it also helps us handle future data changes. Additionally, we can use these schemas with our own custom Kafka clients.

- Kafka Connect provides existing connectors to write to and from various data sources.

References

1 J. MSV. "Apache Kafka: The Cornerstone of an Internet-of-Things Data Platform" (February 15, 2017). https://thenewstack.io/apache-kafka-cornerstone -iot-data-platform/ (accessed August 10, 2017).

2 "Quickstart." Confluent documentation (n.d.). https://docs.confluent.io/ 3.1.2/connect/quickstart.html (accessed November 22, 2019).

3 "JDBC Source Connector for Confluent Platform." Confluent documentation (n.d.). https://docs.confluent.io/kafka-connect-jdbc/current/source-connector/index.html (accessed October 15, 2021).

4 "Running Kafka in Production: Memory." Confluent documentation (n.d.). https://docs.confluent.io/platform/current/kafka/deployment.html#memory (accessed June 16, 2021).

5 "Download." Apache Software Foundation (n.d.). https://kafka.apache.org/downloads (accessed November 21, 2019).

6 J. Kreps. "Why Avro for Kafka Data?" Confluent blog (February 25, 2015). https://www.confluent.io/blog/avro-kafka-data/ (accessed November 23, 2017).

7 "Apache Avro 1.8.2 Documentation." Apache Software Foundation (n.d.). https://avro.apache.org/docs/1.8.2/index.html (accessed November 19, 2019).

8 "Apache Avro 1.8.2 Getting Started (Java)): Serializing and deserializing without code generation." Apache Software Foundation (n.d.). https://avro.apache.org/docs/1.8.2/gettingstartedjava.html#download_install (accessed November 19, 2019).

9 "Apache Avro 1.8.2 Getting Started (Java): Serializing and deserializing without code generation." Apache Software Foundation (n.d.). https://avro.apache.org/docs/1.8.2/gettingstartedjava.html#Serializing+and+deserializing+without+code+generation (accessed November 19, 2019).

10 "Application Development: Java." Confluent documentation (n.d.). https://docs.confluent.io/platform/current/app-development/index.html#java (accessed November 20, 2019).

11 "Installation: Maven repository for jars." Confluent documentation (n.d.). https://docs.confluent.io/3.1.2/installation.html#maven-repository-for-jars (accessed November 20, 2019).

Producers: Sourcing data 4

This chapters covers

- Sending messages and the producer
- Creating our own producer serializers and partitioners
- Examining configuration options to solve a company's requirements

In the previous chapter, we looked at the requirements that an organization might have regarding their data. Some design decisions we made have practical impacts on how we send data to Kafka. Let's now enter the world of an event-streaming platform through the portal gate of a Kafka producer. After reading this chapter, you will be well on your way to solving fundamental requirements of a Kafka project by producing data in a couple of different ways.

The producer, despite its importance, is only one part of this system. In fact, we can change some producer configuration options or set these at the broker or topic level. We will discover those options as we get further along, but getting data into Kafka is our first concern in this chapter.

4.1 An example

The producer provides the way to push data into the Kafka system for our example project. As a refresher, figure 4.1 illustrates where producers fit into Kafka.

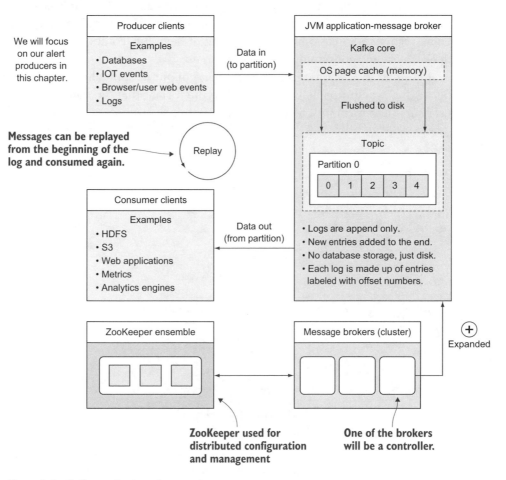

Figure 4.1 Kafka producers

Looking at figure 4.1, let's focus on the top-left corner (the producer clients), which shows examples of data being produced into Kafka. This data could be the IoT events we are using in our fictional company. To make the idea of producing data more concrete, let's imagine a practical example that we might have written for one of our projects. Let's look at an application that takes user feedback on how a website is working for its customers.

Currently, the user submits a form on the website that generates email to a support account or chatbot. Every now and then, one of our support staff checks the inbox to see what suggestions or issues customers have encountered. Looking to the future, we want to keep this information coming to us but in a way that allows the data to be more accessible than in an email inbox. If we instead send this message into a Kafka topic, we could produce more robust and varied replies, rather than just reactive email responses to customers. The benefit of flexibility comes from having the event in Kafka for any consuming applications to use.

Let's first look at what using email as part of our data pipeline impacts. Looking at figure 4.2, it might be helpful to focus on the format that the data is stored in once a user submits a form with feedback on our website.

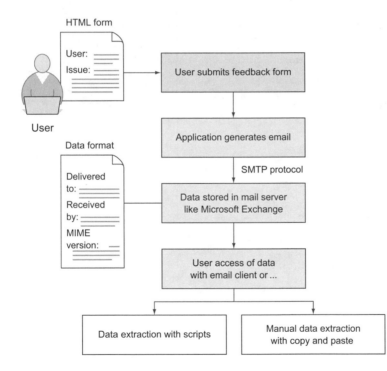

Figure 4.2   Sending data in email

A traditional email uses Simple Mail Transfer Protocol (SMTP), and we will see that reflected in how the email event itself is presented and sometimes stored. We can use email clients like Microsoft® Outlook® to retrieve the data quickly, but rather than just reading email, how else can we pull data out of that system for other uses? Copy and paste are common manual steps, as well as email-parsing scripts. (Parsing scripts includes using a tool or programming language and libraries or frameworks to get the parsing correct.) In comparison, although Kafka uses its own protocol, it does not impose any specific format for our message data. We should be able to write the data in whatever format we choose.

> **NOTE** In the previous chapter, we looked at the Apache Avro format as one of the common formats that the Kafka community uses. Protobuf and JSON are also widely popular [1].

Another usage pattern that comes to mind is to treat notifications of customer issues or website outages as temporary alerts that we can delete after replying to the customer. However, this customer input might serve more than one purpose. What if we are able to look for trends in outages that customers report? Does the site always slow to a crawl after sale coupon codes go out in mass-marketing emails? Could this data help us find features that our users are missing from our site? Do 40% of our user emails involve having trouble finding the Privacy settings for their account? Having this data present in a topic that can be replayed or read by several applications with different purposes can add more value to the customer than an automated support or bot email that is then deleted.

Also, if we have retention needs, those would be controlled by the teams running our email infrastructure versus a configuration setting we can control with Kafka. Looking again at figure 4.3, notice that the application has an HTML form but writes to a

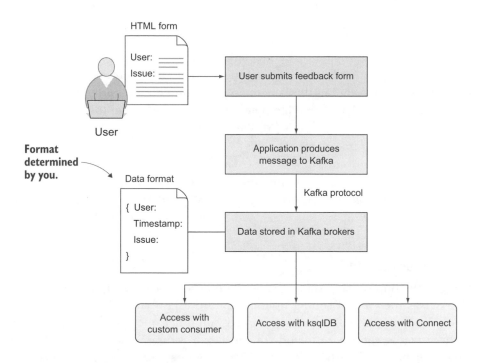

Figure 4.3 Sending data to Kafka

Kafka topic, not to an email server. With this approach, we can extract the information that is important for us in whatever format we need, and it can be used in many ways. Consuming applications can use schemes to work with the data and not be tied to a single protocol format. We can retain and reprocess these messages for new use cases because we control the retention of those events. Now that we have looked at why we might use a producer, let's quickly check out some details of a producer interacting with the Kafka brokers.

4.1.1 Producer notes

The producer's job includes fetching metadata about the cluster [2]. Because producers can only write to the replica leader of the partition they are assigned to, the metadata helps the producer determine which broker to write to as the user might have only included a topic name without any other details. This is nice because the producer's end user does not have to make a separate call to get that information. The end user, however, needs to have at least one running broker to connect to, and the Java client library figures out the rest.

Because this distributed system is designed to account for momentary errors such as a network blip, the logic for retries is already built in. However, if the ordering of the messages is essential, like for our audit messages, then besides setting the `retries` to a number like 3, we also need to set the `max.in.flight.requests.per.connection` value to `1` and set `acks` (the number of brokers that send acknowledgments back) to all [3] [4]. In our opinion, this is one of the safest methods to ensure that your producer's messages arrive in the order you intend [4]. We can set the values for both `acks` and `retries` as configuration parameters.

Another option to be aware of is using an idempotent producer. The term *idempotent* refers to how sending the same message multiple times only results in producing the message once. To use an idempotent producer, we can set the configuration property `enable.idempotence=true` [5]. We will not be using the idempotent producer in our following examples.

One thing we do not have to worry about is one producer getting in the way of another producer's data. Thread safety is not an issue because data will not be overwritten but handled by the broker itself and appended to the broker's log [6]. Now it is time to look at how to enable the values like `max.in.flight.requests.per.connection` in code.

4.2 Producer options

One of the things that was interesting when we started working with sending data into Kafka was the ease of setting options using the Java clients that we will specifically focus on in this book. If you have worked with other queue or messaging systems, the other systems' setups can include things like providing remote and local queues lists, manager hostnames, starting connections, connection factories, sessions, and more.

Although far from being set up totally hassle free, the producer works from the configuration on its own to retrieve much of the information it needs, such as a list of all of our Kafka brokers. Using the value from the property bootstrap.servers as a starting point, the producer fetches metadata about brokers and partitions that it uses for all subsequent writes.

As mentioned earlier, Kafka allows you to change key behaviors just by changing some configuration values. One way to deal with all of the producer configuration key names is to use the constants provided in the Java class ProducerConfig when developing producer code (see http://mng.bz/ZYdA) and by looking for the Importance label of "high" in the Confluent website [7]. However, in our examples, we will use the property names themselves for clarity.

Table 4.1 lists some of the most crucial producer configurations that support our specific examples. In the following sections, we'll look at what we need to complete our factory work.

Table 4.1 Important producer configurations

Key	Purpose
acks	Number of replica acknowledgments that a producer requires before success is established
bootstrap.servers	One or more Kafka brokers to connect for startup
value.serializer	The class that's used for serialization of the value
key.serializer	The class that's used for serialization of the key

4.2.1 Configuring the broker list

From our examples of writing messages to Kafka, it is clear that we have to tell the producer which topic to send messages to. Recall that topics are made up of partitions, but how does Kafka know where a topic partition resides? We, however, do not have to know the details of those partitions when we send messages. Perhaps an illustration will help clarify this conundrum. One of the required configuration options for producers is bootstrap.servers. Figure 4.4 shows an example of a producer that has only broker 0 in its list of bootstrap servers, but it will be able to learn about all three brokers in the cluster by starting with one only.

The bootstrap.servers property can take many or just one initial broker as in figure 4.4. By connecting to this broker, the client can discover the metadata it needs, which includes data about other brokers in the cluster as well [8].

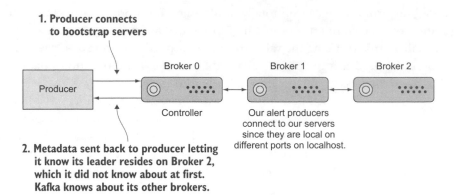

1. **Producer connects to bootstrap servers**

Broker 0   Broker 1   Broker 2

Producer

Controller

Our alert producers connect to our servers since they are local on different ports on localhost.

2. **Metadata sent back to producer letting it know its leader resides on Broker 2, which it did not know about at first. Kafka knows about its other brokers.**

Figure 4.4   Bootstrap servers

This configuration is key to helping the producer find a broker to talk to. Once the producer is connected to the cluster, it can obtain the metadata it needs to get the details (such as where the leader replica for the partition resides on disk) we did not previously provide. Producer clients can also overcome a failure of the partition leader they are writing to by using the information about the cluster to find a new leader. You might have noticed that ZooKeeper's information is not part of the configuration. Any metadata the producer needs will be handled without the producer client having to provide ZooKeeper cluster details.

4.2.2   *How to go fast (or go safer)*

Asynchronous message patterns are one reason that many use queue-type systems, and this powerful feature is also available in Kafka. We can wait in our code for the result of a producer send request, or we can handle success or failure asynchronously with callbacks or Future objects. If we want to go faster and not wait for a reply, we can still handle the results at a later time with our own custom logic.

Another configuration property that applies to our scenario is the acks key, which stands for *acknowledgments*. This controls how many acknowledgments the producer needs to receive from the partition leader's followers before it returns a completed request. The valid values for this property are all, -1, 1, and 0 [9].

Figure 4.5 shows how a message with ack set to 0 behaves. Setting this value to 0 will probably get us the lowest latency but at the cost of safety. Additionally, guarantees are not made if any broker receives the message and, also, retries are not attempted [9]. As a sample use case, say that we have a web-tracking platform that collects the clicks on a page and sends these events to Kafka. In this situation, it might not be a big deal to lose a single link press or hover event. If one is lost, there is no real business impact.

In essence, the event in figure 4.5 was sent from the producer and forgotten. The message might have never made it to the partition. If the message did, by chance, make it to the leader replica, the producer will not know if any follower replica copies were successful.

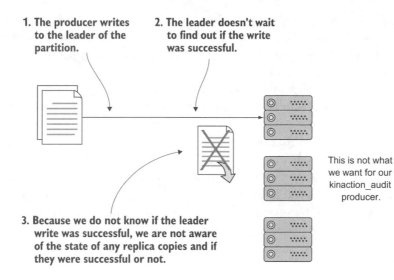

1. The producer writes to the leader of the partition.

2. The leader doesn't wait to find out if the write was successful.

This is not what we want for our kinaction_audit producer.

3. Because we do not know if the leader write was successful, we are not aware of the state of any replica copies and if they were successful or not.

Figure 4.5 The property `acks` **equals** 0.

What we would consider the opposite setting to that used previously would be `acks` with values `all` or `-1`. The values `all` or `-1` are the strongest available option for this configuration setting. Figure 4.6 shows how the value `all` means that a partition leader's replica waits on the entire list of its in-sync replicas (ISRs) to acknowledge completion [9]. In other words, the producer will not get an acknowledgment of success until after all replicas for a partition are successful. It is easy to see that it won't be the quickest due to the dependencies it has on other brokers. In many cases, it is

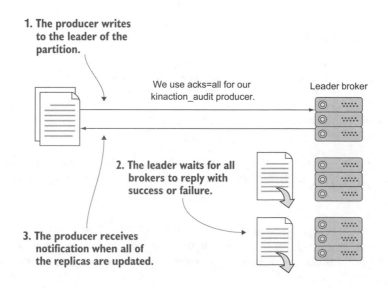

1. The producer writes to the leader of the partition.

We use acks=all for our kinaction_audit producer.

Leader broker

2. The leader waits for all brokers to reply with success or failure.

3. The producer receives notification when all of the replicas are updated.

Figure 4.6 The property `acks` **equals** `all`.

worth paying the performance price in order to prevent data loss. With many brokers in a cluster, we need to be aware of the number of brokers the leader has to wait on. The broker that takes the longest to reply is the determining factor for how long until a producer receives a success message.

Figure 4.7 shows the impact of setting the `acks` value to `1` and asking for an acknowledgment. An acknowledgment involves the receiver of the message (the leader replica of the specific partition) sending confirmation back to the producer. The producer client waits for that acknowledgment. However, the followers might not have copied the message before a failure brings down the leader. If that situation occurs before a copy is made, the message never appears on the replica followers for that partition [9]. Figure 4.7 shows that while the message was acknowledged by the leader replica and sent to the producer, a failure of any replica to make a copy of the message would appear as if the message never made it to the cluster.

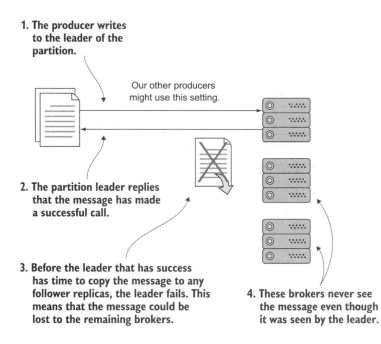

1. The producer writes to the leader of the partition.

Our other producers might use this setting.

2. The partition leader replies that the message has made a successful call.

3. Before the leader that has success has time to copy the message to any follower replicas, the leader fails. This means that the message could be lost to the remaining brokers.

4. These brokers never see the message even though it was seen by the leader.

Figure 4.7　The property `acks` equals `1`.

> **NOTE**　This is closely related to the ideas of at-most and at-least semantics that we covered in chapter 1 [10]. The `acks` setting is a part of that larger picture.

4.2.3　*Timestamps*

Recent versions of the producer record contain a timestamp on the events you send. A user can either pass the time into the constructor as a Java type `long` when sending a `ProducerRecord` Java object or the current system time. The actual time that is used in the message can stay as this value, or it can be a broker timestamp that occurs when the message is logged. Setting the topic configuration `message.timestamp.type` to `CreateTime` uses the time set by the client, whereas setting it to `LogAppendTime` uses the broker time [11].

Why would you want to choose one over the other? You might want to use the created time in order to have the time that a transaction (like a sales order) takes place rather than when it made its way to the broker. Using the broker time can be useful when the created time is handled inside the message itself or an actual event time is not business or order relevant.

As always, timestamps can be tricky. For example, we might get a record with an earlier timestamp than that of a record before it. This can happen in cases where a failure occurred and a different message with a later timestamp was committed before the retry of the first record completed. The data is ordered in the log by offsets and not by timestamp. Although reading timestamped data is often thought of as a consumer client concern, it is also a producer concern because the producer takes the first steps in ensuring message order.

As discussed earlier, this is also why `max.in.flight.requests.per.connection` is important when considering whether you want to allow retries or many inflight requests at a time. If a retry happens and other requests succeed on their first attempt, earlier messages might be added after the later ones. Figure 4.8 provides an example of when a message can get out of order. Even though message 1 was sent first, it does not make it into the log in an ordered manner because retries were enabled.

As a reminder, with Kafka versions before 0.10, timestamp information is not available as that feature was not included in earlier releases. We can still include a timestamp, though, but we would need to store it in the value of the message itself.

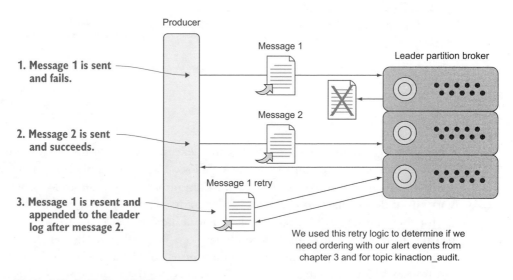

Figure 4.8   Retry impact on order

Another option when using a producer is to create producer interceptors. These were introduced in KIP-42 (Kafka Improvement Proposal). Its main goal was to help support measuring and monitoring [12]. In comparison to using a Kafka Streams workflow to filter or aggregate data, or even creating different topics specifically for modified data, the usage of these interceptors might not be our first choice. At present, there are no default interceptors that run in the life cycle. In chapter 9, we will show a use case for tracing messages from producer clients to consumer clients with interceptors adding a trace ID.

4.3   Generating code for our requirements

Let's try to use the information we gathered about how producers work on our own solutions. We'll start with the audit checklist that we designed in chapter 3 for use with Kafka in our e-bike factory. As noted in chapter 3, we want to make sure that we do not lose any audit messages when operators complete commands against the sensors. One requirement was that there was no need to correlate (or group together) any events. Another requirement was to make sure we don't lose any messages. The following listing shows how we would start our producer configuration and how to make sure that we are safe for message acknowledgment by setting `acks` to `all`.

Listing 4.1   Configuring the audit producer

```
public class AuditProducer {
                                                    Creates properties as before
...                                                   for our configuration
private static final Logger log = LoggerFactory.getLogger
(AuditProducer.class);Properties kaProperties = new Properties();  <-

kaProperties.put( "bootstrap.servers",
   "localhost:9092,localhost:9093,localhost:9094");    Sets acks to all to get
kaProperties.put("acks", "all");                   <-  the strongest guarantee
kaProperties.put("retries", "3");                  <-
kaProperties.put("max.in.flight.requests.per.connection", "1");
...
                                                    Lets the client retry in case of
                                                    failure so we don't have to
                                                    implement our own failure logic
```

Notice that we did not have to touch anything except the configuration we send to the producer to address the concern of message loss. The `acks` configuration change is a small but powerful feature that has a significant impact on if a message arrives or not. Because we do not have to correlate (group) any events together, we are not using a key for these messages. However, there is a foundational part that we want to change in order to wait for the result before moving on. The following listing shows the `get` method, which is how we can bring about waiting for the response to complete synchronously before moving on in the code. Note that the following listing was informed by examples located at: https://docs.confluent.io/2.0.0/clients/producer .html#examples.

Listing 4.2 Waiting for a result

```
RecordMetadata result =                              Waits on the response
  producer.send(producerRecord).get();              from the send call
log.info("kinaction_info offset = {}, topic = {}, timestamp = {}",
        result.offset(), result.topic(), result.timestamp());
  producer.close();
```

Waiting on the response directly in a synchronous way ensures that the code is handling each record's results as they come back before another message is sent. The focus is on delivering the messages without loss, more than on speed!

So far, we have used a couple of prebuilt serializers in earlier chapters. For plain text messages, our producer uses a serializer called `StringSerializer`. And when we talked about Avro in chapter 3, we reached for the class `io.confluent.kafka` `.serializers.KafkaAvroSerializer`. But what if we have a specific format we want to produce? This often happens when trying to work with custom objects. We'll use serialization to translate data into a format that can be transmitted, stored, and then retrieved to achieve a clone of our original data. The following listing shows the code for our `Alert` class.

Listing 4.3 `Alert` class

```
public class Alert implements Serializable {

  private final int alertId;
  private String stageId;
  private final String alertLevel;
  private final String alertMessage;

  public Alert(int alertId,
    String stageId,
    String alertLevel,              Holds the alert's ID,
    String alertMessage) {          level, and messages

    this.alertId = alertId;
    this.stageId = stageId;
    this.alertLevel = alertLevel;
    this.alertMessage = alertMessage;
  }

  public int getAlertId() {
    return alertId;
  }

  public String getStageId() {
    return stageId;
  }
```

```
    public void setStageId(String stageId) {
      this.stageId = stageId;
    }

  public String getAlertLevel() {
    return alertLevel;
  }

  public String getAlertMessage() {
    return alertMessage;
  }
}
```

Listing 4.3 shows code that we use to create a bean named `Alert` to hold the information we want to send. Those familiar with Java will notice that the listing is nothing more than getters and setters and a constructor for the `Alert` class. Now that there is a format for the `Alert` data object, it is time to use it in making a simple alert `Serializer` called `AlertKeySerde` as the following listing shows.

Listing 4.4   Our `Alert` serializer

```
public class AlertKeySerde implements Serializer<Alert>,
                                       Deserializer<Alert> {

  public byte[] serialize(String topic, Alert key) {     ◁─┐ Sends the topic and the
    if (key == null) {                                      │ Alert object to our method
      return null;
    }
    return key.getStageId()
      .getBytes(StandardCharsets.UTF_8);     ◁─┐ Converts objects to
  }                                             │ bytes (our end goal)

  public Alert deserialize
    (String topic, byte[] value) {            ◁─┐ The rest of the interface methods do
    //could return Alert in future if needed    │ not need any logic at this point.
    return null;
  }

  //...
}
```

In listing 4.5, we use this custom class only as the key serializer for the moment, leaving the value serializer as a `StringSerializer`. It is interesting to note that we can serialize keys and values with different serializers on the same message. But we should be mindful of our intended serializers and the configuration values for both. The code implements the `Serializer` interface and only pulls out the field `stageId` to use as a key for our message. This example should be straightforward because the focus is on the technique of using a serde. Other options for serdes that are often used are JSON and Avro implementations.

> **NOTE** If you see or hear the term *serde*, it means that the serializer and deserializer are both handled by the same implementation of that interface [13].

However, it is still common to see each interface defined separately. Just watch when you use `StringSerializer` versus `StringDeserializer`; the difference can be hard to spot!

Another thing to keep in mind is that knowing how to deserialize the values involves the consumers in relation to how the values were serialized by the producer. Some sort of agreement or coordinator is needed for the data formats for clients even though Kafka does not care what data it stores on the brokers.

Another goal of our design for the factory was to capture the alert trend status of our stages to track their alerts over time. Because we care about the information for each stage (and not all sensors at a time), it might be helpful to think of how we are going to group these events. In this case, as each stage ID is unique, it makes sense that we can use that ID as a key. The following listing shows the `key.serializer` property that we'll set, as well as sending a `CRITICAL` alert.

Listing 4.5 Alert trending producer

```java
public class AlertTrendingProducer {

  private static final Logger log =
      LoggerFactory.getLogger(AlertTrendingProducer.class);

  public static void main(String[] args)
      throws InterruptedException, ExecutionException {

    Properties kaProperties = new Properties();
    kaProperties.put("bootstrap.servers",
      "localhost:9092,localhost:9093,localhost:9094");
    kaProperties.put("key.serializer",                    // Tells our producer client
      AlertKeySerde.class.getName());                     // how to serialize our custom
    kaProperties.put("value.serializer",                  // Alert object into a key
      "org.apache.kafka.common.serialization.StringSerializer");

    try (Producer<Alert, String> producer =
      new KafkaProducer<>(kaProperties)) {

      Alert alert = new Alert(0, "Stage 0", "CRITICAL", "Stage 0 stopped");
      ProducerRecord<Alert, String> producerRecord =
          new ProducerRecord<>("kinaction_alerttrend",
            alert, alert.getAlertMessage());

      RecordMetadata result = producer.send(producerRecord).get();
      log.info("kinaction_info offset = {}, topic = {}, timestamp = {}",
              result.offset(), result.topic(), result.timestamp());
    }
  }
}
```

Tells our producer client how to serialize our custom Alert object into a key

Instead of null for the second parameter, uses the actual object we want to populate the key

In general, the same key should produce the same partition assignment, and nothing will need to be changed. In other words, the same stage IDs (the keys) are grouped together just by using the correct key. We will keep an eye on the distribution of the size of the partitions to note if they become uneven in the future, but for now, we will go along with this. Also, note that for our specific classes that we created in the manuscript, we are setting the class properties in a different way to show a different option. Instead of hardcoding the entire path of the class, you can use something like `AlertKey-Serde.class.getName()` or even `AlertKeySerde.class` for the value of the property.

Our last requirement was to have alerts quickly processed to let operators know about any critical outages so we can group by the stage ID in this case as well. One reason for doing this is that we can tell if a sensor failed or recovered (any state change) by looking at only the last event for that stage ID. We do not care about the history of the status checks, only the current scenario. In this case, we also want to partition our alerts.

So far in our examples of writing to Kafka, the data was directed to a topic with no additional metadata provided from the client. Because the topics are made up of partitions that sit on the brokers, Kafka provides a default way to send messages to a specific partition. The default for a message with no key (which we used in the examples thus far) was a round-robin assignment strategy prior to Kafka version 2.4. In versions after 2.4, messages without keys use a sticky partition strategy [14]. However, sometimes we have specific ways that we want our data to be partitioned. One way to take control of this is to write our own unique partitioner class.

The client also has the ability to control what partition it writes to by configuring a unique partitioner. One example to think about is the alert levels from our sensor-monitoring service that was discussed in chapter 3. Some sensors' information might be more important than others; these might be on the critical path of our e-bike, which would cause downtime if not addressed. Let's say we have four levels of alerts: Critical, Major, Minor, and Warning. We could create a partitioner that places the different levels in different partitions. Our consumer clients would always make sure to read the critical alerts before processing the others.

If our consumers keep up with the messages being logged, critical alerts probably would not be a huge concern. However, listing 4.6 shows that we could change the partition assignment with a class to make sure that our critical alerts are directed to a specific partition (like partition 0). (Note that other alerts could end up on partition 0 as well due to our logic, but that critical alerts will always end up there.) The logic mirrors an example of the `DefaultPartitioner` used in Kafka itself [15].

Listing 4.6   Partitioner for alert levels

```
public int partition(final String topic                    ◁—— AlertLevelPartitioner needs
                     # ...                                      to implement the partition
                                                                method for its core logic.
    int criticalLevelPartition = findCriticalPartitionNumber(cluster, topic);
```

```
    return isCriticalLevel(((Alert) objectKey).getAlertLevel()) ?
      criticalLevelPartition :
        findRandomPartition(cluster, topic, objectKey);
}
//...
```

Critical alerts should end up the partition returned from findCriticalPartitionNumber

By implementing the `Partitioner` interface, we can use the `partition` method to send back the specific partition we want our producer to write to. In this case, the value of the key ensures that any `CRITICAL` event makes it to a specific place, partition 0 can be imagined to be sent back from the method `findCriticalPartitionNumber`, for example. In addition to creating the class itself, listing 4.7 shows how we need to set the configuration key, `partitioner.class`, for our producer to use the specific class we created. The configuration that powers Kafka is used to leverage our new class.

Listing 4.7 Configuring the `partitioner` class

```
Properties kaProperties = new Properties();
//...
kaProperties.put("partitioner.class",
        AlertLevelPartitioner.class.getName());
```

Updates the producer configuration to reference and use the custom partitioner AlertLevelPartitioner

This example, in which a specific partition number is always sent back, can be expanded on or made even more dynamic. We can use custom code to accomplish the specific logic of our business needs.

Listing 4.8 shows the configuration of the producer to add the `partitioner.class` value to use as our specific partitioner. The intention is for us to have the data available in a specific partition, so consumers that process the data can have access to the critical alerts specifically and can go after other alerts (in other partitions) when they are handled.

Listing 4.8 Alert producer

```
public class AlertProducer {
  public static void main(String[] args) {

    Properties kaProperties = new Properties();
    kaProperties.put("bootstrap.servers",
      "localhost:9092,localhost:9093");
    kaProperties.put("key.serializer",
      AlertKeySerde.class.getName());
    kaProperties.put("value.serializer",
      "org.apache.kafka.common.serialization.StringSerializer");
    kaProperties.put("partitioner.class",
      AlertLevelPartitioner.class.getName());

    try (Producer<Alert, String> producer =
      new KafkaProducer<>(kaProperties)) {
```

Reuses the Alert key serializer

Uses the property partitioner.class to set our specific partitioner class

```
        Alert alert = new Alert(1, "Stage 1", "CRITICAL", "Stage 1 stopped");
        ProducerRecord<Alert, String>
            producerRecord = new ProducerRecord<>
                ("kinaction_alert", alert, alert.getAlertMessage());

        producer.send(producerRecord,
                    new AlertCallback());
      }
    }
}
```

⟵ **This is the first time we've used a callback to handle the completion or failure of a send.**

One addition we see in listing 4.8 is how we added a callback to run on completion. Although we said that we are not 100% concerned with message failures from time to time, due to the frequency of events, we want to make sure that we do not see a high failure rate that could be a hint at application-related errors. The following listing shows an example of implementing a `Callback` interface. The callback would log a message only if an error occurs. Note that the following listing was informed by examples located at https://docs.confluent.io/2.0.0/clients/producer.html#examples.

Listing 4.9   Alert callback

```
public class AlertCallback implements Callback {
```
⟵ **Implements the Kafka Callback interface**
```
  private static final Logger log =
    LoggerFactory.getLogger(AlertCallback.class);

  public void onCompletion
    (RecordMetadata metadata,
     Exception exception) {
```
⟵ **The completion can have success or failure.**
```
    if (exception != null) {
      log.error("kinaction_error", exception);
    } else {
      log.info("kinaction_info offset = {}, topic = {}, timestamp = {}",
              metadata.offset(), metadata.topic(), metadata.timestamp());
    }
  }
}
```

Although we will focus on small samples in most of our material, we think that it is helpful to look at how to use a producer in a real project as well. As mentioned earlier, Apache Flume can be used alongside Kafka to provide various data features. When we use Kafka as a sink, Flume places data into Kafka. You might (or might not) be familiar with Flume, but we are not interested in its feature set for this. We want to see how it leverages Kafka producer code in a real situation.

In the following examples, we reference Flume version 1.8 (located at https://github.com/apache/flume/tree/flume-1.8, if you want to view more of the complete source code). The following listing shows a configuration snippet that would be used by a Flume agent.

Listing 4.10 Flume sink configuration

```
a1.sinks.k1.kafka.topic = kinaction_helloworld
a1.sinks.k1.kafka.bootstrap.servers = localhost:9092
a1.sinks.k1.kafka.producer.acks = 1
a1.sinks.k1.kafka.producer.compression.type = snappy
```

Some configuration properties from listing 4.10 seem familiar: `topic`, `acks`, `bootstrap.servers`. In our previous examples, we declared the configurations as properties inside our code. However, listing 4.10 shows an example of an application that externalizes the configuration values, which is something we could do on our projects as well. The `KafkaSink` source code from Apache Flume, found at http://mng.bz/JvpZ, provides an example of taking data and placing it inside Kafka with producer code. The following listing is a different example of a producer using a similar idea, taking a configuration file like that in listing 4.10 and loading those values into a producer instance.

Listing 4.11 Reading the Kafka producer configuration from a file

```
...
Properties kaProperties = readConfig();
String topic = kaProperties.getProperty("topic");
kaProperties.remove("topic");

try (Producer<String, String> producer =
                    new KafkaProducer<>(kaProperties)) {
  ProducerRecord<String, String> producerRecord =
    new ProducerRecord<>(topic, null, "event");
  producer.send(producerRecord,
            new AlertCallback());          ⟵┐ Our familiar producer.send
}                                           │  with a callback

private static Properties readConfig() {
  Path path = Paths.get("src/main/resources/kafkasink.conf");

  Properties kaProperties = new Properties();       ┐ Reads an external file
  try (Stream<String>  lines = Files.lines(path))  ⟵┘ for configuration
      lines.forEachOrdered(line ->
                    determineProperty(line, kaProperties));
  } catch (IOException e) {
    System.out.println("kinaction_error" + e);
  }
  return kaProperties;
}

private static void determineProperty           ┐ Parses configuration properties
  (String line, Properties kaProperties) {     ⟵┘ and sets those values
  if (line.contains("bootstrap")) {
    kaProperties.put("bootstrap.servers", line.split("=")[1]);
  } else if (line.contains("acks")) {
      kaProperties.put("acks", line.split("=")[1]);
  } else if (line.contains("compression.type")) {
    kaProperties.put("compression.type", line.split("=")[1]);
  } else if (line.contains("topic")) {
```

```
    kaProperties.put("topic", line.split("=")[1]);
  }
  ...
}
```

Although some code is omitted in listing 4.11, the core Kafka producer pieces might be starting to look familiar. Setting the configuration and the producer send method should all look like the code we wrote in this chapter. And now, hopefully, you have the confidence to dig into which configuration properties were set and what impacts they will have.

One exercise left for the reader would be to compare how AlertCallback.java stacks up to the Kafka Sink callback class SinkCallback, located in the source code at http://mng.bz/JvpZ. Both examples uses the RecordMetadata object to find more information about successful calls. This information can help us learn more about where the producer message was written, including the partition and offset within that specific partition.

It is true that you can use applications like Flume without ever having to dig into its source code and still be successful. However, we think that if you want to know what is going on internally or need to do some advanced troubleshooting, it is important to know what the tools are doing. With your new foundational knowledge of producers, it should be apparent that you can make powerful applications using these techniques yourself.

4.3.1   *Client and broker versions*

One important thing to note is that Kafka broker and client versions do not always have to match. If you are running a broker that is at Kafka version 0.10.0 and the Java producer client you are using is at 0.10.2, the broker will handle this upgrade in the message version [16]. However, because you can does not mean you should do it in all cases. To dig into more of the bidirectional version compatibility, take a peek at KIP-97 (http://mng.bz/7jAQ).

We crossed a significant hurdle by starting to get data into Kafka. Now that we are deeper into the Kafka ecosystem, we have other concepts to conquer before we are done with our end-to-end solution. The next question is, how can we start to pull this data back out so our other applications can consume it? We now have some ideas about *how* we get data into Kafka, so we can start to work on learning more about making that data useful to other applications by getting it out in the correct ways. Consumer clients are a vital part of this discovery and, as with producers, there are various configuration-driven behaviors that we can use to help us satisfy different requirements for consumption.

Summary

- Producer clients provide developers a way to get data into Kafka.
- A large number of configuration options are available to control client behavior without custom code.

- Data is stored on the brokers in what is known as partitions.
- The client can control which partition the data gets written to by providing their own logic with the `Partitioner` interface.
- Kafka generally sees data as a series of bytes. However, custom serializers can be used to deal with specific data formats.

References

1 J. Kreps. "Why Avro for Kafka Data?" Confluent blog (February 25, 2015). https://www.confluent.io/blog/avro-kafka-data/ (accessed November 23, 2017).

2 "Sender.java." Apache Kafka. GitHub (n.d.). https://github.com/apache/kafka/blob/299eea88a5068f973dc055776c7137538ed01c62/clients/src/main/java/org/apache/kafka/clients/producer/internals/Sender.java (accessed August 20, 2021).

3 "Producer Configurations: Retries." Confluent documentation (n.d.). https://docs.confluent.io/platform/current/installation/configuration/producer-configs.html#producerconfigs_retries (accessed May 29, 2020).

4 "Producer Configurations: max.in.flight.requests.per.connection." Confluent documentation (n.d.). https://docs.confluent.io/platform/current/installation/configuration/producer-configs.html#max.in.flight.requests.per.connection (accessed May 29, 2020).

5 "Producer Configurations: enable.idempotence." Confluent documentation (n.d.). https://docs.confluent.io/platform/current/installation/configuration/producer-configs.html#producerconfigs_enable.idempotence (accessed May 29, 2020).

6 "KafkaProducer." Apache Software Foundation (n.d.). https://kafka.apache.org/10/javadoc/org/apache/kafka/clients/producer/KafkaProducer.html (accessed July 7, 2019).

7 "Producer Configurations." Confluent documentation (n.d.). https://docs.confluent.io/platform/current/installation/configuration/producer-configs.html (accessed May 29, 2020).

8 "Producer Configurations: bootstrap.servers." Confluent documentation (n.d.). https://docs.confluent.io/platform/current/installation/configuration/producer-configs.html #bootstrap.servers (accessed May 29, 2020).

9 "Producer Configurations: acks." Confluent documentation (n.d.). https://docs.confluent.io/platform/current/installation/configuration/producer-configs.html#acks (accessed May 29, 2020).

10 "Documentation: Message Delivery Semantics." Apache Software Foundation (n.d.). https://kafka.apache.org/documentation/#semantics (accessed May 30, 2020).

11 "Topic Configurations: message.timestamp.type." Confluent documentation (n.d.). https://docs.confluent.io/platform/current/installation/configuration/ topic-configs.html#topicconfigs_message.timestamp.type (accessed July 22, 2020).

12   KIP-42: "Add Producer and Consumer Interceptors," Wiki for Apache Kafka, Apache Software Foundation. https://cwiki.apache.org/confluence/display/ KAFKA/KIP-42%3A+Add+Producer+and+Consumer+Interceptors   (accessed April 15, 2019).

13   "Kafka Streams Data Types and Serialization." Confluent documentation (n.d.). https://docs.confluent.io/platform/current/streams/developer-guide/data types.html (accessed August 21, 2021).

14   J. Olshan. "Apache Kafka Producer Improvements with the Sticky Partitioner." Confluent blog (December 18, 2019). https://www.confluent.io/blog/apache -kafka-producer-improvements-sticky-partitioner/ (accessed August 21, 2021).

15   "DefaultPartitioner.java," Apache Software Foundation. GitHub (n.d.). https:// github.com/apache/kafka/blob/trunk/clients/src/main/java/org/apache/ kafka/clients/producer/internals/DefaultPartitioner.java (accessed March 22, 2020).

16   C. McCabe. "Upgrading Apache Kafka Clients Just Got Easier." Confluent blog (July 18, 2017). https://www.confluent.io/blog/upgrading-apache-kafka-clients -just-got-easier/ (accessed August 21, 2021).

Consumers:
Unlocking data

5

This chapters covers

- Exploring the consumer and how it works
- Using consumer groups to coordinate reading data from topics
- Learning about offsets and how to use them
- Examining various configuration options that change consumer behavior

In our previous chapter, we started writing data into our Kafka system. However, as you know, that is only one part of the story. Consumers get the data from Kafka and provide those values to other systems or applications. Because consumers are clients that exist outside of brokers, they can be written in various programming languages just like producer clients. Take note that when we look at how things work in this chapter, we will try to lean towards the defaults of the Java consumer client. After reading this chapter, we will be on our way to solving our previous business requirements by consuming data in a couple of different ways.

87

5.1   *An example*

The consumer client is the program that subscribes to the topic or topics that interest them [1]. As with producer clients, the actual consumer processes can run on separate machines and are not required to run on a specific server. In fact, most consumer clients in production settings are on separate hosts. As long as the clients can connect to the Kafka brokers, they can read messages. Figure 5.1 reintroduces the broad scope of Kafka and shows consumers running outside the brokers to get data from Kafka.

Why is it important to know that the consumer is subscribing to topics (pulling messages) and not being pushed to instead? The power of processing control shifts to the consumer in this situation. Figure 5.1 shows where consumer clients fit into the overall Kafka ecosystem. Clients are responsible for reading data from topics and

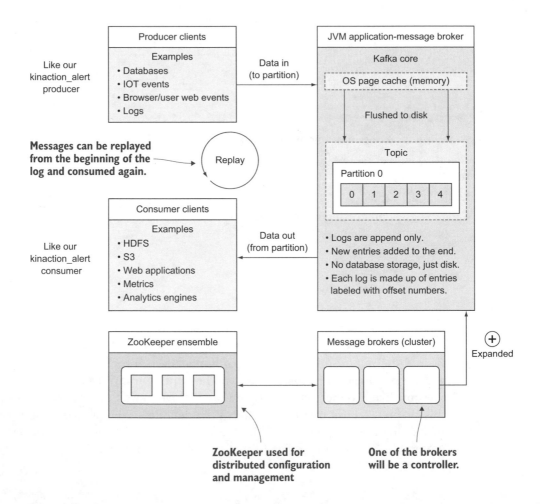

Figure 5.1   Overview of Kafka consumer clients

making it available to application (like metrics dashboards or analytics engines) or storing it in other systems. Consumers themselves control the rate of consumption.

With consumers in the driver's seat, if a failure occurs and the consumer applications come back online, they can start pulling again. There's no need to always have the consumers up and running to handle (or miss) notifications. Although you can develop applications that are capable of handling this constant data flow or even a buildup of back pressure due to volume, you need to know that you are not a listener for the brokers; consumers are the ones pulling the data. For those readers that have used Kafka before, you might know that there are reasons why you probably will not want to have your consumers down for extended periods. When we discuss more details about topics, we will look at how data might be removed from Kafka due to size or time limits that users can define.

5.1.1 Consumer options

In our discussion, you will notice a couple of properties that are related to the ones that were needed for the producer clients as well. We always need to know the brokers we can attempt to connect to on client startup. One minor "gotcha" is to make sure you use the deserializers for the keys and values that match the serializers you produced the message with. For example, if you produce using a `StringSerializer` but try to consume using the `LongDeSerializer`, you will get an exception that you will need to fix.

Table 5.1 lists some of the configuration values that we should know as we start writing our own consumers [2].

Table 5.1 Consumer configuration

Key	Purpose
bootstrap.servers	One or more Kafka brokers to connect on startup
value.deserializer	Needed for deserialization of the value
key.deserializer	Needed for deserialization of the key
group.id	A name that's used to join a consumer group
client.id	An ID to identify a user (we will use this in chapter 10)
heartbeat.interval.ms	Interval for consumer's pings to the group coordinator

One way to deal with all of the consumer configuration key names is to use the constants provided in the Java class `ConsumerConfig` (see http://mng.bz/oGgy) and by looking for the Importance label of "high" in the Confluent website (http://mng.bz/drdv). However, in our examples, we will use the property names themselves for clarity. Listing 5.1 shows four of these keys in action. The values for the configurations in table 5.1 determine how our consumer interacts with the brokers as well as other consumers.

We will now switch to reading from a topic with one consumer as we did in chapter 2. For this example, we have an application similar to how Kafka could have started in LinkedIn, dealing with user activity events (mentioned in chapter 1) [3]. Let's say that we have a specific formula that uses the time a user spends on the page as well as the number of interactions they have, which is sent as a value to a topic to project future click rates with a new promotion. Imagine that we run the consumer and process all of the messages on the topic and that we are happy with our application of the formula (in this case, multiplying by a magic number).

Listing 5.1 shows an example of looking at the records from the topic `kinaction _promos` and printing a value based on the data from each event. This listing has many similarities to the producer code that we wrote in chapter 4, where properties are used to determine the behavior of the consumer. This use of deserializers for the keys and values is different than having serializers for producers, which varies depending on the topic we consume.

> **NOTE** Listing 5.1 is not a complete code listing but is meant to highlight spe-
> cific consumer lines. Remember, a consumer can subscribe to multiple topics,
> but in this instance, we are only interested in the `kinaction_promos` topic.

In the listing, a loop is also used to poll the topic partitions that our consumer is assigned in order to process messages. This loop is toggled with a Boolean value. This sort of loop can cause errors, especially for beginner programmers! Why this loop then? Part of the streaming mindset encompasses events as a continuous stream, and this is reflected in the logic. Notice that this example uses `250` for the value of the poll dura-tion, which is in milliseconds. This timeout indicates how long the call blocks a main application thread by waiting, but it can return immediately when records are ready for delivery [4]. This value is something that you can fine-tune and adjust, based on the needs of your applications. The reference (and more details) for the Java 8 style of using `addShutdownHook` we use in the following listing can be seen at https://docs .confluent.io/platform/current/streams/developer-guide/write-streams.html.

Listing 5.1   Promotion consumer

```
...
  private volatile boolean keepConsuming = true;

  public static void main(String[] args) {                    Defines group.id. (We'll
    Properties kaProperties = new Properties();               discuss this with
    kaProperties.put("bootstrap.servers",                     consumer groups.)
            "localhost:9092,localhost:9093,,localhost:9094");
    kaProperties.put("group.id",
            "kinaction_webconsumer");
    kaProperties.put("enable.auto.commit", "true");
    kaProperties.put("auto.commit.interval.ms", "1000");      Defines
    kaProperties.put("key.deserializer",                      deserializers for
"org.apache.kafka.common.serialization.StringDeserializer");  the key and values
    kaProperties.put("value.deserializer",
"org.apache.kafka.common.serialization.StringDeserializer");
```

```
    WebClickConsumer webClickConsumer = new WebClickConsumer();
    webClickConsumer.consume(kaProperties);

    Runtime.getRuntime()
      .addShutdownHook(
        new Thread(webClickConsumer::shutdown)
      );
}

private void consume(Properties kaProperties) {        Passes the properties
    try (KafkaConsumer<String, String> consumer =       into the KafkaConsumer
      new KafkaConsumer<>(kaProperties)) {         ◁──┘ constructor
      consumer.subscribe(
        List.of("kinaction_promos")           ◁─┐  Subscribes to one topic,
      );                                        └  kinaction_promos

      while (keepConsuming) {                  ◁─┐  Uses a loop to poll
         ConsumerRecords<String, String> records =  └ for topic records
          consumer.poll(Duration.ofMillis(250));
        for (ConsumerRecord<String, String> record : records) {
          log.info("kinaction_info offset = {}, key = {}",
                      record.offset(),
                      record.key());
          log.info("kinaction_info value = {}",
            Double.parseDouble(record.value()) * 1.543);
        }
      }
    }
}

private void shutdown() {
    keepConsuming = false;
}
}
```

After generating a value for every message in the topic in listing 5.1, we find out that our modeling formula isn't correct! So what should we do now? Attempt to recalculate the data we have from our end results (assuming the correction would be harder than in the example) and then apply a new formula?

This is where we can use our knowledge of consumer behavior in Kafka to replay the messages we already processed. By having the raw data retained, we do not have to worry about trying to recreate the original data. Developer mistakes, application logic mistakes, and even dependent application failures can be corrected because the data is not removed from our topics once it is consumed. This also explains how time travel, in a way, is possible with Kafka.

Let's switch to looking at how to stop our consumer. You already saw where you used Ctrl-C to end your processing or stopped the process on the terminal. However, the proper way includes calling a `close` method on the consumer [23].

Listing 5.2 shows a consumer that runs on a thread and a different class controls shutdown. When the code in listing 5.2 is started, the thread runs with a consumer instance. By calling the public method `shutdown`, a different class can flip the Boolean and stop our consumer from polling for new records. The stopping variable is our guard, which decides whether to continue processing or not. Calling the `wakeup` method also causes a `WakeupException` to be thrown that leads to the final block closing the consumer resource correctly [5]. Listing 5.2 used https://kafka.apache.org/26/javadoc/index.html?org/apache/kafka/clients/consumer/KafkaConsumer.html as a reference documentation.

Listing 5.2   Closing a consumer

```
public class KinactionStopConsumer implements Runnable {
    private final KafkaConsumer<String, String> consumer;
    private final AtomicBoolean stopping =
                            new AtomicBoolean(false);

    ...

    public KinactionStopConsumer(KafkaConsumer<String, String> consumer) {
      this.consumer = consumer;
    }

    public void run() {
        try {
            consumer.subscribe(List.of("kinaction_promos"));
            while (!stopping.get()) {                        ◁─┐  The variable stopping
                ConsumerRecords<String, String> records =        │  determines whether to
                  consumer.poll(Duration.ofMillis(250));         │  continue processing.
                ...
            }
        } catch (WakeupException e) {                        ◁─┐  The client shutdown hook
            if (!stopping.get()) throw e;                        │  triggers WakeupException.
        } finally {
            consumer.close();                                ◁─┐  Stops the client and informs
        }                                                        │  the broker of the shutdown
    }

    public void shutdown() {                                ◁─┐  Calls shutdown from a different
        stopping.set(true);                                     │  thread to stop the client properly
        consumer.wakeup();
    }
 }
```

As we move on to the next topic, to go further, we need to understand offsets and how they can be used to control how consumers will read data.

5.1.2   *Understanding our coordinates*

One of the items that we have only talked about in passing so far is the concept of *offsets*. We use offsets as index positions in the log that the consumer sends to the broker.

This lets the log know which messages it wants to consume and from where. If you think back to our console consumer example, we used the flag `--from-beginning`. This sets the consumer's configuration parameter `auto.offset.reset` to `earliest` behind the scenes. With that configuration, you should see all the records for that topic for the partitions you are connected to, even if they were sent before you started the console consumer. The top part of figure 5.2 shows reading from the start of the log every time you run in this mode.

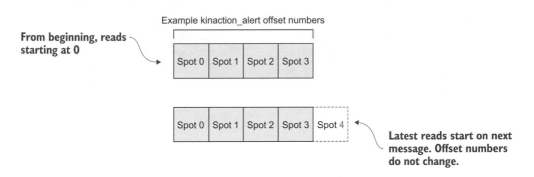

Figure 5.2   Kafka offsets [6]

If you don't add the option `auto.offset.reset`, the default is `latest`. Figure 5.2 shows this mode as well. In this case, you will not see any messages from the producer unless you send them after you start the consumer. This option says to disregard processing the messages that already are in the topic partition your consumer is reading from; we only want to process what comes in after the consumer client starts polling the topic. You can think of this as an infinite array that has an index starting at 0. However, there are no updates allowed for an index. Any changes need to be appended to the end of the log.

Note that offsets always increase for each partition. Once a topic partition has seen offset 0, even if that message is removed at a later point, the offset number is not used again. Some of you might have run into the issue of numbers that keep increasing until they hit the upper bound of a data type. Each partition has its own offset sequence, so the hope is that the risk will be low.

For a message written to a topic, what are the coordinates to find the message? First, we would find the partition within the topic that it was written to, and then we would find the index-based offset. As figure 5.3 shows, consumers usually read from the consumer's partition leader replica. This consumer leader replica could be different from any producer's leader replica due to changes in leadership over time; however, they are generally similar in concept.

Topic: 3 partitions, 2 replicas

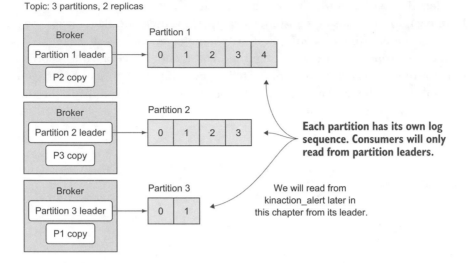

Figure 5.3   **Partition leaders**

Also, when we talk about partitions, it is okay to have the same offset number across partitions. The ability to tell messages apart needs to include the details of which partition we are talking about within a topic, as well as the offset.

As a side note, if you do need to fetch from a follower replica due to an issue like network latency concerns (for example, having a cluster that stretches across data centers), KIP-392 introduced this ability in version 2.4.0 [7]. As you are starting out with your first clusters, we recommend starting with the default behavior and only reaching for this feature as it becomes necessary to impart a real impact. If you do not have your cluster across different physical sites, you likely will not need this feature at the current time.

Partitions play an important role in how we can process messages. Although the topic is a logical name for what your consumers are interested in, they will read from the leader replicas of their assigned partitions. But how do consumers figure out which partition to connect to? And not just which partition, but where does the leader exist for that partition? For each group of consumers, a specific broker takes on the role of being a group coordinator [8]. The consumer client talks to this coordinator in order to get a partition assignment along with other details it needs in order to consume messages.

The number of partitions also comes into play when talking about consumption. Some consumers will not get any work with more consumers than partitions. An example would be four consumers and only three partitions. Why might you be okay with that? In some instances, you might want to make sure that a similar rate of consumption occurs if a consumer dies unexpectedly. The *group coordinator* is not only in charge of assigning which consumers read which partitions at the beginning of group startup but also when consumers are added or fail and exit the group [8]. And, in an instance where there are more partitions than consumers, consumers handle more than one partition if needed.

Figure 5.4 shows a generic view of how four consumers read all of the data on the brokers where the subscribed topic has partition leader replicas spread evenly, with one on each of the three brokers. In this figure, the data is roughly the same size, which might not always be the case. One consumer sits ready without work because each partition leader replica is handled by one consumer only.

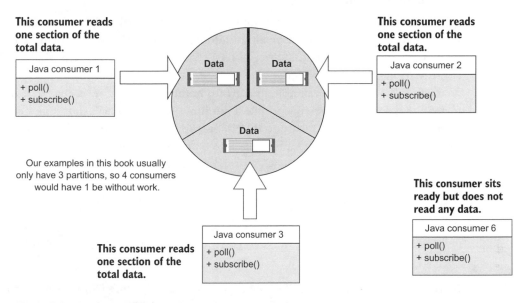

This consumer reads one section of the total data.

Java consumer 1
+ poll() + subscribe()

This consumer reads one section of the total data.

Java consumer 2
+ poll() + subscribe()

Our examples in this book usually only have 3 partitions, so 4 consumers would have 1 be without work.

This consumer sits ready but does not read any data.

Java consumer 6
+ poll() + subscribe()

This consumer reads one section of the total data.

Java consumer 3
+ poll() + subscribe()

Figure 5.4   An extra Kafka consumer

Because the number of partitions determines the amount of parallel consumers you can have, some might ask why you don't always choose a large number such as 500 partitions. This quest for higher throughput is not free [9]. This is why you need to choose what best matches the shape of your data flow.

One key consideration is that many partitions might increase end-to-end latency. If milliseconds count in your application, you might not be able to wait until a partition is replicated between brokers [9]. This is key to having in-sync replicas, and it is done before a message is available for delivery to a consumer. You would also need to make sure that you watch the memory usage of your consumers. If you do not have a 1-to-1 mapping of partitions to consumers, each consumer's memory requirements can increase as it is assigned more partitions [9].

If you run across older documentation for Kafka, you might notice consumer client configurations for Apache ZooKeeper. Unless one is using an old consumer client,

Kafka does not have consumers rely directly on ZooKeeper. Although consumers used ZooKeeper to store the offsets that they consume to a certain point, now the offsets are often stored inside a Kafka internal topic [10]. As a side note, consumer clients do not have to store their offsets in either of these locations, but this will likely be the case. If you want to manage your own offset storage you can! You can either store it in a local file, in cloud storage with a provider like AWS™, or a database. One of the advantages of moving away from ZooKeeper storage was to reduce the clients' dependency on ZooKeeper.

5.2   How consumers interact

Why is the concept of consumer groups paramount? Probably the most important reason is that scaling is impacted by either adding customers to or removing consumers from a group. Consumers that are not part of the same group do not share the same coordination of offset knowledge.

Listing 5.3 shows an example of a group named `kinaction_team0group`. If you instead make up a new `group.id` (like a random GUID), you will start a new consumer with no stored offsets and with no other consumers in your group [11]. If you join an existing group (or one that had offsets stored already), your consumer can share work with others or can even resume where it left off reading from any previous runs [1].

Listing 5.3   Consumer configuration for consumer group

```
Properties kaProperties = new Properties();
kaProperties.put("group.id", "kinaction_team0group");   ◁──  group.id determines
                                                              consumer behavior
                                                              with other consumers.
```

It is often the case that you will have many consumers reading from the same topic. An important detail to decide on if you need a new group ID is whether your consumers are working as part of one application or as separate logic flows. Why is this important?

Let's think of two use cases for data that come from a human resource system. One team wonders about the number of hires from specific states, and the other team is more interested in the data for the impact on travel budgets for interviews. Would anyone on the first team care about what the other team is doing or would either of the teams want to consume only a portion of the messages? Likely not! How can we keep this separation? The answer is to assign a separate `group.id` to each application. Each consumer that uses the same `group.id` as another consumer will be considered to be working together to consume the partitions and offsets of the topic as one logical application.

5.3   Tracking

Going through our usage patterns so far, we have not talked too much about how we keep a record of what each client has read. Let's briefly talk about how some message brokers handle messages in other systems. In some systems, consumers do not record what they have read. They pull the message and then it does not exist on a queue after acknowledgment. This works well for a single message that needs to have exactly one application process it. Some systems use topics in order to publish the message to all those that are subscribers. And often, future subscribers will have missed this message entirely because they were not actively part of the receiver list when the event happened.

Figure 5.5 shows non-Kafka message broker scenarios, including how messages are often removed after consumption. It also shows a second pattern where a message might come from the original source and then be replicated to other queues. In systems where the message would be consumed and not available for more than one consumer, this approach is needed so that separate applications each get a copy.

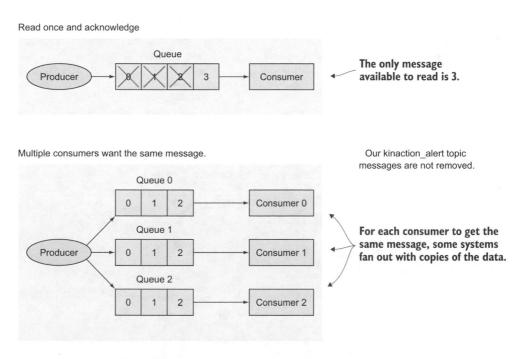

Figure 5.5   Other broker scenarios

You can imagine that the copies grow in number as an event becomes a popular source of information. Rather than have entire copies of the queue (besides those for replication or failover), Kafka can serve multiple applications from the same partition leader replica.

Kafka, as we mentioned in the first chapter, is not limited to having only one consumer. Even if a consuming application does not exist when a message is first created on a topic, as long as Kafka retains the message in its log, then it can still process the data. Because messages are not removed from other consumers or delivered once, consumer clients need a way to keep a record of where they have read in the topic. In addition, because many applications can read the same topic, it is important that the offsets and partitions are specific to a certain consumer group. The key coordinates to let your consumer clients work together is a unique blend of the following: group, topic, and partition number.

5.3.1 Group coordinator

As mentioned earlier, the group coordinator works with the consumer clients to keep a record of where inside the topic that specific group has read [8]. The partition's coordinates of a topic and group ID make it specific to an offset value.

Looking at figure 5.6, notice that we can use the offset commits as coordinates to find out where to read from next. For example, in the figure, a consumer that is part of a group called `kinaction_teamoffka0` and is assigned partition 0 would be ready to read offset 3 next.

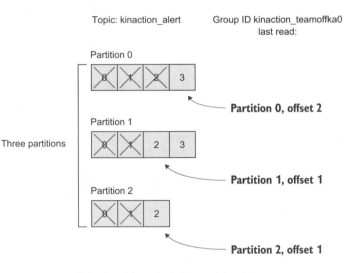

Figure 5.6 Coordinates

Figure 5.7 shows a scenario where the same partitions of interest exist on three separate brokers for two different consumer groups, `kinaction_teamoffka0` and `kinaction_teamsetka1`. The consumers in each group will get their own copy of the data from the partitions on each broker. They do not work together unless they are part of the same group. Correct group membership is important for each group to have their metadata managed accurately.

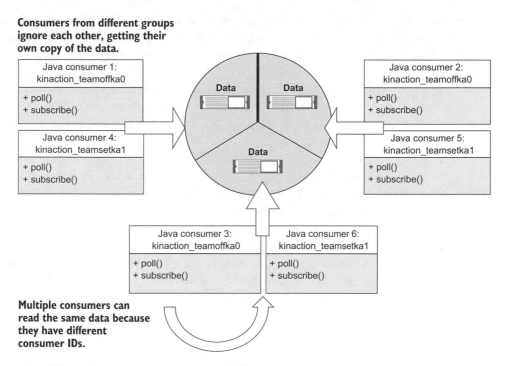

Consumers from different groups ignore each other, getting their own copy of the data.

Multiple consumers can read the same data because they have different consumer IDs.

Figure 5.7   Consumers in separate groups [12]

As a general rule, only one consumer per consumer group can read one partition. In other words, whereas a partition might be read by many consumers, it can only be read by one consumer from each group at a time. Figure 5.8 highlights how one consumer can read two partitions leader replicas, where the second consumer can only read the data from a third partition leader [8]. A single partition replica is not to be divided or shared between more than one consumer with the same ID.

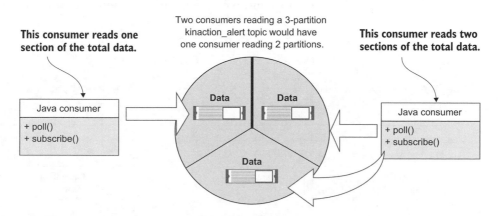

This consumer reads one section of the total data.

Two consumers reading a 3-partition kinaction_alert topic would have one consumer reading 2 partitions.

This consumer reads two sections of the total data.

Figure 5.8   Kafka consumers in a group

One of the neat things about being part of a consumer group is that when a consumer fails, the partitions that it was reading are reassigned [8]. An existing consumer takes the place of reading a partition that was once read by the consumer that dropped out of the group.

Table 5.1 listed `heartbeat.interval.ms`, which determines the amount of pings to the group coordinator [13]. This heartbeat is the way that the consumer communicates with the coordinator to let it know it is still replying in a timely fashion and working away diligently [8].

Failure by a consumer client to send a heartbeat over a period of time can happen in a couple of ways, like stopping the consumer client by either termination of the process or failure due to a fatal exception. If the client isn't running, it cannot send messages back to the group coordinator [8].

5.3.2   *Partition assignment strategy*

One item that we will want to be aware of is how consumers get assigned to partitions. This matters since it will help you figure out how many partitions each of your consumers might be taxed with processing. The property `partition.assignment.strategy` is what determines which partitions are assigned to each consumer [14]. `Range` and `RoundRobin` are provided, as are `Sticky` and `CooperativeSticky` [15].

The *range assigner* uses a single topic to find the number of partitions (ordered by number) and then is broken down by the number of consumers. If the split is not even, then the first consumers (using alphabetical order) get the remaining partitions [16]. Make sure that you employ a spread of partitions that your consumers can handle and consider switching the assignment strategy if some consumer clients use all their resources, though others are fine. Figure 5.9 shows how three clients will grab three out of seven total partitions and end up with more partitions than the last client.

The *round-robin* strategy is where the partitions are uniformly distributed down the row of consumers [1]. Figure 5.9 is a modified figure from the article "What I have learned from Kafka partition assignment strategy," which shows an example of three clients that are part of the same consumer group and assigned in a round-robin fash-

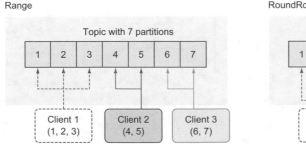
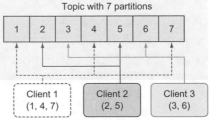

Figure 5.9   Partition assignments

ion for one topic made of seven partitions [17]. The first consumer gets the first partition, the second consumer the second, and so on until the partitions run out.

The *sticky* strategy was added in version 0.11.0 [18]. However, since we will use range assigner in most of our examples internally and already looked at round-robin as well, we will not dig into `Sticky` and `CooperativeSticky`.

5.4 Marking our place

One of the important things to think about is your need for assuring that your applications read all messages from your topic. Is it okay to miss a few, or do you need each message confirmed as it's read? The real decision comes down to your requirements and any trade-offs you are willing to make. Are you okay with sacrificing some speed in order to have a safer method of seeing each message? These choices are discussed in this section.

One option is to use `enable.auto.commit` set to `true`, the default for consumer clients [19]. Offsets are committed on our behalf. One of the nicest parts of this option is that we do not have to make any other calls to commit the offsets that are consumed.

Kafka brokers resend messages if they are not automatically acknowledged due to a consumer client failure. But what sort of trouble can we get into? If we process messages that we get from our latest poll, say, in a separate thread, the automatic commit offset can be marked as being read even if everything is not actually done with those specific offsets. What if we had a message fail in our processing that we would need to retry? With our next poll, we could get the next set of offsets after what was already committed as being consumed [8]. It is possible and easy to lose messages that look like they have been consumed despite not being processed by your consumer logic.

When looking at what you commit, notice that timing might not be perfect. If you do not call a commit method on a consumer with metadata noting your specific offset to commit, you might have some undefined behavior based on the timing of polls, expired timers, or even your own threading logic. If you need to be sure to commit a record at a specific time as you process it or a specific offset in particular, you should make sure that you send the offset metadata into the commit method.

Let's explore this topic more by talking about using code-specific commits enabled by `enable.auto.commit` set to `false`. This method can be used to exercise the most management over when your application actually consumes a message and commits it. At-least-once delivery guarantees can be achieved with this pattern.

Let's talk about an example in which a message causes a file to be created in Hadoop in a specific location. As you get a message, you poll a message at offset 999. During processing, the consumer stops because of an error. Because the code never actually committed offset 999, the next time a consumer of that same group starts reading from that partition, it gets the message at offset 999 again. By receiving the message twice, the client was able to complete the task without missing the message. On the flip side, you did get the message twice! If for some reason your processing actually works and you achieve a successful write, your code has to handle the fact that you might have duplicates.

Now let's look at some of the code that we would use to control our offsets. As we did with a producer when we sent a message earlier, we can also commit offsets in a synchronous or asynchronous manner. Listing 5.4 shows a synchronous commit. Looking at that listing for `commitSync`, it is important to note that the commit takes place in a manner that blocks any other progress in the code until a success or failure occurs [20].

Listing 5.4   Waiting on a commit

```
      consumer.commitSync();                    ◁─┐  commitSync waits for
#// Any code here will wait on line before       │  a success or fail.
```

As with producers, we can also use a callback. Listing 5.5 shows how to create an asynchronous commit with a callback by implementing the `OffsetCommitCallback` interface (the `onComplete` method) with a lambda expression [21]. This instance allows for log messages to determine our success or failure even though our code does not wait before moving on to the next instruction.

Listing 5.5   Commit with a callback

```
public static void commitOffset(long offset,
                                int partition,
                                String topic,
                                KafkaConsumer<String, String> consumer) {
  OffsetAndMetadata offsetMeta = new OffsetAndMetadata(++offset, "");

  Map<TopicPartition, OffsetAndMetadata> kaOffsetMap = new HashMap<>();
  kaOffsetMap.put(new TopicPartition(topic, partition), offsetMeta);

  consumer.commitAsync(kaOffsetMap, (map, e) -> {      ◁─┐  A lambda that creates an
    if (e != null) {                                      │  OffsetCommitCallback instance
      for (TopicPartition key : map.keySet()) {
        log.info("kinaction_error: offset {}", map.get(key).offset());
      }
    } else {
      for (TopicPartition key : map.keySet()) {
        log.info("kinaction_info: offset {}", map.get(key).offset());
      }
    }
  });
}
```

If you think back to chapter 4, this is similar to how we used asynchronous sends with a callback for acknowledgments. To implement your own callback, you need to use the interface `OffsetCommitCallback`. You can define an `onComplete` method definition to handle exceptions or successes as needed.

Why would you want to choose synchronous or asynchronous commit patterns? Keep in mind that your latency is higher if you wait for a blocking call. This time factor might be worth the delay if your requirements include needs for data consistency [21]. These decisions help determine the amount of control you need to exercise when informing Kafka which messages your logic considers as processed.

5.5 Reading from a compacted topic

Consumers should be made aware of reading from a compacted topic. Kafka compacts the partition log in a background process, and records with the same key might be removed except for the last one. Chapter 7 will go further into how these topics work, but in short, we need to update records that have the same key value. If you do not need a history of messages, but rather just the last value, you might wonder how this concept works with an immutable log that only adds records to the end. The biggest "gotcha" for consumers that might cause an error is that when reading records from a compacted topic, consumers can still get multiple entries for a single key [22]! How is this possible? Because compaction runs on the log files that are on disk, compaction may not see every message that exists in memory during cleanup.

Clients need to handle this case, where there is more than one value per key. We should have the logic in place to handle duplicate keys and, if needed, ignore all but the last value. To pique your interest about compacted topics, note that Kafka uses its own compacted internal topic, called `__consumer_offsets`, which relates directly to your consumer offsets themselves [23]. Compaction makes sense here because for a specific combination of a consumer group, partition, and topic, only the latest value is needed as it will have the latest offset consumed.

5.6 Retrieving code for our factory requirements

Let's try to use the information we gathered about how consumers work to see if we can start working on our own solutions designed in chapter 3 for use with Kafka in our e-bike factory but from the consumer client perspective. As noted in chapter 3, we want to ensure that we do not lose any audit messages when operators complete commands against the sensors. First, let's look at the options we have in reading our offsets.

5.6.1 Reading options

Although there is no lookup of a message by a key option in Kafka, it is possible to seek to a specific offset. Thinking about our log of messages being an ever increasing array with each message having an index, we have a couple of options for this, including starting from the beginning, going to the end, or finding offsets based on specific times. Let's take a look at these options.

One issue that we might run into is that we want to read from the beginning of a topic even if we have already done so. Reasons could include logic errors and a desire to replay the entire log or a failure in our data pipeline after starting with Kafka. The important configuration to set for this behavior is `auto.offset.reset` to `earliest`[24]. Another technique that we can use is to run the same logic but use a different group ID. In effect, this means that the commit offset topics that Kafka uses internally will not be able to find an offset value but will be able to start at the first index found because the commit offset topic does not have any data on the new consumer group.

Listing 5.6 is an example of setting the property `auto.offset.reset` to `"earliest"` to seek to a specific offset [24]. Setting a group ID to a random UUID also helps to achieve starting with no offset history for a consumer group. This is the type of reset we could use to look at `kinaction_alerttrend` with different code logic to determine trends against all of the data in that topic.

Listing 5.6   Earliest offset

```
Properties kaProperties = new Properties();          Creates a group ID for
kaProperties.put("group.id",                         which Kafka does not
             UUID.randomUUID().toString());    ←──   have a stored offset
kaProperties.put("auto.offset.reset", "earliest");  ←── Uses the earliest offset
                                                        retained in our logs
```

Sometimes you just want to start your logic from when the consumers start up and forget about past messages [24]. Maybe the data is already too old to have business value in your topic. Listing 5.7 shows the properties you would set to get this behavior of starting with the latest offset. If you want to make sure that you don't find a previous consumer offset and want to instead default to the latest offset Kafka has for your subscriptions, using a UUID isn't necessary except for testing. If we are only interested about new alerts coming into our `kinaction_alert` topic, this might be a way for a consumer to see only those alerts.

Listing 5.7   Latest offset

```
Properties kaProperties = new Properties();          Creates a group ID for
kaProperties.put("group.id",                         which Kafka does not
             UUID.randomUUID().toString());    ←──   have a stored offset
kaProperties.put("auto.offset.reset", "latest");    ←── Uses the latest
                                                        record offset
```

One of the trickier offset search methods is `offsetsForTimes`. This method allows you to send a map of topics and partitions as well as a timestamp for each in order to get a map back of the offset and timestamp for the given topics and partitions [25]. This can be useful in situations where a logical offset is not known, but a timestamp is known. For example, if you have an exception related to an event that was logged, you might be able to use a consumer to determine the data that was processed around your specific timestamp. Trying to locate an audit event by time might be used for our topic `kinaction_audit` to locate commands happening as well.

As listing 5.8 shows, we have the ability to retrieve the offset and timestamps per a topic or partition when we map each to a timestamp. After we get our map of metadata returned from the `offsetsForTimes` call, we then can seek directly to the offset we are interested in by seeking to the offset returned for each respective key.

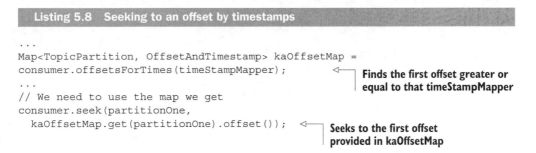

Listing 5.8 Seeking to an offset by timestamps

```
...
Map<TopicPartition, OffsetAndTimestamp> kaOffsetMap =
consumer.offsetsForTimes(timeStampMapper);          ◁──┐ Finds the first offset greater or
...                                                      │ equal to that timeStampMapper
// We need to use the map we get
consumer.seek(partitionOne,
  kaOffsetMap.get(partitionOne).offset());    ◁──┐ Seeks to the first offset
                                                 │ provided in kaOffsetMap
```

One thing to be aware of is that the offset returned is the first message with a timestamp that meets your criteria. However, due to the producer resending messages on failures or variations in when timestamps are added (by consumers, perhaps), times might appear out of order.

Kafka also gives you the ability to find other offsets as can be referenced in the consumer Javadoc [26]. With all of these options, let's see how they apply to our use case.

5.6.2 Requirements

One requirement for our audit example was that there is no need to correlate (or group together) any events across the individual events. This means that there are no concerns on the order or need to read from specific partitions; any consumer reading any partition should be good. Another requirement was to not lose any messages. A safe way to make sure that our logic is executed for each audit event is to specifically commit the offset per record after it is consumed. To control the commit as part of the code, we can set `enable.auto.commit` to `false`.

Listing 5.9 shows an example of leveraging a synchronous commit after each record is processed for the audit feature. Details of the next offset to consume in relation to the topic and partition of the offset that was just consumed are sent as a part of each loop through the records. One "gotcha" to note is that it might seem odd to add 1 to the current offset, but the offset sent to your broker is supposed to be your future index. The method `commitSync` is called and passed the offset map containing the offset of the record that was just processed [20].

Listing 5.9 Audit consumer logic

```
...
kaProperties.put("enable.auto.commit", "false");     ◁──┐ Sets autocommit
                                                          │ to false
try (KafkaConsumer<String, String> consumer =
     new KafkaConsumer<>(kaProperties)) {

    consumer.subscribe(List.of("kinaction_audit"));

    while (keepConsuming) {
      var records = consumer.poll(Duration.ofMillis(250));
      for (ConsumerRecord<String, String> record : records) {
        // audit record process ...
```

```
        OffsetAndMetadata offsetMeta =                    ◁──┐  Adding a record to the
          new OffsetAndMetadata(++record.offset(), "");        current offset determines
                                                                the next offset to read.
        Map<TopicPartition, OffsetAndMetadata> kaOffsetMap =
          new HashMap<>();
        kaOffsetMap.put(
          new TopicPartition("kinaction_audit",          ◁──┐  Allows for a topic
                             record.partition()), offsetMeta);  and partition key
                                                                to be related to a
        consumer.commitSync(kaOffsetMap);      ◁──┐ Commits    specific offset
      }                                             the offsets
    }
  }
...
```

Another goal of the design for our e-bike factory was to capture our alert status and monitor the alert trend over time. Even though we know our records have a key that is the stage ID, there is no need to consume one group at a time or worry about the order. Listing 5.10 shows how to set the `key.deserializer` property so the consumer knows how to deal with the binary data that was stored in Kafka when we produced the message. In this example, `AlertKeySerde` is used for the key to deserialize. Because message loss isn't a huge concern in our scenario, allowing autocommit of messages is good enough in this situation.

Listing 5.10   Alert trending consumer

```
...                                               Uses autocommit as lost
kaProperties.put("enable.auto.commit", "true");  ◁── messages are not an issue
kaProperties.put("key.deserializer",
  AlertKeySerde.class.getName());                ◁──┐  AlertKeySerde
kaProperties.put("value.deserializer",                key deserializer
  "org.apache.kafka.common.serialization.StringDeserializer");

KafkaConsumer<Alert, String> consumer =
  new KafkaConsumer<Alert, String>(kaProperties);
consumer.subscribe(List.of("kinaction_alerttrend"));

while (true) {
    ConsumerRecords<Alert, String> records =
    consumer.poll(Duration.ofMillis(250));
    for (ConsumerRecord<Alert, String> record : records) {
      // ...
    }
}
...
```

Another large requirement is to have any alerts quickly processed to let operators know about critical issues. Because the producer in chapter 4 used a custom `Partitioner`, we will assign a consumer directly to that same partition to alert us to critical issues. Because a delay in case of other alerts is not desirable, the commit will be for each offset in an asynchronous manner.

Listing 5.12 shows the consumer client logic focused on critical alerts assigning themselves to the specific topic and partition that is used for producing alerts when the custom partitioner class `AlertLevelPartitioner` is used. In this case, it is partition 0 and topic `kinaction_alert`.

We use `TopicPartition` objects to tell Kafka which specific partitions we are interested in for a topic. Passing the `TopicPartition` objects to the `assign` method takes the place of allowing a consumer to be at the discretion of a group coordinator assignment [27].

For listing 5.11, each record that comes back from the consumer poll, an asynchronous commit is used with a callback. A commit of the next offset to consume is sent to the broker and should not block the consumer from processing the next record, per our requirements. The options in the following listing seem to satisfy our core design requirements from chapter 3.

Listing 5.11 Alert consumer

```
kaProperties.put("enable.auto.commit", "false");

KafkaConsumer<Alert, String> consumer =
  new KafkaConsumer<Alert, String>(kaProperties);
TopicPartition partitionZero =                            Uses TopicPartition
  new TopicPartition("kinaction_alert", 0);              for critical messages
consumer.assign(List.of(partitionZero));                 Consumer assigns itself
                                                          the partition rather than
while (true) {                                            subscribing to the topic
    ConsumerRecords<Alert, String> records =
      consumer.poll(Duration.ofMillis(250));
    for (ConsumerRecord<Alert, String> record : records) {
        // ...
        commitOffset(record.offset(),
          record.partition(), topicName, consumer);       Commits each record
    }                                                      asynchronously
}

...
public static void commitOffset(long offset,int part, String topic,
  KafkaConsumer<Alert, String> consumer) {
    OffsetAndMetadata offsetMeta = new OffsetAndMetadata(++offset, "");

    Map<TopicPartition, OffsetAndMetadata> kaOffsetMap =
      new HashMap<TopicPartition, OffsetAndMetadata>();
    kaOffsetMap.put(new TopicPartition(topic, part), offsetMeta);

    OffsetCommitCallback callback = new OffsetCommitCallback() {
    ...
    };
    consumer.commitAsync(kaOffsetMap, callback);           The asynchronous commit
}                                                          uses the kaOffsetMap and
                                                           callback arguments.
```

Overall, the consumer can be a complex piece of our interactions with Kafka. Some options can be done with property configurations alone, but if not, you can use your knowledge of topics, partitions, and offsets to navigate your way to the data you need.

Summary

- Consumer clients provide developers with a way to get data out of Kafka. As with producer clients, consumer clients have a large number of available configuration options we can set rather than using custom coding.
- Consumer groups allow more than one client to work as a group to process records. With grouping, clients can process data in parallel.
- Offsets represent the position of a record in the commit log that exists on a broker. By using offsets, consumers can control where they want to start reading data.
- An offset can be a previous offset that consumers have already seen, which gives us the ability to replay records.
- Consumers can read data in a synchronous or an asynchronous manner.
- If asynchronous methods are used, the consumer can use code in callbacks to run logic once data is received.

References

1 S. Kozlovski. "Apache Kafka Data Access Semantics: Consumers and Membership." Confluent blog (n.d.). https://www.confluent.io/blog/apache-kafka-data-access-semantics-consumers-and-membership (accessed August 20, 2021).

2 "Consumer Configurations." Confluent documentation (n.d.). https://docs.confluent.io/platform/current/installation/configuration/consumer-configs.html (accessed June 19, 2019).

3 N. Narkhede. "Apache Kafka Hits 1.1 Trillion Messages Per Day – Joins the 4 Comma Club." Confluent blog (September 1, 2015). https://www.confluent.io/blog/apache-kafka-hits-1-1-trillion-messages-per-day-joins-the-4-comma-club/ (accessed October 20, 2019).

4 "Class KafkaConsumer<K,V>." Kafka 2.7.0 API. Apache Software Foundation (n.d.). https://kafka.apache.org/27/javadoc/org/apache/kafka/clients/consumer/KafkaConsumer.html#poll-java.time.Duration- (accessed August 24, 2021).

5 "Class WakeupException." Kafka 2.7.0 API. Apache Software Foundation (n.d.). https://kafka.apache.org/27/javadoc/org/apache/kafka/common/errors/WakeupException.html (accessed June 22, 2020).

6 "Documentation: Topics and Logs." Confluent documentation (n.d.). https://docs.confluent.io/5.5.1/kafka/introduction.html#topics-and-logs (accessed October 20, 2021).

7 "KIP-392: Allow consumers to fetch from closest replica." Wiki for Apache Kafka. Apache Software Foundation (November 05, 2019). https://cwiki.apache.org/confluence/display/KAFKA/KIP-392%3A+Allow+consumers+to+fetch+from+closest+replica (accessed December 10, 2019).

8   J. Gustafson. "Introducing the Kafka Consumer: Getting Started with the New Apache Kafka 0.9 Consumer Client." Confluent blog (January 21, 2016). https://www.confluent.io/blog/tutorial-getting-started-with-the-new-apache-kafka-0-9-consumer-client/ (accessed June 01, 2020).

9   J. Rao. "How to choose the number of topics/partitions in a Kafka cluster?" Confluent blog (March 12, 2015). https://www.confluent.io/blog/how-choose-number-topics-partitions-kafka-cluster/ (accessed May 19, 2019).

10 "Committing and fetching consumer offsets in Kafka." Wiki for Apache Kafka. Apache Software Foundation (March 24, 2015). https://cwiki.apache.org/confluence/pages/viewpage.action?pageId=48202031 (accessed December 15, 2019).

11 "Consumer Configurations: group.id." Confluent documentation (n.d.). https://docs.confluent.io/platform/current/installation/configuration/consumer-configs.html#consumerconfigs_group.id (accessed May 11, 2018).

12 "Documentation: Consumers." Apache Software Foundation (n.d.). https://kafka.apache.org/23/documentation.html#intro_consumers (accessed December 11, 2019).

13 "Consumer Configurations: heartbeat.interval.ms." Confluent documentation (n.d.). https://docs.confluent.io/platform/current/installation/configuration/consumer-configs.html#consumerconfigs_heartbeat.interval.ms (accessed May 11, 2018).

14 "Consumer Configurations: partition.assignment.strategy." Confluent documentation (n.d.). https://docs.confluent.io/platform/current/installation/configuration/consumer-configs.html#consumerconfigs_partition.assignment.strategy (accessed December 22, 2020).

15 S. Blee-Goldman. "From Eager to Smarter in Apache Kafka Consumer Rebalances." Confluent blog (n.d.). https://www.confluent.io/blog/cooperative-rebalancing-in-kafka-streams-consumer-ksqldb/ (accessed August 20, 2021).

16 "RangeAssignor.java." Apache Kafka GitHub (n.d.). https://github.com/apache/kafka/blob/c9708387bb1dd1fd068d6d8cec2394098d5d6b9f/clients/src/main/java/org/apache/kafka/clients/consumer/RangeAssignor.java (accessed August 25, 2021).

17 A. Li. "What I have learned from Kafka partition assignment strategy." Medium (December 1, 2017). https://medium.com/@anyili0928/what-i-have-learned-from-kafka-partition-assignment-strategy-799fdf15d3ab (accessed October 20, 2021).

18 "Release Plan 0.11.0.0." Wiki for Apache Kafka. Apache Software Foundation (June 26, 2017). https://cwiki.apache.org/confluence/display/KAFKA/Release+Plan+0.11.0.0 (accessed December 14, 2019).

19 "Consumer Configurations: enable.auto.commit." Confluent documentation (n.d.). https://docs.confluent.io/platform/current/installation/configuration/consumer-configs.html#consumerconfigs_enable.auto.commit (accessed May 11, 2018).

20 Synchronous Commits. Confluent documentation (n.d.). https://docs.confluent .io/3.0.0/clients/consumer.html#synchronous-commits (accessed August 24, 2021).

21 Asynchronous Commits. Confluent documentation (n.d.). https://docs.conflu ent.io/3.0.0/clients/consumer.html#asynchronous-commits (accessed August 24, 2021).

22 Kafka Design. Confluent documentation (n.d.). https://docs.confluent.io/ platform/current/kafka/design.html (accessed August 24, 2021).

23 Kafka Consumers. Confluent documentation (n.d.). https://docs.confluent.io/ 3.0.0/clients/consumer.html (accessed August 24, 2021).

24 "Consumer Configurations: auto.offset.reset." Confluent documentation (n.d.). https://docs.confluent.io/platform/current/installation/configura tion/consumer-configs.html#consumerconfigs_auto.offset.reset (accessed May 11, 2018).

25 offsetsForTimes. Kafka 2.7.0 API. Apache Software Foundation (n.d.). https://kafka.apache.org/27/javadoc/org/apache/kafka/clients/consumer/ Consumer.html#offsetsForTimes-java.util.Map- (accessed June 22, 2020).

26 seek. Kafka 2.7.0 API. Apache Software Foundation (n.d.). https:// kafka.apache.org/27/javadoc/org/apache/kafka/clients/consumer/Consumer .html#seek-org.apache.kafka.common.TopicPartition-long- (accessed June 22, 2020).

27 assign. Kafka 2.7.0 API. Apache Software Foundation (n.d.). https:// kafka.apache.org/27/javadoc/org/apache/kafka/clients/consumer/Kafka Consumer.html#assign-java.util.Collection- (accessed August 24, 2021).

Brokers

6

This chapters covers

- The role of brokers and their duties
- Evaluating options for certain broker configuration values
- Explaining replicas and how they stay up to date

So far in our discussions, we have dealt with Kafka from the view of an application developer interacting from external applications and processes. However, Kafka is a distributed system that deserves attention in its own right. In this chapter, let's look at the parts that make the Kafka brokers work.

6.1 Introducing the broker

Although we have focused on the client side of Kafka so far, our focus will now shift to another powerful component of the ecosystem: brokers. Brokers work together with other brokers to form the core of the system.

111

As we start to discover Kafka, those who are familiar with big data concepts or who have worked with Hadoop before might see familiar terminologies such as *rack awareness* (knowing which physical server rack a machine is hosted on) and *partitions*. Kafka has a rack awareness feature that makes replicas for a partition exist physically on separate racks [1]. Using familiar data terms should make us feel at home as we draw new parallels between what we've worked with before and what Kafka can do for us. When setting up our own Kafka cluster, it is important to know that we have another cluster to be aware of: Apache ZooKeeper. This then is where we'll begin.

6.2   *Role of ZooKeeper*

ZooKeeper is a key part of how the brokers work and is a requirement to run Kafka. Because Kafka needs to be running and exist before the brokers do, we will start our discussion there.

> **NOTE** As mentioned in chapter 2, to simplify the requirements of running Kafka, there was a proposal for the replacement of ZooKeeper with its own managed quorum [2]. Because this work was not yet complete at the time of publication, ZooKeeper is discussed in this work. But look for an early access release of the managed quorum, arriving in version 2.8.0.

As ZooKeeper needs to have a minimum number in order to elect leaders and reach a decision, this cluster is indeed important for our brokers [3]. ZooKeeper itself holds information such as topics in our cluster [4]. ZooKeeper helps the brokers by coordinating assignments and notifications [5].

With all of this interaction with the brokers, it is important that we have Zoo-Keeper running before starting our brokers. The health of the ZooKeeper cluster impacts the health of our Kafka brokers. For instance, if our ZooKeeper instances are damaged, topic metadata and configuration could be lost.

Usually, we won't need to expose the details (IP addresses and ports) of our Zoo-Keeper cluster to our producer and consumer applications. Certain legacy frameworks we use might also provide a means of connecting our client application with our ZooKeeper cluster. One example of this is version 3.1.*x* of Spring Cloud Stream, which allowed us to set the `zkNodes` property [6]. The value defaulted to `localhost` and should be left alone in most cases to avoid a ZooKeeper dependency. The `zkNodes` property is marked as deprecated, but you never know if you will encounter older code for maintenance, so you want to keep an eye out for it. Why is this not needed currently and in the future? Besides the fact that Kafka will not always require ZooKeeper, it is also important for us to avoid unnecessary external dependencies in our applications. In addition, it gives us fewer ports to expose if we are working with firewalls for Kafka and our client to communicate directly.

Using the Kafka tool `zookeeper-shell.sh`, which is located in the bin folder of our Kafka installation, we can connect to a ZooKeeper host in our cluster and look at how the data is stored [7]. One way to find the paths that Kafka uses is to look at the class ZkData.scala [8]. In this file, you will find paths like /controller, /controller _epoch, /config, and /brokers, for example. If we look at the /brokers/topics path, we will see a list of the topics that we have created. At this point, we should, hopefully, at least have the kinaction_helloworld topic in the list.

> **NOTE** We can also use a different Kafka tool, kafka-topics.sh, to see the list of topics, getting the same results! Commands in the following listings connect to ZooKeeper and Kafka, respectively, for their data but do so with a different command interface. The output should include the topic we created in chapter 2, [kinaction_helloworld].

Listing 6.1 Listing our topics

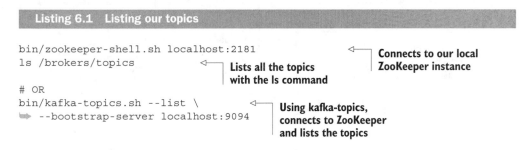

```
bin/zookeeper-shell.sh localhost:2181              ◁─── Connects to our local
ls /brokers/topics        ◁──┐ Lists all the topics       ZooKeeper instance
                              │ with the ls command
# OR
bin/kafka-topics.sh --list \                ◁───┐ Using kafka-topics,
⮕ --bootstrap-server localhost:9094              │ connects to ZooKeeper
                                                 │ and lists the topics
```

Even when ZooKeeper no longer helps to power Kafka, we might need to work with clusters that have not migrated yet, and we will likely see ZooKeeper in documentation and reference material for quite a while. Overall, being aware of the tasks that Kafka used to rely on ZooKeeper to perform and the shift to handling those inside a Kafka cluster with internal metadata nodes provides insight into the moving pieces of the entire system.

Being a Kafka broker means being able to coordinate with the other brokers as well as talking to ZooKeeper. In testing or working with proof-of-concept clusters, we might have only one broker node. However, in production, we will almost always have multiple brokers.

Turning away from ZooKeeper for now, figure 6.1 shows how brokers exist in a cluster and how they are home to Kafka's data logs. Clients will be writing to and reading from brokers to get information into and out of Kafka, and they will demand broker attention [9].

6.3 *Options at the broker level*

Configuration is an important part of working with Kafka clients, topics, and brokers. If you looked at the setup steps to create our first brokers in appendix A, we modified the server.properties file there, which we then passed as a command line argument to the broker startup shell script. This file is a common way to pass a specific configuration to a broker instance. For example, the log.dirs configuration property in that file should always be set to a log location that makes sense for your setup.

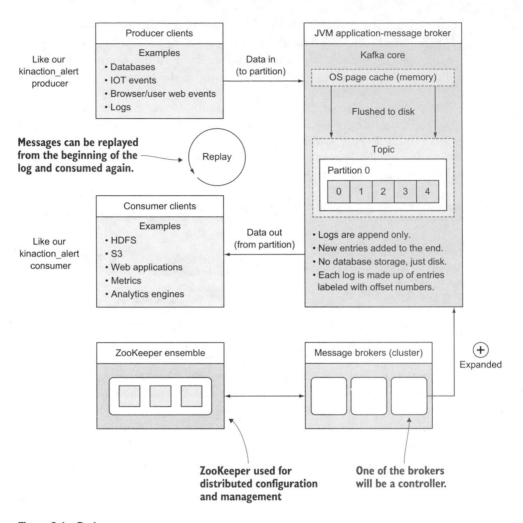

Figure 6.1   Brokers

This file also deals with configurations related to listeners, log locations, log retention, ZooKeeper, and group coordinator settings [10]. As with the producer and consumer configurations, look for the Importance label of "high" in the documentation at http://mng.bz/p9p2.

The following listing provides an example of what happens when we have only one copy of our data and the broker it is on goes down. This can happen when we allow the broker defaults and do not pick them with purpose. To begin, make sure that your local test Kafka cluster is running with three nodes, and create a topic like listing 6.2 presents.

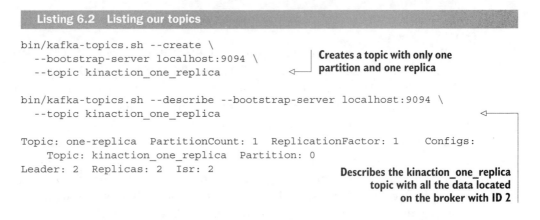

Listing 6.2 Listing our topics

```
bin/kafka-topics.sh --create \
  --bootstrap-server localhost:9094 \
  --topic kinaction_one_replica
```
Creates a topic with only one
partition and one replica

```
bin/kafka-topics.sh --describe --bootstrap-server localhost:9094 \
  --topic kinaction_one_replica
```

```
Topic: one-replica  PartitionCount: 1  ReplicationFactor: 1   Configs:
    Topic: kinaction_one_replica  Partition: 0
Leader: 2  Replicas: 2  Isr: 2
```
Describes the kinaction_one_replica
topic with all the data located
on the broker with ID 2

When we run the commands in listing 6.2 to create and describe the topic
kinaction_one_replica, we'll see that there is only one value in the fields Partition,
Leader, Replicas, and Isr (in-sync replicas). Further, the broker uses the same ID
value. This means that the entire topic depends on that one broker being up and
working.

If we terminate the broker with ID 2 in this example and then try to consume a message for that topic, we would get a message such as "1 partitions have leader brokers
without a matching listener." Because there are no replica copies for the topic's partition, there is no easy way to keep producing or consuming that topic without recovering
that broker. Although this is just one example, it illustrates the importance that broker
configuration can have when users create their topics manually as in listing 6.2.

Another important configuration property to define sets the location for our application logs and errors during normal operation. Let's look at this next.

6.3.1 *Kafka's other logs: Application logs*

As with most applications, Kafka provides logs for letting us know what is going on
inside the application. In the discussion that follows, the term *application logs* refers to
the logs that we usually think of when working with any application, whether debug-
ging or auditing. These application logs are not related to the record logs that form
the backbone of Kafka's feature set.

The location where these application logs are stored is also entirely different than
those for records. When we start a broker, we will find the application log directory in
the Kafka base installation directory under the folder logs/. We can change this location by editing the config/log4j.properties file and the value for kafka.logs.dir [11].

6.3.2 *Server log*

Many errors and unexpected behaviors can be traced back to configuration issues on
startup. The server log file, server.log, is where we would look if there is a startup error
or an exception that terminates the broker. It seems to be the most natural place to

check first for any issues. Look (or use the `grep` command) for the heading `Kafka-Config` values.

If you are overwhelmed when you first look at the directory that holds this file, note that you will likely see other files like controller.log (if the broker was ever in that role) and older dated files with the same name. One tool that you can use for log rotation and compression is `logrotate` (https://linux.die.net/man/8/logrotate), but there are many other tools available as well to manage older server logs.

Something else to mention in regard to these logs is that they are located on each broker. They are not aggregated by default into one location. Various platforms might do this on our behalf, or we can gather them with a tool like Splunk™ (https://www.splunk.com/). It is especially important to know when we are trying to analyze logs to gather them when using something like a cloud environment in which the broker instance might not exist.

6.3.3 *Managing state*

As we discussed in chapter 2, each partition has a single leader replica. A leader replica resides on a single broker at any given time. A broker can host the leader replica of multiple partitions, and any broker in a cluster can host leader replicas. Only one broker in the cluster, however, acts as the controller. The role of the controller is to handle cluster management [12]. The controller also performs other administrative actions like partition reassignment [13].

When we consider a rolling upgrade of a cluster, shutting down and restarting one broker at a time, it is best to do the controller last [14]. Otherwise, we might end up restarting the controller multiple times.

To figure out which broker is the current controller, we can use the zookeeper-shell script to look up the ID of the broker, as listing 6.3 shows. The path /controller exists in ZooKeeper, and in the listing, we run one command to look at the current value. Running that command for my cluster showed my broker with ID 0 as the controller.

Listing 6.3 Listing the current controller

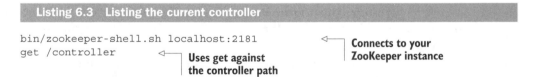

```
bin/zookeeper-shell.sh localhost:2181          ◁──┐  Connects to your
get /controller            ◁──┐                     ZooKeeper instance
                               │  Uses get against
                               │  the controller path
```

Figure 6.2 shows all of the output from ZooKeeper, including the `brokerid` value, `"brokerid":0`. If we migrate or upgrade this cluster, we would upgrade this broker last due to this role.

We will also find a controller log file with the name controller.log that serves as an application log on broker 0 in this case. This log file can be important when we look at broker actions and failures.

```
Connecting to localhost:2181
Welcome to ZooKeeper!
JLine support is disabled

WATCHER::

WatchedEvent state:SyncConnected type:None path:null
get /controller
{"version":1,"brokerid":0,"timestamp":"1540874053577"}
cZxid = 0x2f
ctime = Mon Oct 29 23:34:13 CDT 2018
mZxid = 0x2f
mtime = Mon Oct 29 23:34:13 CDT 2018
pZxid = 0x2f
cversion = 0
dataVersion = 0
aclVersion = 0
ephemeralOwner = 0x166c33ffa650000
dataLength = 54
numChildren = 0
```

Figure 6.2   Example controller output

6.4   *Partition replica leaders and their role*

As a quick refresher, topics are made up of partitions, and partitions can have replicas for fault tolerance. Also, partitions are written on the disks of the Kafka brokers. One of the replicas of the partition will have the job of being the leader. The leader is in charge of handling writes from external producer clients for that partition. Because the leader is the only one with newly written data, it also has the job of being the source of data for the replica followers [15]. And because the ISR list is maintained by the leader, it knows which replicas are up to date and have seen all the current messages. Replicas act as consumers of the leader partition and will fetch the messages [15].

Figure 6.3 shows a three-node cluster with broker 3 as its leader and broker 2 and broker 1 as its followers, using `kinaction_helloworld` as a topic that might have been

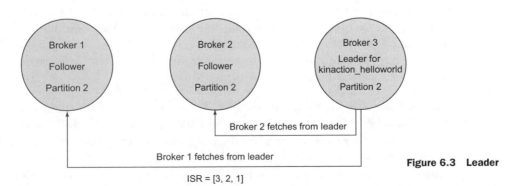

Figure 6.3   Leader

created in this manner. Broker 3 holds the leader replica for partition 2. As the leader, broker 3 handles all of the reads and writes from external producers and consumers. It also handles requests it receives from broker 2 and broker 1 as they pull new messages into their copies. The ISR list [3,2,1] includes the leader in the first position (3) and then the remaining followers (2,1), who stay current with their copies of the messages from the leader.

In some cases, a broker that fails may have hosted the leader replica for a partition. In figure 6.4, the previous example in figure 6.3 experiences a failure. Because broker 3 is not available, a new leader is elected. Figure 6.4 shows the new leader broker 2. Once a follower, it was elected as a leader replica to keep Kafka serving and receiving data for that partition. The ISR list is now [2,1] with the first position reflecting the new leader replica hosted on broker 2.

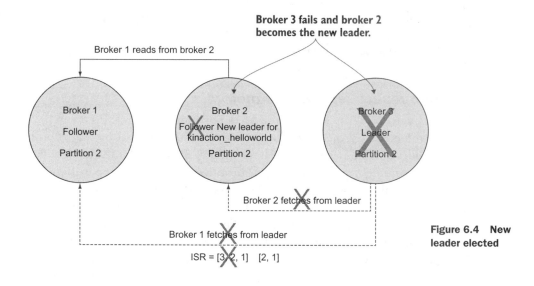

Figure 6.4   New leader elected

NOTE In chapter 5 we discussed a Kafka Improvement Proposal, KIP-392, which allows consumer clients to fetch from the closest replica [16]. Reading from a preferred follower rather than the leader replica is something that might make sense if our brokers span physical data centers. However, when discussing leaders and followers in this book, unless stated otherwise, we will focus on the default leader read and write behaviors.

In-sync replicas (ISRs) are a key piece to really understanding Kafka. For a new topic, a specific number of replicas are created and added to the initial ISR list [17]. This number can be either from a parameter or, as a default, from the broker configuration.

One of the details to note with Kafka is that replicas do not heal themselves by default. If you lose a broker on which one of your copies of a partition exists, Kafka does not (currently) create a new copy. We mention this because some users are used to filesystems like HDFS that maintain their replication number (self-heal) if a block is seen as corrupted or failed. An important item to look at when monitoring the health of our systems is how many of our ISRs are indeed matching our desired number.

Why is watching this number so important? It is good to keep aware of how many copies you have before it hits 0! Let's say that we have a topic that is only one partition and that partition is replicated three times. In the best-case scenario, we would have two copies of the data that is in our lead partition replica. This, of course, means that the follower replicas are caught up with the leader. But what if we lose another ISR?

It is also important to note that if a replica starts to get too far behind in copying messages from the leader, it can be removed from the ISR list. The leader notices if a follower is taking too long and drops it from its list of followers [17]. Then the leader continues to operate with a new ISR list. The result of this "slowness" to the ISR list is the same as in figure 6.4, in which a broker failed.

6.4.1 Losing data

What if we have no ISRs and lose our lead replica due to a failure? When `unclean .leader.election.enable` is `true`, the controller selects a leader for a partition even if it is not up to date so that the system keeps running [15]. The problem with this is that data could be lost because none of the replicas have all the data at the time of the leader's failure.

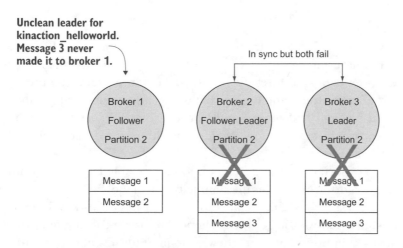

Figure 6.5   Unclean leader election

Figure 6.5 shows data loss in the case of a partition with three replicas. In this case, both brokers 3 and 2 failed and are not online. Because unclean leader election was enabled, broker 1 is made the new leader even though it is not in sync with the other brokers. Broker 1 never sees message 3, so it cannot present that data to clients. At the cost of missing data, this option allows us to keep serving clients.

6.5   *Peeking into Kafka*

There are many tools we can use to capture and view data from our applications. We will look at Grafana® (https://grafana.com/) and Prometheus® (https://prometheus .io/) as examples of tools that can be used to help set up a simple monitoring stack that can be used for Confluent Cloud [18].[1] We'll use Prometheus to extract and store Kafka's metrics data. Then we'll send that data to Grafana to produce helpful graphical views. To fully understand why we are setting up all of the following tools, let's quickly review the components and the work each one does (figure 6.6).

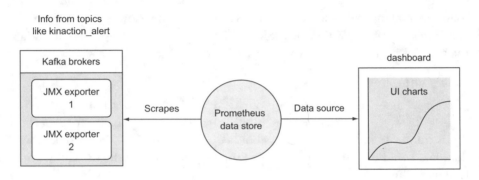

Figure 6.6   Graph flow

In figure 6.6, we use JMX to look inside the Kafka applications. The Kafka exporter takes the JMX notifications and exports them into the Prometheus format. Prometheus scrapes the exporter data and stores the metrics data. Various tools can then take the information from Prometheus and display that information in a visual dashboard.

There are many Docker™ images and Docker Compose files that bundle all of these tools, or you can install each tool to a local machine in order to explore this process in greater detail.

For the Kafka exporter, an outstanding option is available at https://github.com/ danielqsj/kafka_exporter. We prefer the simplicity of this tool because we can just run it and give it one or a list of Kafka servers to watch. It might work well for your use cases as well. Notice that we will get many client and broker-specific metrics because there are quite a few options that we might want to monitor. Even so, this is not a complete list of the metrics available to us.

Figure 6.7 shows a query against a local data store, such as a local instance of Prometheus, that gathers metrics from our Kafka exporter tool. As we discussed about partitions, Kafka replicas do not heal themselves automatically, so one of the things we

---

[1] The Grafana Labs Marks are trademarks of Grafana Labs, and are used with Grafana Labs' permission. We are not affiliated with, endorsed or sponsored by Grafana Labs or its affiliates.

want to monitor is under-replicated partitions. If this number is greater than 0, we might want to look at what is going on in the cluster to determine why there is a replica issue. We might display the data from this query in a chart or dashboard, or we can, potentially, send an alert.

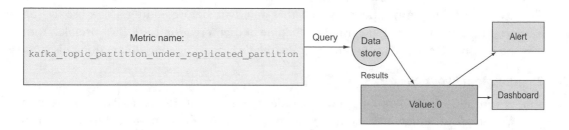

kafka_topic_partition_under_replicated_partition{instance="localhost:9308",job="kafka_exporter",partition="0",topic=kinaction_helloworld)0

Figure 6.7 Metric query example

As noted, the Kafka exporter does not expose every JMX metric. To get more JMX metrics, we can set the `JMX_PORT` environment variable when starting our Kafka processes [19]. Other tools are available that use a Java agent to produce the metrics to an endpoint or port, which Prometheus can scrape.

Listing 6.4 shows how we would set the variable `JMX_PORT` when starting a broker [19]. If we already have a broker running and do not have this port exposed, we will need to restart the broker to affect this change. We may also want to automate the setting of this variable to ensure that it is enabled on all future broker restarts.

Listing 6.4   Starting a broker with a JMX port

```
JMX_PORT=$JMX_PORT bin/kafka-server-start.sh \          ⟵  Adds the JMX_PORT variable
   config/server0.properties                                when starting the cluster
```

6.5.1   Cluster maintenance

As we consider moving to production, we will want to configure more than one server. Another item to note is that various pieces of the ecosystem such as Kafka and Connect clients, Schema Registry, and the REST Proxy do not usually run on the same servers as the brokers themselves. Although we might run all of these on a laptop for testing (and we can run this software on one server), for safety and efficiency, we definitely don't want all of these processes running on a single server when we handle production workloads. To draw a parallel to similarities with tools from the Hadoop ecosystem, Kafka scales well horizontally with more servers. Let's look at adding a server to a cluster.

6.5.2   *Adding a broker*

Beginning with a small cluster is a great way to start, as we can always add brokers to grow our footprint. To add a Kafka broker to our cluster, we just start a new Kafka broker with a unique ID. This ID can either be created with the configuration `broker.id` or with `broker.id.generation.enable` set to `true` [10]. That is pretty much it. But, there is something to be aware of in this situation—the new broker will not be assigned to any partitions! Any topic partitions that we create before adding a new broker still persist on the brokers that existed at the time of their creation [20]. If we are okay with the new broker only handling new topics, then we don't need to do anything else.

6.5.3   *Upgrading your cluster*

As with all software, updates and upgrades are a part of life. Not all systems can be brought down simultaneously and upgraded due to production workloads or business impact. One technique that can be used to avoid downtime for our Kafka applications is the *rolling restart* [14]. This means just upgrading one broker at a time. Figure 6.8 shows each broker being upgraded one at a time before moving on to the next broker for our cluster.

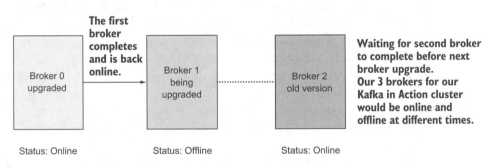

Figure 6.8   Rolling restart

An important broker configuration property for rolling restarts is `controlled.shutdown.enable`. Setting this to `true` enables the transfer of partition leadership before a broker shuts down [21].

6.5.4   *Upgrading your clients*

As mentioned in chapter 4, although Kafka does its best to decouple the clients from the broker, it's beneficial to know the versions of clients with respect to brokers. This bidirectional client compatibility feature was new in Kafka 0.10.2, and brokers version 0.10.0 or later support this feature [22]. Clients can usually be upgraded *after* all of the Kafka brokers in a cluster are upgraded. As with any upgrade, though, take a peek at the version notes to make sure newer versions are compatible.

6.5.5 *Backups*

Kafka does not have a backup strategy like one would use for a database; we don't take a snapshot or disk backup per se. Because Kafka logs exist on disk, why not just copy the entire partition directories? Although nothing is stopping us from doing that, one concern is making a copy of all of the data directories across all locations. Rather than performing manual copies and coordinating across brokers, one preferred option is for a cluster to be backed by a second cluster [23]. Between the two clusters, events are then replicated between topics. One of the earliest tools that you might have seen in production settings is MirrorMaker. A newer version of this tool (called Mirror-Maker 2.0) was released with Kafka version 2.4.0 [24]. In the bin subdirectory of the Kafka install directory, we will find a shell script named kafka-mirror-maker as well as a new MirrorMaker 2.0 script, connect-mirror-maker.

There are also some other open source as well as enterprise offerings for mirroring data between clusters. Confluent Replicator (http://mng.bz/Yw7K) and Cluster Link-ing (http://mng.bz/OQZo) are also options to be aware of [25].

6.6 *A note on stateful systems*

Kafka is an application that definitely works with stateful data stores. In this book, we will work on our own nodes and not with any cloud deployments. There are some great resources, including Confluent's site on using the Kubernetes Confluent Operator API (https://www.confluent.io/confluent-operator/) as well as Docker images available to do what you need done. Another interesting option is Strimzi™ (https://github.com/strimzi/strimzi-kafka-operator), if you are looking at running your cluster on Kubernetes. At the time of this writing, Strimzi is a Cloud Native Computing Foundation® (https://www.cncf.io/) sandbox project. If you are familiar with these tools, it might be a quick way for you to kick the tires on a proof of concept (PoC) setup if you find some interesting projects out in the Docker Hub. There is not, however, a one-size-fits-all mandate for our infrastructure.

One benefit of Kubernetes that stands out is its ability to create new clusters quickly and with different storage and service communication options that Gwen Shapira explores further in her paper, "Recommendations for Deploying Apache Kafka on Kubernetes" [26]. For some companies, giving each product its own cluster might be easier to manage than having one huge cluster for the entire enterprise. The ability to spin up a cluster quickly rather than adding physical servers can provide the quick turnaround products need.

Figure 6.9 shows a general outline of how Kafka brokers can be set up in Kubernetes with an operator pod, similar to how the Confluent and Strimzi operators might work. The terms in the figure are Kubernetes-specific, and we do not provide much explanation here because we do not want to shift the focus away from learning about Kafka itself. We, rather, provide a general overview. Note that this is how a cluster *could* work, not a specific setup description.

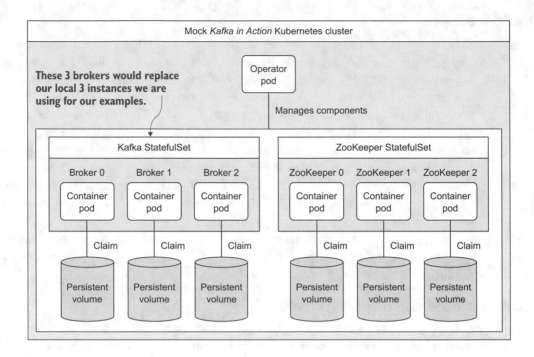

Figure 6.9   Kafka on Kubernetes

The Kubernetes operator is its own pod that lives inside of the Kubernetes cluster. As well, each broker is in its own pod as a part of a logical group called a StatefulSet. The purpose of the StatefulSet is to manage the Kafka pods and help guarantee ordering and an identity for each pod. If the pod that hosts a broker (the JVM process) with ID 0 fails, for example, a new pod is created with that identity (and not a random ID) and attaches to the same persistent storage volume as before. Because these volumes hold the messages of the Kafka partitions, the data is maintained. This statefulness helps overcome the sometimes short lives of containers. Each ZooKeeper node would also be in its own pod and part of its own StatefulSet.

For those who are new to Kubernetes or are anxious about the transition to such a platform, one migration strategy that can be helpful is to run Kafka clients and applications on a Kubernetes cluster before the Kafka brokers. Besides being stateless, running our clients in this manner can help us get a feel for Kubernetes at the start of our learning path. However, we should not neglect the need to understand Kubernetes well in order to run Kafka on top of this platform.

One developer team of four that one of the authors worked with recently focused half of the team on Kubernetes and half on running Kafka. Of course, this ratio might not be what every team encounters. The developer time required to focus on Kubernetes depends on your team and overall experience.

6.7 Exercise

Because it can be hard to apply some of our new learning in a hands-on manner and because this chapter is heavier on commands than code, it might be helpful to have a quick exercise to explore a different way to discover the metric under-replicated partitions rather than the exporter we saw earlier. Besides using something like a dashboard to see this data, what command line options can we use to discover this information?

Let's say that we want to confirm the health of one of our topics named `kinaction_replica_test`. We created this topic with each partition having three replicas. We want to make sure we have three brokers listed in the ISR list in case there is ever a broker failure. What command should we run to look at that topic and see its current status? Listing 6.5 shows an example describing that topic [27]. Notice that the `ReplicationFactor` is 3 and the `Replicas` list shows three broker IDs as well. However, the ISR list only shows two values when it should show three!

Listing 6.5 Describing the topic replica: a test for ISR count

Note the topic parameter and the describe flag in use.

```
$ bin/kafka-topics.sh --describe --bootstrap-server localhost:9094 \
  --topic kinaction_replica_test

Topic:kinaction_replica_test  PartitionCount:1  ReplicationFactor:3    Configs:
    Topic: kinaction_replica_test  Partition: 0

  Leader: 0  Replicas: 1,0,2  Isr: 0,2
```

Topic-specific information about leader, partition, and replicas

---

Although we can notice the under-replicated partitions issue by looking at the details of the command output, we could have also used the `--under-replicated-partitions` flag to see any problems quickly [27]. Listing 6.6 shows how to use this flag, which quickly filters out the hard-to-see ISR data and only outputs under-replicated partitions to the terminal.

Listing 6.6 Using the `under-replicated-partitions` flag

```
bin/kafka-topics.sh --describe --bootstrap-server localhost:9094 \
  --under-replicated-partitions

Topic: kinaction_replica_test  Partition: 0
⇒  Leader: 0  Replicas: 1,0,2  Isr: 0,2
```

Note the under-replicated-partition flag in use.

The ISR only lists two brokers!

Listing 6.6 shows that when using the `--describe` flag, we do not have to limit the check for under-replicated partitions to a specific topic. We can run this command to display issues across topics and to quickly find issues on our cluster. We will explore more of the out-of-the-box tools included with Kafka when we talk about administration tools in chapter 9.

> **TIP** When using any of the commands in this chapter, it is always a good idea to run the command without any parameters and read the command options that are available for troubleshooting.

As we examined more about Kafka in this chapter, we've come to realize we are running a complex system. However, there are various command line tools as well as metrics to help us monitor the health of our cluster. In our next chapter, we will continue to use commands to complete specific tasks for this dynamic system throughout its lifetime.

Summary

- Brokers are the centerpiece of Kafka and provide the logic with which external clients interface with our applications. Clusters provide not only scale but also reliability.
- We can use ZooKeeper to provide agreement in a distributed cluster. One example is to elect a new controller between multiple available brokers.
- To help manage our cluster, we can set configurations at the broker level, which our clients can override for specific options.
- Replicas allow for a number of copies of data to span across a cluster. This helps in the event a broker fails and cannot be reached.
- In-sync replicas (ISRs) are current with the leader's data and that can take over leadership for a partition without data loss.
- We can use metrics to help produce graphs to visually monitor a cluster or alert on potential issues.

References

1 "Post Kafka Deployment." Confluent documentation (n.d.). https://docs.confluent.io/platform/current/kafka/post-deployment.html#balancing-replicas-across-racks (accessed September 15, 2019).

2 "KIP-500: Replace ZooKeeper with a Self-Managed Metadata Quorum." Wiki for Apache Kafka. Apache Software Foundation (July 09, 2020). https://cwiki.apache.org/confluence/display/KAFKA/KIP-500%3A+Replace+ZooKeeper+with+a+Self-Managed+Metadata+Quorum (accessed August 22, 2020).

3 F. Junqueira and N. Narkhede. "Distributed Consensus Reloaded: Apache ZooKeeper and Replication in Apache Kafka." Confluent blog (August 27, 2015). https://www.confluent.io/blog/distributed-consensus-reloaded-apache-zookeeper-and-replication-in-kafka/ (accessed September 15, 2019).

4 "Kafka data structures in Zookeeper [sic]." Wiki for Apache Kafka. Apache Software Foundation (February 10, 2017). https://cwiki.apache.org/confluence/display/KAFKA/Kafka+data+structures+in+Zookeeper (accessed January 19, 2020).

5 C. McCabe. "Apache Kafka Needs No Keeper: Removing the Apache Zoo-Keeper Dependency." Confluent blog. (May 15, 2020). https://www.confluent .io/blog/upgrading-apache-kafka-clients-just-got-easier (accessed August 20, 2021).

6 Apache Kafka Binder (n.d.). https://docs.spring.io/spring-cloud-stream -binder-kafka/docs/3.1.3/reference/html/spring-cloud-stream-binder-kafka .html#_apache_kafka_binder (accessed July 18, 2021).

7 "CLI Tools for Confluent Platform." Confluent documentation (n.d.). https:// docs.confluent.io/platform/current/installation/cli-reference.html (accessed August 25, 2021).

8 "ZkData.scala." Apache Kafka GitHub. https://github.com/apache/kafka/ blob/99b9b3e84f4e98c3f07714e1de6a139a004cbc5b/core/src/main/scala/ kafka/zk/ZkData.scala (accessed August 27, 2021).

9 "A Guide To The Kafka Protocol." Wiki for Apache Kafka. Apache Software Foundation (June 14, 2017). https://cwiki.apache.org/confluence/display/ KAFKA/A+Guide+To+The+Kafka+Protocol (accessed September 15, 2019).

10 "Kafka Broker Configurations." Confluent documentation (n.d.). https://docs .confluent.io/platform/current/installation/configuration/broker-configs .html (accessed August 21, 2021).

11 "Logging." Confluent documentation (n.d.). https://docs.confluent.io/platform/ current/kafka/post-deployment.html#logging (accessed August 21, 2021).

12 "Controller." Confluent documentation (n.d.). https://docs.confluent.io/ platform/current/kafka/post-deployment.html#controller (accessed August 21, 2021).

13 "Kafka Controller Internals." Wiki for Apache Kafka. Apache Software Founda-tion (January 26, 2014). https://cwiki.apache.org/confluence/display/ KAFKA/Kafka+Controller+Internals (accessed September 15, 2019).

14 "Post Kafka Deployment." Confluent documentation (n.d.). https://docs .confluent.io/platform/current/kafka/post-deployment.html#rolling-restart (accessed July 10, 2019).

15 "Replication." Confluent documentation (n.d.). https://docs.confluent.io/plat-form/current/kafka/design.html#replication (accessed August 21, 2021).

16 "KIP-392: Allow consumers to fetch from closest replica." Wiki for Apache Kafka. Apache Software Foundation (November 5, 2019). https://cwiki.apache .org/confluence/display/KAFKA/KIP-392%3A+Allow+consumers+to+fetch+ from+closest+replica (accessed December 10, 2019).

17 N. Narkhede. "Hands-free Kafka Replication: A lesson in operational simplicity." Confluent blog (July 1, 2015). https://www.confluent.io/blog/hands-free-kafka -replication-a-lesson-in-operational-simplicity/ (accessed October 02, 2019).

18 "Observability Overview and Setup." Confluent documentation (n.d.). https:// docs.confluent.io/platform/current/tutorials/examples/ccloud-observability/ docs/observability-overview.html (accessed August 26, 2021).

19   "Kafka Monitoring and Metrics Using JMX". Confluent documentation. (n.d.). https://docs.confluent.io/platform/current/installation/docker/operations/ monitoring.html (accessed June 12, 2020).

20   "Scaling the Cluster (Adding a node to a Kafka cluster)." Confluent documentation (n.d.). https://docs.confluent.io/platform/current/kafka/post-deploy ment.html#scaling-the-cluster-adding-a-node-to-a-ak-cluster (accessed August 21, 2021).

21   "Graceful shutdown." Apache Software Foundation (n.d.). https://kafka.apache .org/documentation/#basic_ops_restarting (accessed May 11, 2018).

22   C. McCabe. "Upgrading Apache Kafka Clients Just Got Easier." Confluent blog. (July 18, 2017). https://www.confluent.io/blog/upgrading-apache-kafka-cli ents-just-got-easier (accessed October 02, 2019).

23   "Backup and Restoration." Confluent documentation (n.d.). https://docs .confluent.io/platform/current/kafka/post-deployment.html#backup-and -restoration (accessed August 21, 2021).

24   Release Notes, Kafka Version 2.4.0. Apache Software Foundation (n.d.). https:// archive.apache.org/dist/kafka/2.4.0/RELEASE_NOTES.html (accessed May 12, 2020).

25   "Multi-DC Solutions." Confluent documentation (n.d.). https://docs.confluent .io/platform/current/multi-dc-deployments/index.html#multi-dc-solutions (accessed August 21, 2021).

26   G. Shapira. "Recommendations_for_Deploying_Apache_Kafka_on_Kuberne tes." White paper (2018). https://www.confluent.io/resources/recommenda tions-for-deploying-apache-kafka-on-kubernetes (accessed December 15, 2019).

27   "Replication tools." Wiki for Apache Kafka. Apache Software Foundation (February 4, 2019). https://cwiki.apache.org/confluence/display/kafka/replica tion+tools (accessed January 19, 2019).

Topics and partitions

7

This chapters covers

- Creation parameters and configuration options
- How partitions exist as log files
- How segments impact data inside partitions
- Testing with `EmbeddedKafkaCluster`
- Topic compaction and how data can be retained

In this chapter, we will look further into how we might store our data across topics as well as how to create and maintain topics. This includes how partitions fit into our design considerations and how we can view our data on the brokers. All of this information will help us as we also look at how to make a topic update data rather than appending it to a log.

7.1 Topics

To quickly refresh our memory, it is important to know that a topic is a non-concrete concept rather than a physical structure. It does not usually exist on only one broker. Most applications consuming Kafka data view that data as being in a single topic; no other details are needed for them to subscribe. However, behind the topic name are one or more partitions that actually hold the data [1]. Kafka writes the data that makes up a topic in the cluster to logs, which are written to the broker filesystems.

Figure 7.1 shows partitions that make up one topic named `kinaction _helloworld`. A single partition's copy is not split between brokers and has a physical footprint on each disk. Figure 7.1 also shows how those partitions are made up of messages that are sent to the topic.

If writing to a topic is so simple in getting-started examples, why do we need to understand the role and pieces that make up a topic? At the highest level, this impacts how our consumers get to the data. Let's say that our company is selling spots for a training class

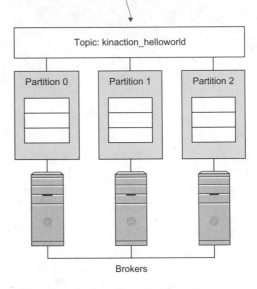

The topic kinaction_helloworld is made up of three partitions that will likely be spread out among different brokers.

Figure 7.1   Example topic with partitions

using a web-based application that sends the events of user actions into our Kafka cluster. Our overall application process could generate droves of events. For example, there would be an event for the initial search on the location, one for the specific training being selected by the customer, and a third for classes that are confirmed. Should the producing applications send all of this data to a single topic or several topics? Is each message a specific type of event, and should each remain separated in different topics? There are adjustments with each approach and some things to consider that will help us determine the best method to take in every situation.

We see topic design as a two-step process. The first looks at the events we have. Do they belong in one topic or more than one? The second considers each topic. What is the number of partitions we should use? The biggest takeaway is that partitions are a per-topic design question and not a cluster-wide limitation or mandate. Although we can set a default number of partitions for topic creation, in most cases, we should consider how the topic will be used and what data it will hold.

We should have a solid reason to pick a specific number of partitions. Jun Rao wrote a fantastic article titled "How to choose the number of topics/partitions in a Kafka cluster?" on the Confluent blog about this very subject [2]! Let's say that we want to have a partition for each server as a generic rule. However, because we have one partition on each server does not mean producers will write evenly among them. To do so, we would have to ensure that each partition leader is spread out in that manner and stays that way.

We also need to get familiar with our data. Let's take a look at a list of items to think about, both in general and in this training class scenario:

- Data correctness
- The volume of messages of interest per consumer
- How much data you will have or need to process

Data correctness is at the top of most data concerns in real-world designs. This term could be considered vague, so our defintion is explained here as our opinion. With regard to topics, this involves making sure that events that must be ordered end up in the same partition and, thus, the same topic. Although we can place events by our consumers in an order based on a timestamp, it is more trouble (and error prone) to handle cross-topic event coordination than it is worth, in our opinion. If we use keyed messages and need those in order, we should care about partitions and any future changes to those partitions [1].

For data correctness with our three previous example events, it might be helpful to place the events with a message key (including the student ID) in two separate topics for the actual booked and confirmed/billed events. These events are student-specific, and this approach would be helpful to ensure that confirmation of a class occurs for that specific student. The search events themselves, however, may not be of interest or need to be ordered for a specific student if, for example, our analytics team is looking for the most popular searched cities rather than student information.

Next, we should consider the *volume of messages* of interest per consumer. For our theoretical training system, let's look at the number of events as we consider the topic placement. The search events themselves would far outnumber the other events. Let's say that a training location near a large city gets 50,000 searches a day but only has room for 100 students. Traffic on most days produces 50,000 search events and fewer than 100 actual booked training events. Will our confirmation team have an application that would want to subscribe to a generic event topic in which it uses or cares about less than 1% of the total messages? Most of the consumer's time would be, in effect, filtering out the mass of events to process only a select few.

Another point to account for is *the quantity of data* we will be processing. Will the number of messages require multiple consumers to be running in order to process within the time constraints required by our applications? If so, we have to be aware of how the number of consumers in a group is limited by the partitions in our topic [2]. It is easier at this point to create more partitions than we think we might require. Having more capacity for consumers to grow allows us to increase in volume without having to deal with repartitioning data. However, it is important to know that partitions are not an unlimited free resource, as talked about in Rao's article that we mentioned earlier. It also means having more brokers to migrate in case of a broker failure, which could be a potential headache in the making.

It's best to find a happy medium and to go with that as we design our systems. Figure 7.2 shows how our design might be best suited to two topics for the three event

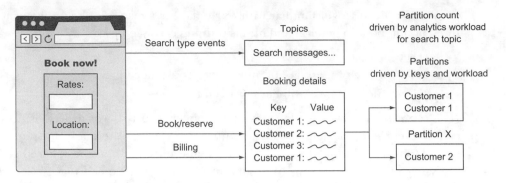

Figure 7.2   Example training event topic design

types we used in our scenario. As always, more requirements or details can change our future implementations.

A last thing to consider when deciding on the number of partitions for a topic is that reducing that number is not currently supported [3]. There may be ways to do this, but it is definitely not advised! Let's take a moment to think about why this would not be desirable.

When consumers subscribe to a topic, they really are attached to a partition. The removal of a partition could lose its current position when or if a consumer starts reading from a reassigned partition. This is where we need to make sure our keyed messages and consuming clients can follow any changes we make at the broker level. We impact consumers with our actions. Now that we've discussed topic design, let's dig a little deeper into the options that we can set when creating topics. We touched on these briefly when we created topics to produce messages in chapter 3, so we'll dive a bit deeper here.

7.1.1   *Topic-creation options*

Kafka topics have a couple of core options that must be set in order to create a topic. Although we have created topics since chapter 2 (with our `kinaction_helloworld` topic), we need to make sure we dig into the basic parameters that were glossed over. For these parameters, it's best to treat these decisions with thought and care and be intentional [4].

Another important decision to make at creation time is if you will ever need to delete a topic. Because this operation is significant, we want to make sure it cannot happen without a logical confirmation. For this, Kafka requires us to enable the `delete.topic.enable` option. If this is switched to `true`, we will be able to successfully delete the topic and it will then be removed [5].

It is nice to know that Kafka scripts have good usage documentation in general. We recommend running the command `kafka-topics.sh` first to see what various actions you can attempt. The following listing shows an incomplete command to get help.

Listing 7.1   Listing our topic options

```
bin/kafka-topics.sh
```
⊲┐ **Runs the generic Kafka topic-related command**

In the output that we'll see, one obvious command stands out: `--create`. Adding that parameter helps us get further information related to the `create` action itself (for example, "Missing required argument `"[topic]"`"). The following listing shows our still incomplete generic command built a little further.

Listing 7.2   Listing our topic options with `--create`

```
bin/kafka-topics.sh --create
```
⊲┐ **Lists command-specific errors and the help documentation**

Why spend time even talking about these steps, as some users are familiar with manual (man) pages as part of their Linux® work? Even though Kafka does not present data about how to use the tooling in that manner, this command is available before you have to search on Google.

Once we have a name that does not have over 249 characters (it's been attempted before), we can create our topic [6]. For our examples, we'll create `kinaction _topicandpart` with a replication factor of 2 and with two partitions. The next listing shows the syntax to use in the command prompt [3].

Listing 7.3   Creating another topic

```
bin/kafka-topics.sh
    --create --bootstrap-server localhost:9094 \
    --topic kinaction_topicandpart \
    --partitions 2 \
    --replication-factor 2
```
Adds the create option to our command
Names our topic
Ensures that we have two copies of our data
Creates our topic with two partitions

After we create our topic, we can `describe` that topic to make sure our settings look correct. Notice in figure 7.3 how our partition and replication factor match the command we just ran.

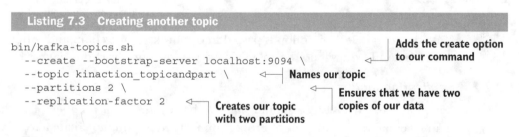

```
) bin/kafka-topics.sh --bootstrap-server localhost:9092 --describe --topic kinaction_topicandpart
Topic: kinaction_topicandpart    PartitionCount: 2        ReplicationFactor: 2    Configs:
        Topic: kinaction_topicandpart    Partition: 0    Leader: 1    Replicas: 1,0    Isr: 1,0
        Topic: kinaction_topicandpart    Partition: 1    Leader: 0    Replicas: 0,2    Isr: 0,2
```

Figure 7.3   Describing a topic with two partitions

In our opinion, another option that is good to take care of at the broker level is to set `auto.create.topics.enable` to `false` [7]. Doing this ensures that we create our topics on purpose and not from a producer sending a message to a topic name that was mistyped and never actually existed before a message was attempted. Although not tightly coupled, usually producers and consumers do need to know the correct topic name of where their data should live. This automatic topic creation can cause confusion. But while testing and learning Kafka, autocreated topics can be helpful. For a concrete example, if we run the command

```
kafka-console-producer.sh --bootstrap-server localhost:9094 --topic notexisting
```

without that topic existing, Kafka creates that topic for us. And if we run

```
kafka-topics.sh --bootstrap-server localhost:9094 --list
```

we would now have that topic in our cluster.

Although we usually focus on not removing data from production environments, as we continue in our own exploration of topics, we might run across some mistakes. It's good to know that we can indeed remove a topic if needed [3]. When we do that, all the data in the topic is removed. This is not something we would do unless we're ready to get rid of that data for good! Listing 7.4 shows how to use the `kafka-topic` command we used before, but this time to delete a topic named `kinaction_topicandpart` [3].

Listing 7.4   **Deleting a topic**

```
bin/kafka-topics.sh --delete --bootstrap-server localhost:9094
  --topic kinaction_topicandpart            <──┐  Removes topic
                                               │  kinaction_topicandpart
```

Note that the `--delete` option is passed to our Kafka topics command. After running this command, you will not be able to work with this topic for your data as before.

7.1.2   *Replication factors*

For practical purposes, we should plan on having the total number of replicas less than or equal to the number of brokers. In fact, attempting to create a topic with the number of replicas being greater than the total number of brokers results in an error: `InvalidReplicationFactorException` [8]. We may imagine why this is an error. Imagine, we only have two brokers, and we want three replicas of a partition. One of those replicas would exist on one broker and two on the other broker. In this case, if we lost the broker that was hosting two of the replicas, we would be down to only one copy of the data. Losing multiple replicas of your data at once is not the ideal way to provide recovery in the face of failure.

7.2   *Partitions*

Moving on from dealing with Kafka commands at a (mostly) topic level, let's start to look deeper at partitions. From a consumer standpoint, each partition is an immutable log of messages. It should only grow and append messages to our data store. Although this data does not grow forever in practice, thinking of the data as being added to rather than modified in place is a good mental model to maintain. Also, consumer clients cannot directly delete messages. This is what makes it possible to replay messages from a topic, which is a feature that can help us in many scenarios.

7.2.1 *Partition location*

One thing that might be helpful is to look at how the data is stored on our brokers. To start, let's find the location of the log.dirs (or log.dir) directory. Its location can be found by looking for log.dirs in your server.properties file if you followed along from appendix A. Under that directory, we should be able to see subfolders with a topic name and a partition number. If we pick one of those folders and look inside, we will see a couple of different files with these extensions: .index, .log, and .timeindex. Figure 7.4 shows how a single partition (in this case, 1) in our test topic looks by issuing a directory listing (ls).

```
) ls /tmp/kafkainaction/kafka-logs-0/kinaction_topicandpart-1
00000000000000000000.index    00000000000000000000.log    00000000000000000000.timeindex  leader-epoch-checkpoint
```

Figure 7.4 Partition directory listing

Sharp-eyed readers might see the file named leader-epoch-checkpoint and maybe even files with a .snapshot extension (not shown above) in their own directory. The leader-epoch-checkpoint file and snapshot files are those that we will not spend time looking at.

The files with the .log extension are where our data payload is stored. Other important information in the log file includes the offset of the message as well as the CreateTime field. Why the need for any other files then? Because Kafka is built for speed, it uses the .index and .timeindex files to store a mapping between the logical message offset and a physical position inside the index file [9].

As shown so far, partitions are made up of many files. In essence, this means that on a physical disk, a partition is not one single file but is rather split into several segments [10]. Figure 7.5 shows how multiple segments might make up a partition.

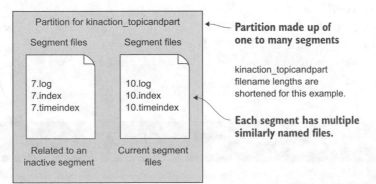

Figure 7.5 Segments make up a partition.

An active segment is the file to which new messages are currently written [11]. In our illustration, 10.log is where messages are being written in the partition directory. Older segments are managed by Kafka in various ways in which the active segment will not be; this includes being governed for retention based on the size of the messages or time configuration. These older segments (like 7.log in figure 7.5) can be eligible for topic compaction, which we will touch on later in this chapter.

To recap what we now know about segments, we know why we might have multiple files with the same name in a partition directory but with an .index, .timeindex, or .log extension. For example, if we have 4 segments, we would have a set of 4 files, each with one of the previous 3 extensions, for a total of 12 files. If we only see 1 of each file extension, we only have 1 segment.

7.2.2   *Viewing our logs*

Let's try to take a peek at a log file to see the messages we have produced for our topic so far. If we open it in a text editor, we will not see those messages in a human-readable format. Confluent has a script that we can use to look at those log segments [12]. Listing 7.5 shows us passing the command to awk and grep to look at a segment log file for partition 1 of the topic kinaction_topicandpart.

Listing 7.5   Looking at a dump of a log segment

```
bin/kafka-dump-log.sh --print-data-log \          ⟵ Prints data that cannot be
  --files /tmp/kafkainaction/kafka-logs-0/             viewed easily with a text editor
⟹ kinaction_topicandpart-1/*.log \
| awk -F: '{print $NF}' | grep kinaction          ⟵ Passes a file
                                                       to read
```

By using the --files option, which is required, we chose to look at a segment file. Assuming the command is successful, we should see a list of messages printed to the screen. Without using awk and grep, you would also see offsets as well as other related metadata like compression codecs. This is definitely an interesting way to see how Kafka places messages on the broker and the data it retains around those messages. The ability to see the actual messages is empowering as it really helps you see the log in action that drives Kafka.

Looking at figure 7.6, we can see a payload in text that is a little easier to read than when we tried to cat the log file directly. For example, we can see a message in the segment file with the payload kinaction_helloworld. Hopefully, you will have more valuable data!

```
⟩ bin/kafka-dump-log.sh --print-data-log --files /tmp/kafkainaction/kafka-logs-0/kinaction_topicandpart-1/*.
log | awk -F: '{print $NF}' | grep kinaction
Dumping /tmp/kafkainaction/kafka-logs-0/kinaction_topicandpart-1/00000000000000000000.log
 kinaction_helloworld
```

Figure 7.6   Viewing a log segment

As for the large number in the log filename, it is not random. The segment name should be the same as the first offset in that file.

One of the impacts of being able to see this data is that we now have to be concerned with who else can see it. Because data security and access controls are common concerns with most data that holds values, we will look at ways you can secure Kafka and topics in chapter 10. Facts about the segment log and index files are details that we would not normally rely on in our applications. However, knowing how to look at these logs might be helpful when understanding how our logs really exist.

It helps to imagine Kafka as a living and complex system (it is distributed, after all) that might need some care and feeding from time to time. In this next section, we will tackle testing our topic.

7.3 *Testing with EmbeddedKafkaCluster*

With all of the configuration options we have, it might be nice to test them as well. What if we could spin up a Kafka cluster without having a real production-ready cluster handy? Kafka Streams provides an integration utility class called `EmbeddedKafka-Cluster` that serves as a middle ground between mock objects and a full-blown cluster. This class provides an in-memory Kafka cluster [13]. Although built with Kafka Streams in mind, we can use it to test our Kafka clients.

Listing 7.6 is set up like the tests found in the book *Kafka Streams in Action* by William P. Bejeck Jr., for example, his `KafkaStreamsYellingIntegrationTest` class [14]. That book and his following book, *Event Streaming with Kafka Streams and ksqlDB*, show more in-depth testing examples. We recommend checking those out, including his suggestion of using Testcontainers (https://www.testcontainers.org/). The following listing shows testing with `EmbeddedKafkaCluster` and JUnit 4.

Listing 7.6 Testing with `EmbeddedKafkaCluster`

```
@ClassRule
public static final EmbeddedKafkaCluster embeddedKafkaCluster
    = new EmbeddedKafkaCluster(BROKER_NUMBER);          ◁── Uses JUnit-specific annotation
                                                            to create the cluster with a
private Properties kaProducerProperties;                     specific number of brokers
private Properties kaConsumerProperties;

@Before
public void setUpBeforeClass() throws Exception {
    embeddedKafkaCluster.createTopic(TOPIC,
        PARTITION_NUMBER, REPLICATION_NUMBER);
    kaProducerProperties = TestUtils.producerConfig(
        embeddedKafkaCluster.bootstrapServers(),
        AlertKeySerde.class,
        StringSerializer.class);                        ◁─

    kaConsumerProperties = TestUtils.consumerConfig(        Sets the consumer
        embeddedKafkaCluster.bootstrapServers(),            configuration to point to the
        AlertKeySerde.class,                                embedded cluster brokers
        StringDeserializer.class);                      ◁─
}
```

```
@Test
public void testAlertPartitioner() throws InterruptedException {
    AlertProducer alertProducer =  new AlertProducer();
    try {
        alertProducer.sendMessage(kaProducerProperties);
    } catch (Exception ex) {
        fail("kinaction_error EmbeddedKafkaCluster exception"
        ➥ + ex.getMessage());
    }

    AlertConsumer alertConsumer = new AlertConsumer();
    ConsumerRecords<Alert, String> records =
        alertConsumer.getAlertMessages(kaConsumerProperties);
    TopicPartition partition = new TopicPartition(TOPIC, 0);
    List<ConsumerRecord<Alert, String>> results = records.records(partition);
    assertEquals(0, results.get(0).partition());
}
```

Calls the client without any changes, which is clueless of the underlying cluster being embedded

Asserts that the embedded cluster handled the message from production to consumption

When testing with `EmbeddedKafkaCluster`, one of the most important parts of the setup is to make sure that the embedded cluster is started before the actual testing begins. Because this cluster is temporary, another key point is to make sure that the producer and consumer clients know how to point to this in-memory cluster. To discover those endpoints, we can use the method `bootstrapServers()` to provide the needed configuration to the clients. Injecting that configuration into the client instances is again up to your configuration strategy, but it can be as simple as setting the values with a method call. Besides these configurations, the clients should be able to test away without the need to provide mock Kafka features!

The test in listing 7.6 verifies that the `AlertLevelPartitioner` logic was correct. Using that custom partitioner logic with a critical message should have landed the alert on partition 0 with our example code in chapter 4. By retrieving the messages for `Topic-Partition(TOPIC, 0)` and looking at the included messages, the message partition location was confirmed. Overall, this level of testing is usually considered integration testing and moves you beyond just a single component under test. At this point, we have tested our client logic together with a Kafka cluster, integrating more than one module.

> **NOTE** Make sure that you reference the pom.xml changes in the source code for chapter 7. There are various JARs that were not needed in previous chapters. Also, some JARs are only included with specific classifiers, noting that they are only needed for test scenarios.

7.3.1 *Using Kafka Testcontainers*

If you find that you are having to create and then tear down your infrastructure, one option that you can use (especially for integration testing) is Testcontainers (https://www.testcontainers.org/modules/kafka/). This Java library uses Docker and one of a variety of JVM testing frameworks like JUnit. Testcontainers depends on Docker images to provide you with a running cluster. If your workflow is Docker-based or a development technique your team uses well, Testcontainers is worth looking into to get a Kafka cluster set up for testing.

NOTE One of the coauthors of this book, Viktor Gamov, maintains a repository (https://github.com/gAmUssA/testcontainers-java-module-confluent-platform) of integration testing Confluent Platform components (including Kafka, Schema Registry, ksqlDB).

7.4 Topic compaction

Now that we have a solid foundation on topics being made up of partitions and partitions being made up of segments, it is time to talk about the details of log compaction. With compaction, the goal is not to expire messages but rather to make sure that the latest value for a key exists and not to maintain any previous state. As just referenced, compaction depends on a key being part of the messages and that key not being `null` [10].

The configuration option that we used to create a compacted topic is `cleanup.policy=compact` [15]. This differs from the default configuration value that was set to `delete` before our override. In other words, we have to choose to create a compacted topic or the topic won't exist in that way. The following listing adds the configuration option needed for this new compacted topic.

Listing 7.7 Creating a compacted topic

```
bin/kafka-topics.sh --create --bootstrap-server localhost:9094 \    ◁── Creates the topic like any other topic
  --topic kinaction_compact --partitions 3 --replication-factor 3 \
  --config cleanup.policy=compact    ◁── Creates our topic type to be compacted
```

One of the easiest comparisons for how a compacted topic presents data can be seen in how code would update an array's existing field rather than appending more data. Let's say that we want to keep a current membership status for an online membership. A user can only be in one state at a time, either a Basic or a Gold membership. At first, a user enrolls in the Basic plan, but over time, upgrades to the Gold plan for more features. Although this is still an event that Kafka stores, in our case, we only want the most recent membership level for a specific customer (our key). Figure 7.7 shows an example using three customers.

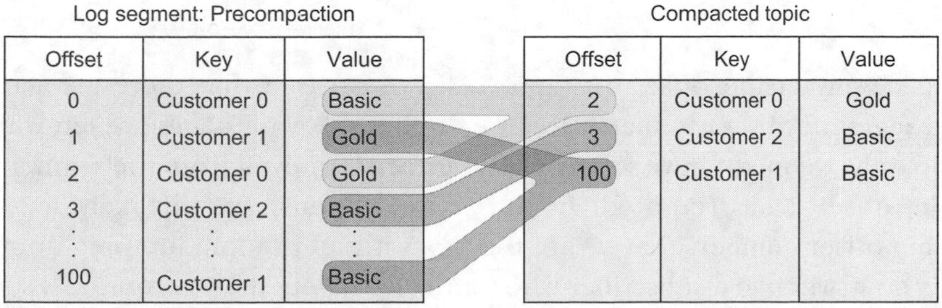

Log segment: Precompaction

Offset	Key	Value
0	Customer 0	Basic
1	Customer 1	Gold
2	Customer 0	Gold
3	Customer 2	Basic
⋮	⋮	⋮
100	Customer 1	Basic

Compacted topic

Offset	Key	Value
2	Customer 0	Gold
3	Customer 2	Basic
100	Customer 1	Basic

Figure 7.7 Compaction in general

After compaction is done, the latest customer 0 update (in our example) is all that exists in the topic. A message with offset 2 replaces the old value of `Basic` (message offset 0) for customer 0 with `Gold`. Customer 1 has a current value of `Basic` because the latest key-specific offset of 100 updates the previous offset 1 `Gold` state. As customer 2 only has one event, that event carries over to the compacted topic without any changes.

Another real-world example of why one would want to use a compacted topic is Kafka's internal topic, `__consumer_offsets`. Kafka does not need a history of offsets that a consumer group consumes; it just needs the latest offset. By storing the offsets in a compacted topic, the log, in effect, gets an updated view of the current state of its world.

When a topic is marked for compaction, we can view a single log in a couple of different states: compacted or not. For older segments, duplicate values for each key should have been reduced to just one value once compaction is completed. The active segment messages are those that have not yet been through compaction [11]. Multiple values can exist for a message for a specific key until all the messages are cleaned. Figure 7.8 illustrates how a pointer is used to show which messages have been processed with compaction and which messages have yet to be visited [16].

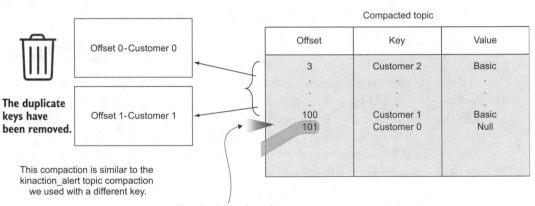

Figure 7.8 Compaction cleaning

Looking closely at the offsets in figure 7.8, we can see that there are gaps in the cleaned segment offset numbers. Because duplicate key messages are left with the latest value only, we might have some offset numbers removed from the segment file, for example, offset 2 was removed. In the active sections, we will likely see the ever-increasing offset numbers that we are used to, without random jumping numbers.

Let's now switch to a subscriber who wanted to delete their account. By sending an event with the subscriber key, like Customer 0, with a message value of `null`, this message will be treated as a delete. This message is considered a `tombstone` [10]. If you have used other systems like Apache HBase™, the notion is similar. Figure 7.9 shows that the null value does not remove a message but is served like any other message [10].

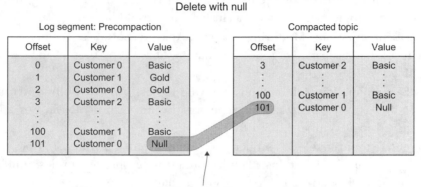

Figure 7.9 Compaction for a deleted value

With delete rules that an application may or may not have to deal with, Kafka can help us fulfill those data requirements with its core feature set.

Throughout this chapter, we have looked at the various details of topics, partitions, and segments. Although broker-specific, they can indeed impact our clients. Because we have experience now with how Kafka stores some of its own data, we are going to spend some time in our next chapter discussing how we can store our data. This includes longer-term storage options for data.

Summary

- Topics are non-concrete rather than physical structures. To understand the topic's behavior, a consumer of that topic needs to know about the number of partitions and the replication factors in play.
- Partitions make up topics and are the basic unit for parallel processing of data inside a topic.
- Log file segments are written in partition directories and are managed by the broker.
- Testing can be used to help validate partition logic and may use an in-memory cluster.
- Topic compaction is a way to provide a view of the latest value of a specific record.

References

1   "Main Concepts and Terminology." Confluent documentation (n.d.). https:// docs.confluent.io/platform/current/kafka/introduction.html#main-concepts- and-terminology (accessed August 28, 2021).

2   J. Rao. "How to choose the number of topics/partitions in a Kafka cluster?" (March 12, 2015). Confluent blog. https://www.confluent.io/blog/how-choose -number-topics-partitions-kafka-cluster/ (accessed May 19, 2019).

3   "Documentation: Modifying topics." Apache Software Foundation (n.d.). https://kafka.apache.org/documentation/#basic_ops_modify_topic (accessed May 19, 2018).

4   "Documentation: Adding and removing topics." Apache Software Foundation (n.d.).   https://kafka.apache.org/documentation/#basic_ops_add_topic (accessed December 11, 2019).

5   "delete.topic.enable." Confluent documentation (n.d.). https://docs.confluent .io/platform/current/installation/configuration/broker-configs.html#broker configs_delete.topic.enable (accessed January 15, 2021).

6   Topics.java. Apache Kafka GitHub. https://github.com/apache/kafka/blob/ 99b9b3e84f4e98c3f07714e1de6a139a004cbc5b/clients/src/main/java/org/ apache/kafka/common/internals/Topic.java (accessed August 27, 2021).

7   "auto.create.topics.enable." Apache Software Foundation (n.d.). https://docs. confluent.io/platform/current/installation/configuration/broker-configs .html#brokerconfigs_auto.create.topics.enable (accessed December 19, 2019).

8   AdminUtils.scala. Apache Kafka GitHub. https://github.com/apache/kafka/ blob/d9b898b678158626bd2872bbfef883ca60a41c43/core/src/main/scala/ kafka/admin/AdminUtils.scala (accessed August 27, 2021).

9   "Documentation: index.interval.bytes." Apache Kafka documentation. https:// kafka.apache.org/documentation/#topicconfigs_index.interval.bytes (accessed August 27, 2021).

10 "Log Compaction." Confluent documentation (n.d.). https://docs.confluent.io/ platform/current/kafka/design.html#log-compaction (accessed August 20, 2021).

11 "Configuring The Log Cleaner." Confluent documentation (n.d.). https:// docs.confluent.io/platform/current/kafka/design.html#configuring-the-log -cleaner (accessed August 27, 2021).

12 "CLI Tools for Confluent Platform." Confluent documentation (n.d.). https:// docs.confluent.io/platform/current/installation/cli-reference.html (accessed August 25, 2021).

13 EmbeddedKafkaCluster.java. Apache Kafka GitHub. https://github.com/ apache/kafka/blob/9af81955c497b31b211b1e21d8323c875518df39/streams/ src/test/java/org/apache/kafka/streams/integration/utils/EmbeddedKafka Cluster.java (accessed August 27, 2021).

14   W. P. Bejeck Jr. *Kafka Streams in Action.* Shelter Island, NY, USA: Manning, 2018.

15   "cleanup.policy." Confluent documentation (n.d.). https://docs.confluent.io/ platform/current/installation/configuration/topic-configs.html#topicconfigs _cleanup.policy (accessed November 22, 2020).

16   "Log Compaction Basics." Confluent documentation (n.d.). https://docs .confluent.io/platform/current/kafka/design.html#log-compaction-basics (accessed August 20, 2021).

Kafka storage

8

This chapters covers
- How long to retain data
- Data movement into and out of Kafka
- Data architectures Kafka enables
- Storage for cloud instances and containers

So far we have thought of our data as moving into and out of Kafka for brief periods of time. Another decision to consider is where our data should live long term. When you use databases like MySQL or MongoDB®, you may not always think about if or how that data expires. Rather, you know that the data is (likely) going to exist for the majority of your application's entire lifetime. In comparison, Kafka's storage logically sits somewhere between the long-term storage solutions of a database and the transient storage of a message broker, especially if we think of message brokers holding onto messages until they are consumed by a client, as it often is in other message brokers. Let's look at a couple of options for storing and moving data in our Kafka environment.

144

8.1   How long to store data

Currently, the default retention limit for data in Kafka topics is seven days, but we can easily configure this by time or data size [1]. But can Kafka hold data itself for a period of years? One real-world example is how the *New York Times* uses Kafka. The content in their cluster is in a single partition that was less than 100 GB at the time of writing [2]. If you recall from our discussion in chapter 7 about partitions, you know that all of this data exists on a single broker drive (as do any replica copies on their own drives) as partitions are not split between brokers. Because storage is considered to be relatively cheap and the capacity of modern hard drives is way beyond hundreds of gigabytes, most companies would not have any size issues with keeping that data around. Is this a valid use of Kafka or an abuse of its intended purpose and design? As long as you have the space for your planned growth on a disk for future use, you might have found a good pattern for handling your specific workload.

How do we configure retention for brokers? The main considerations are the size of the logs and the length of time the data exists. Table 8.1 shows some of the broker configuration options that are helpful for retention [3].

Table 8.1   Broker retention configuration

Key	Purpose
log.retention.bytes	The largest size threshold in bytes for deleting a log.
log.retention.ms	The length in milliseconds a log will be maintained before being deleted.
log.retention.minutes	Length before deletion in minutes. log.retention.ms is used as well if both are set.
log.retention.hours	Length before deletion in hours. log.retention.ms and log.retention.minutes would be used before this value if either of those are set.

How do we disable log retention limits and allow them to stay forever? By setting both log.retention.bytes and log.retention.ms to −1, we can effectively turn off data deletion [4].

Another thing to consider is how we can get similar retention for the latest values by using keyed events with a compacted topic. Although we can still remove data during compaction cleaning, the most recent keyed messages will always be in the log. This is a good way to retain data in use cases where we do not need every event (or history) of how a key changed state from the current value.

What if we want our data to stick around for a while, but simply do not have the disk space to hold our data on brokers? Another option for long-term storage is to move the data outside of Kafka and not retain it internally to the Kafka brokers themselves. Before data is removed by retention from Kafka, we could store the data in a database, in a Hadoop Distributed File System (HDFS™), or upload our event messages into something like cloud storage. All of these paths are valid options and could provide more cost-effective means of holding onto our data after our consumers process it.

8.2   *Data movement*

Almost all companies seem to have a need for transforming the data that they receive. Sometimes, it is specific to an area within the company or due to third-party integrations. A popular term that many people use in this data transformation space is *ETL* (extract, transform, load). We can use tooling or code to take data in its original format, transform the data, and then place it into a different table or data store. Kafka can play a key role in these data pipelines.

8.2.1   *Keeping the original event*

One thing that we would like to note is our preference for event formats inside of Kafka. Although open to debate and your use case requirements, our preference is to store messages in the original format in a topic. Why keep the original message and not format it immediately before placing it into a topic? Having the original message makes it easier to go back and start over if you inadvertently messed up your transform logic. Instead of having to try to figure out how to fix your mistake on the altered data, you can always just go back to the original data and start again. We know that most of us usually have that experience when trying to format a date or the first time we run a regular expression. Sometimes you need a couple of shots at formatting the data the way you want.

Another plus for getting the entire original message is that data you don't use today might be used in the future. Let's say the year is 1995, and you are getting a field from a vendor called `mobile`. Your business will never need that field, right? Once you see the need to launch your first text marketing campaign, you'll be thanking your past self that you kept that original, "useless" data.

Although the `mobile` field might be a trivial example for some, it is interesting to think about usage for data analysis. What if your models start to see trends on data that you once thought wouldn't matter? By retaining all the data fields, you might be able to go back to that data and find insights you never expected.

8.2.2   *Moving away from a batch mindset*

Does the general topic of ETL or data pipelines bring terms to mind such as *batch, end of day, monthly,* or even *yearly*? One of the shifts from the data transformation processes of the past is the idea that you can continuously stream your data into various systems without delay. With Kafka, for example, you can keep the pipeline running in near-real time, and you can use its stream-processing platform to treat your data as an infinite series of events.

We mention this as a reminder that Kafka can help enable a shift in the way you think of your data altogether. You do not have to wait for a nightly job to run and update a database. You also do not have to wait for a nightly window with less traffic to do intensive ETL tasks; you can do these as they stream into your system and have pipelines that are constantly working for your applications in real time. Let's take a look at tools available that might help you use your pipelines in the future or make better use of your pipelines today.

8.3 Tools

Data movement is a key to many systems, Kafka included. Although you can stay inside the open source Kafka and Confluent offerings like Connect, which was discussed in chapter 3, there are other tools that might fit your infrastructure or are already available in your tool suite. Depending on your specific data source or sinks, the options mentioned in the following sections might help you achieve your goals. Note that although some tools in this section include sample configuration and commands, more setup (not shown) might be required before you can run these commands on your local machines. Hopefully, this section gives you enough information to pique your interest and allow you to start exploring on your own.

8.3.1 Apache Flume

If you were first introduced to Kafka through work in the big data space, it is a strong possibility that you might have used Flume in relation to your cluster. If you have ever heard the term *Flafka*, you have definitely used this Kafka and Flume integration. Flume can provide an easier path for getting data into a cluster and relies more on configuration than on custom code. For example, if you want to ingest data into your Hadoop cluster and already have support from a vendor on these various pieces, Flume is a solid option to get data into your Kafka cluster.

Figure 8.1 shows an example of how a Flume agent runs on a node as its own process. It watches the files local to that server and then uses the configuration for the agent that you provided to send data to a sink.

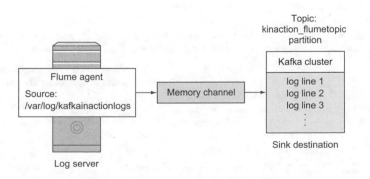

Figure 8.1   Flume agent

Let's take a look again at integrating log files (our source of data) using a Flume agent into a Kafka topic (our data sink). Listing 8.1 shows a sample configuration file that we could use to set up a local Flume agent to watch a directory for changes [5]. The changes are placed in a Kafka topic, titled `kinaction_flumetopic`. To imagine this example, here's a comparison: it is like using a `cat` command on a file in a directory to read the file and send the result to a specific Kafka topic.

Listing 8.1   Flume configuration for watching a directory

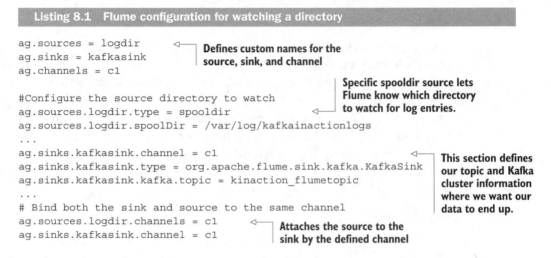

```
ag.sources = logdir              ◁──┐ Defines custom names for the
ag.sinks = kafkasink                 │ source, sink, and channel
ag.channels = c1

#Configure the source directory to watch    Specific spooldir source lets
ag.sources.logdir.type = spooldir        ◁── Flume know which directory
ag.sources.logdir.spoolDir = /var/log/kafkainactionlogs   to watch for log entries.
...
ag.sinks.kafkasink.channel = c1                             ◁─┐ This section defines
ag.sinks.kafkasink.type = org.apache.flume.sink.kafka.KafkaSink │ our topic and Kafka
ag.sinks.kafkasink.kafka.topic = kinaction_flumetopic           │ cluster information
...                                                             │ where we want our
# Bind both the sink and source to the same channel            │ data to end up.
ag.sources.logdir.channels = c1      ◁──┐ Attaches the source to the
ag.sinks.kafkasink.channel = c1          │ sink by the defined channel
```

Listing 8.1 shows how we could configure a Flume agent running on a server. You should notice that the sink configuration looks a lot like the properties we have used before in our Java client producer code.

It is also interesting to note that Flume can use Kafka as not only a source or as a sink, but also as a channel. Because Kafka is seen as a more reliable channel for events, Flume can use Kafka to deliver messages between various sources and sinks.

If you are reviewing Flume configurations and see Kafka mentioned, be sure to notice where and how it is actually used. The following listing shows the Flume agent configuration we can use to provide a reliable channel between various sources and sinks that Flume supports [5].

Listing 8.2   Flume Kafka channel configuration

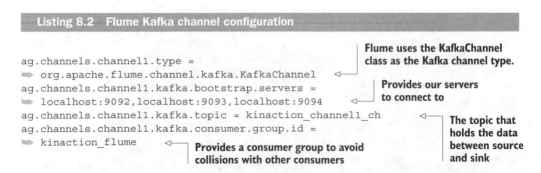

```
                                                          Flume uses the KafkaChannel
                                                          class as the Kafka channel type.
ag.channels.channel1.type =
➥ org.apache.flume.channel.kafka.KafkaChannel     ◁──┐
ag.channels.channel1.kafka.bootstrap.servers =        Provides our servers
➥ localhost:9092,localhost:9093,localhost:9094   ◁──┘ to connect to
ag.channels.channel1.kafka.topic = kinaction_channel1_ch   ◁─┐ The topic that
ag.channels.channel1.kafka.consumer.group.id =              │ holds the data
➥ kinaction_flume     ◁──┐ Provides a consumer group to avoid  between source
                          │ collisions with other consumers     and sink
```

8.3.2 *Red Hat® Debezium™*

Debezium (https://debezium.io) describes itself as a distributed platform that helps turn databases into event streams. In other words, updates to our database can be treated as events! If you have a database background (or not), you may have heard of the term *change data capture* (CDC). As the name implies, the data changes can be tracked and used to react to those changes. At the time of writing this chapter, Debezium supports MySQL, MongoDB, PostgreSQL®, Microsoft SQL Server™, Oracle, and IBM Db2. Cassandra™ and Vitess™ are in an incubating status as well [6]. Please see the current list of connectors at https://debezium.io/documentation/reference/connectors/.

Debezium uses connectors and Kafka Connect to record the events our application consumes from Kafka as a normal client. Figure 8.2 shows an example of Debezium when it is registered as a connector in regard to Kafka Connect.

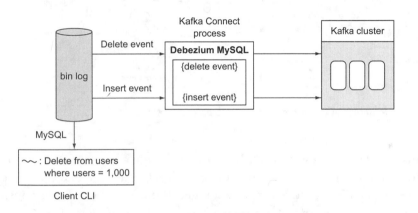

Figure 8.2 Kafka Connect and Debezium used with a MySQL database

In our scenario, a developer uses a command line interface (CLI) and deletes a user against the MySQL database instance that is being monitored for changes. Debezium captures the event written to the database's internal log, and that event goes through the connector service and feeds into Kafka. If a second event, such as a new user, is inserted into the database, a new event is captured.

As an additional note, although not Kafka-specific, there are other examples of using techniques like CDC to provide timely events or changes to your data that might help you draw a parallel to what Debezium is aiming for overall.

8.3.3 *Secor*

Secor (https://github.com/pinterest/secor) is an interesting project from Pinterest that has been around since 2014. It aims to help persist Kafka log data to a variety of storage options, including S3 and Google Cloud Storage™ [7]. The options for output are also various, including sequence, Apache ORC™, and Apache Parquet™ files as well as other formats. As always, one major benefit of projects having source code in a public repository is that we can see how other teams have implemented requirements that might be similar to ours.

Figure 8.3 shows how Secor would act as a consumer of a Kafka cluster, much like any other application. Having a consumer added to a cluster for data backup is not a big deal. It leverages the way Kafka has always handled multiple readers of the events.

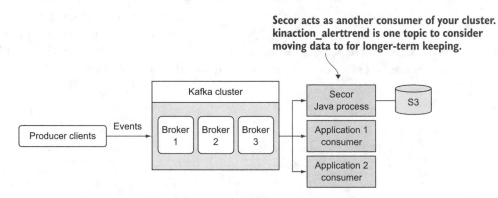

Figure 8.3   Secor acting as a consumer and placing data into storage.

Secor runs as a Java process and can be fed our specific configurations. In effect, it acts as another consumer of our existing topic(s) to gather data to end up in a specific destination like an S3 bucket. Secor does not get in the way of our other consumers, and it allows us to have a copy of our events so that they are not lost once Kafka retention removes data from its logs.

Invoking Secor should be familiar to those who are used to working with JARs in a Java environment. We can pass arguments with the standard -D parameters to the Secor application. In this instance, the most important file to update is the properties file with the configuration options. This file lets us fill in the details about our specific cloud storage bucket, for example.

8.3.4 *Example use case for data storage*

Let's look at an example of how moving data out of Kafka for storage could be used at a later time. First, to clarify, we will break down our usage of the same data between two different areas. One area is working with the data in an operational manner as it comes into Kafka.

Operational data is the events that are produced by our day-to-day operations. We can think of an event to order an item from a website as an example. A purchase event triggers our application into motion and does so in a low-latency way. The value of this data to our real-time applications might warrant keeping the data for a couple of days until the order is completed and mailed. After this timeframe, the event may become more important for our analytical systems.

Analytical data, while based on that same operational data, is usually used more to make business decisions. In traditional systems, this is where processes like a data warehouse, an online analytical processing system (OLAP), and Hadoop shine. That event data can be mined using different combinations of fields in our events in different scenarios to find insights into sales data, for instance. If we notice that sales of cleaning supplies always spike before a holiday, we might use that data to generate better sale options for our business in the future.

8.4   Bringing data back into Kafka

One of the most important things to note is that just because our data has left Kafka does not mean that it can't be put back in again. Figure 8.4 shows an example of data that lived out its normal lifespan in Kafka and was archived in cloud storage like S3. When a new application logic change required the older data be reprocessed, we did not have to create a client to read from both S3 and Kafka. Rather, using a tool like Kafka Connect, we can load that data from S3 back into Kafka! The interface stays the same from the point of view of our applications. Although it might not seem obvious at first glance why we would want to do such a thing, let's consider a situation in which we find value in moving our data back into Kafka after we have processed it and the retention period has passed.

Imagine a team working on trying to find patterns in data that they collected throughout years of handling events. In our example, there are terabytes of data. To serve operational real-time data collection, this data was moved from Kafka into HDFS after real-time consumers dealt with the messages. Does our application logic now have to pull from HDFS directly? Why not just pull it back into Kafka, and our application can process the data as it had before? Loading data into Kafka again is a valid way of reprocessing data that may have aged out of our system. Figure 8.4 shows another example of how we can move data back into Kafka.

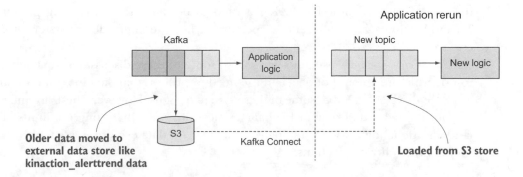

Figure 8.4   Moving data back into Kafka

After some time, events are not available to the applications due to data retention configurations within Kafka. However, we have a copy of all previous events in an S3 bucket. Let's say that we have a new version of our previous application and would prefer to go through all of the previous data events as in our previous application. However, because those events are not in Kafka, do we pull them from S3 now? Do we want our application logic to pull from various sources or just to have one interface (that being Kafka)? We can create a new topic in our existing Kafka cluster and load the data from S3 with Kafka Connect, placing the data into a new Kafka topic. Our application can then run against Kafka, processing events without having to change any processing logic.

The thought process is really to keep Kafka as the interface of our application and not have to create multiple ways to pull data into processing. Why create and maintain custom code to pull from different locations when we can use an existing tool like Connect to move the data to or from Kafka? Once we have our data in that one interface, we can process it the same.

> **NOTE** Keep in mind this technique only applies to data that has been removed from Kafka. If you still have the total timeline of data that you need in Kafka, you can always seek to the earlier offsets.

8.4.1   Tiered storage

A newer option from the Confluent Platform version 6.0.0 on is called Tiered Storage. In this model, local storage is still the broker itself, and remote storage is introduced for data that is older (and stored in a remote location) and controlled by time configuration (`confluent.tier.local.hotset.ms`) [8].

8.5   Architectures with Kafka

Although there are various architectural patterns that view your data as events when building your products, such as model-view-controller (MVC), peer-to-peer (P2P), or service-oriented architecture (SOA) to name a few, Kafka can change the way you think about your entire architectural design. Let's take a peek at a couple of architectures that could be powered by Kafka (and to be fair, other streaming platforms). This will help us get a different perspective on how we might design systems for our customers.

The term *big data* is used in reference to some of these discussions. It is important to note that the amount of data and the need to process that data in a timely manner were the drivers that led to some of these system designs. However, these architectures are not limited to fast data or big data applications only. By hitting the limits of specific traditional database technologies, new views on data evolved. Let's look at two of them in the following sections.

8.5.1   *Lambda architecture*

If you have ever researched or worked with data applications that have included needs for both batch processing and operational workloads, you might have seen references to lambda architecture. The implementation of this architecture can start with Kafka as well, but it is a little more complex.

The real-time view of the data is combined with a historical view to serve end users. The complexity of merging these two data views should not be ignored. For the authors, it was a challenge to rebuild the serving table. Also, you are likely going to have to maintain different interfaces for your data as you work with the results from both systems.

The book *Big Data*, written by Nathan Marz with James Warren, discusses the lambda architecture more fully and goes into details about the batch, serving, and speed layers [9]. Figure 8.5 shows an example of how taking customer orders can be thought of in a batch and a real-time way. The customer totals from the previous days can be integrated with orders happening during the day into a combined data view to end users.

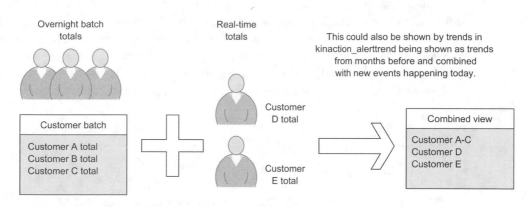

Figure 8.5   Lambda architecture

Taking the concepts from figure 8.5 and to get a feel for this architecture, let's look at each layer at a high level. These layers are discussed in *Big Data* by Marz:

- *Batch*—This layer is similar to the way batch processing with MapReduce occurs in a system like Hadoop. As new data is added to your data stores, the batch layer continues to precompute the view of the data that already lives in the system.
- *Speed*—This layer is similar in concept to the batch layer except it produces views from recent data.
- *Serving*—This layer updates the views it sends to consumers after each update to the batch views.

For the end user, the lambda architecture unites data from the serving layer and the speed layer to answer requests with a complete view of all recent and past data. This real-time streaming layer is the most obvious place for Kafka to play a role, but it can also be used to feed the batch layer.

8.5.2   *Kappa architecture*

Another architectural pattern that can leverage the power of Kafka is kappa architecture. This architecture was proposed by the co-creator of Kafka, Jay Kreps [10]. Think about wanting to maintain a system that impacts your users without disruption. One way to do this is to switch out your updated views like in lambda. Another way to do this is by running the current system in parallel to the new one and cutting over once the new version is ready to serve traffic. Part of this cutover is of course making sure that the data that is being served by the older version will be reflected correctly in the newer version.

You only regenerate the user-facing data when you need to. There is no need to merge old and new data, which is an ongoing process for some lambda implementations. It does not have to be a continuous job, but rather invoked when you need an application logic change. Also, there's no need to change your interface to your data. Kafka can be used by both your new and old application code at the same time. Figure 8.6 shows how customer events are used to create a view without using a batch layer.

Figure 8.6 shows customer events from the past and present being used directly to create a view. Imagine the events being sourced from Kafka and then using Kafka Streams or ksqlDB to read all the events in near-real time and creating a view for end

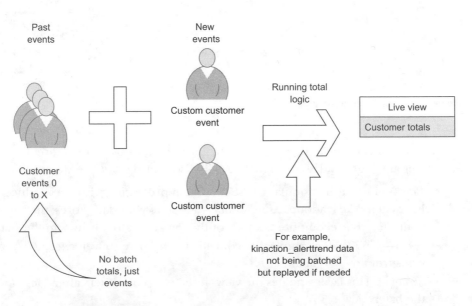

Figure 8.6   Kappa architecture

users. If a change is ever needed to how customer events are processed, a second application can be created with different logic (like a new ksqlDB query), using the same data source (Kafka) as before. There is no need to have a batch layer (and manage it) as there is only streaming logic used for making your end user views.

8.6 Multiple cluster setups

Most of our topics and discussions so far have been from the viewpoint of our data in one cluster. But Kafka scales well, and it is not unheard of to reach hundreds of brokers for a single cluster. However, a one-size cluster does not fit all infrastructures. One of the concerns we run into when talking about cluster storage is where you serve your data in relation to your end user clients. In this section, we will talk about scaling by adding clusters rather than by adding brokers alone.

8.6.1 Scaling by adding clusters

Usually, the first things to scale would be the resources inside your existing cluster. The number of brokers is the first option that makes a straightforward path to growth. Netflix®'s multicluster strategy is a captivating take on how to scale Kafka clusters [11]. Instead of using only the broker number as the way to scale the cluster, they found they could scale by adding clusters themselves!

This design brings to mind the idea of Command Query Responsibility Segregation (CQRS). For more details on CQRS, check out Martin Fowler's site at https://martinfowler.com/bliki/CQRS.html, specifically the idea of separating the load of reading data from that of writing data [12]. Each action can scale in an independent manner without limiting other actions. Although CQRS is a pattern that can add complexity to our systems, it is interesting to note how this specific example helps manage the performance of a large cluster by separating the load of producers sending data into Kafka from the sometimes much larger load of consumers reading the data.

8.7 Cloud- and container-based storage options

Although we talked about Kafka log directories in chapter 6, we did not address the types of instances to use in environments that provide more short-lived storage. For reference, Confluent shared a study on deployments with AWS considerations in which they looked at the storage type trade-offs [13].

Another option is to look at Confluent Cloud (https://www.confluent.io/confluent-cloud/). This option allows you to worry less about the underlying storage used across cloud providers and how it is managed. As always, remember that Kafka itself keeps evolving and reacting to the needs that users run into as daily challenges. KIP-392 shows an item that was accepted at the time of this writing, which seeks to help address the issues of a Kafka cluster spanning data centers. The KIP is titled "Allow consumers to fetch from the closest replica" [14]. Be sure to check out recent KIPs (Kafka Improvement Proposals) from time to time to see how Kafka evolves in exciting ways.

8.7.1   Kubernetes clusters

Dealing with a containerized environment, we might run into challenges similar to what we would in the cloud. If we hit a poorly configured memory limit on our broker, we might find ourselves on an entirely new node without our data unless the data persists correctly. If we are not in a sandbox environment in which we can lose the data, persistent volume claims may be needed by our brokers to ensure that our data survives any restarts, failures, or moves. Although the broker instance container might change, we should be able to claim the previous persistent volume.

Kafka applications will likely use the StatefulSet API in order to maintain the identity of each broker across failures or pod moves. This static identity also helps us claim the same persistent volumes that were used before our pod went down. There are already Helm® charts (https://github.com/confluentinc/cp-helm-charts) to help us get started with a test setup as we explore Kubernetes [15]. Confluent for Kubernetes helps as well with our Kubernetes management [16].

The scope of Kubernetes is relatively large to cover in our discussion, but the key concerns are present regardless of our environment. Our brokers have an identity in the cluster and are tied to the data that each is related to. To keep the cluster healthy, those brokers need the ability to identify their broker-managed logs across failures, restarts, or upgrades.

Summary

- Data retention should be driven by business needs. Decisions to weigh include the cost of storage and the growth rate of our data over time.
- Size and time are the basic parameters for defining how long data is retained on disk.
- Long-term storage of data outside of Kafka is an option for data that might need to be retained for long periods. Data can be reintroduced as needed by producing the data into a cluster at a later time.
- The ability of Kafka to handle data quickly and also replay data can enable architectures such as the lambda and kappa architectures.
- Cloud and container workloads often involve short-lived broker instances. Data that needs to be persisted requires a plan for making sure newly created or recovered instances can utilize that data across all instances.

References

1   "Kafka Broker Configurations." Confluent documentation (n.d.). https://docs.confluent.io/platform/current/installation/configuration/broker-configs.html#brokerconfigs_log.retention.hours (accessed December 14, 2020).

2   B. Svingen. "Publishing with Apache Kafka at The New York Times." Confluent blog (September 6, 2017). https://www.confluent.io/blog/publishing-apache-kafka-new-york-times/ (accessed September 25, 2018).

3 "Kafka Broker Configurations." Confluent documentation (n.d.). https:// docs.confluent.io/platform/current/installation/configuration/broker-configs .html (accessed December 14, 2020).

4 "Kafka Broker Configurations: log.retention.ms." Confluent documentation (n.d.). https://docs.confluent.io/platform/current/installation/configuration/broker-configs.html#brokerconfigs_log.retention.ms (accessed December 14, 2020).

5 "Flume 1.9.0 User Guide: Kafka Sink." Apache Software Foundation (n.d.). https://flume.apache.org/releases/content/1.9.0/FlumeUserGuide.html#kafka -sink (accessed October 10, 2019).

6 "Connectors." Debezium documentation (n.d.). https://debezium.io/docu- mentation/reference/connectors/ (accessed July 20, 2021).

7 "Pinterest Secor." Pinterest. GitHub. https://github.com/pinterest/secor/ blob/master/README.md (accessed June 1, 2020).

8 "Tiered Storage." Confluent documentation (n.d.). https://docs.confluent.io/ platform/current/kafka/tiered-storage.html (accessed June 2, 2021).

9 N. Marz and J. Warren. *Big Data: Principles and best practices of scalable real-time data systems.* Shelter Island, NY, USA: Manning, 2015.

10 J. Kreps. "Questioning the Lambda Architecture." O'Reilly Radar (July 2, 2014). https://www.oreilly.com/radar/questioning-the-lambda-architecture/ (accessed October 11, 2019).

11 A. Wang. "Multi-Tenant, Multi-Cluster and Hierarchical Kafka Messaging Ser- vice." Presented at Confluent's Kafka Summit, San Francisco, USA, 2017 Pre- sentation [online]. https://www.confluent.io/kafka-summit-sf17/multitenant -multicluster-and-hieracrchical-kafka-messaging-service/.

12 M. Fowler. "CQRS" (July 14, 2011). https://martinfowler.com/bliki/CQRS.html (accessed December 11, 2017).

13 A. Loddengaard. "Design and Deployment Considerations for Deploying Apache Kafka on AWS." Confluent blog (July 28, 2016). https://www.conflu- ent.io/blog/design-and-deployment-considerations-for-deploying-apache-kafka -on-aws/ (accessed June 11, 2021).

14 KIP-392: "Allow consumers to fetch from closest replica." Wiki for Apache Kafka. Apache Software Foundation (November 05, 2019). https:// cwiki.apache.org/confluence/display/KAFKA/KIP-392%3A+Allow+consumers +to+fetch+from+closest+replica (accessed December 10, 2019).

15 cp-helm-charts. Confluent Inc. GitHub (n.d.). https://github.com/conflu entinc/cp-helm-charts (accessed June 10, 2020).

16 "Confluent for Kubernetes." Confluent documentation (n.d.). https:// docs.confluent.io/operator/2.0.2/overview.html (accessed August 16, 2021).

Management: Tools and logging

This chapters covers

- Scripting administration client options
- Examining REST APIs, tools, and utilities
- Managing Kafka and ZooKeeper logs
- Finding JMX metrics
- Advertised listeners and clients
- Tracing using interceptors with headers

We have spent some time discussing brokers in depth in chapter 6 and client concerns throughout the earlier chapters. We saw some development practices that can be applied in most situations, but there will always be environments where special handling is required. The best way to keep a cluster moving along is to understand the data that is flowing through it and to monitor that activity at run time. Although operating Apache Kafka may not be the same as writing and running Java applications per se, it still requires monitoring log files and being aware of what is happening with our workloads.

9.1 Administration clients

So far, we have performed most of our cluster management activities with the command line tools that come with Kafka. And, in general, we need to be comfortable with a shell environment to set up and install Kafka. However, there are some helpful options we can use to branch out from these provided scripts.

9.1.1 Administration in code with AdminClient

One useful tool to look at is the AdminClient class [1]. Although the Kafka shell scripts are great to have at hand for quick access or one-off tasks, there are situations such as automation where the Java AdminClient really shines. The AdminClient is in the same kafka-clients.jar that we used for the producer and consumer clients. It can be pulled into a Maven project (see the pom.xml from chapter 2,) or it can be found in the share/ or libs/ directory of the Kafka installation.

Let's look at how we can execute a command we have used before to create a new topic but this time with AdminClient. The following listing shows how we ran this from the command line in chapter 2.

> **Listing 9.1 Creating the `kinaction_selfserviceTopic` topic from the command line**

```
bin/kafka-topics.sh
  --create --topic kinaction_selfserviceTopic \      ◁──┘  Uses the kafka-topic.sh
  --bootstrap-server localhost:9094 \                       script to create a new topic
  --partitions 2 \               Includes our custom integers for the number
  --replication-factor 2         of partitions and replicas for our topic
```

Though this command line example works fine, we don't want it to be called every time someone needs a new topic. Instead, we'll create a self-service portal that other developers can use to create new topics on our development cluster. The form for our application takes a topic name and the numbers for partitions and replicas. Figure 9.1 shows an example of how this application might be set up for end users. Once the user submits the web form, the AdminClient Java code runs, creating a new topic.

In this example, we could add logic to make sure that naming conventions for new topics fit a certain pattern (if we had such a business requirement). This is a way to maintain more control over our cluster rather than users working from the command line tools. To start, we need to create a NewTopic class. The constructor for this class takes three arguments:

- Topic name
- The number of partitions
- The number of replicas

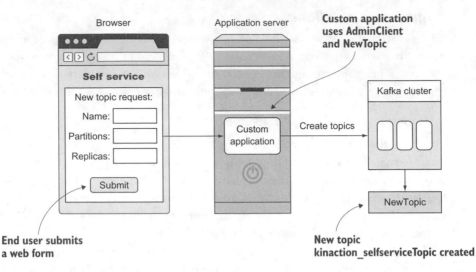

Figure 9.1   Self-service Kafka web application

Once we have this information, we can use the AdminClient object to complete the work. AdminClient takes a Properties object that contains the same properties we've used with other clients, like bootstrap.servers and client.id. Note that the class AdminClientConfig (http://mng.bz/8065) holds constants for configuration values such as BOOTSTRAP_SERVERS_CONFIG as a helper for those names. Then we'll call the method createTopics on the client. Notice that the result, topicResult, is a Future object. The following listing shows how to use the AdminClient class to create a new topic called kinaction_selfserviceTopic.

Listing 9.2   Using AdminClient to create a topic

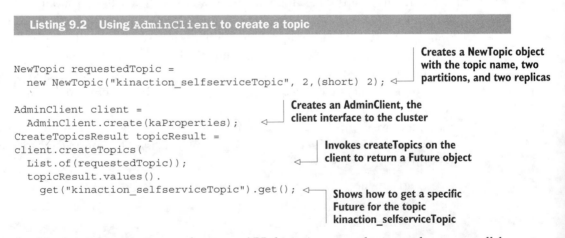

At this time, there is no synchronous API, but we can make a synchronous call by using the get() function. In our case, that would mean starting with the topicResult variable and evaluating the Future object that was returned for the specific topic.

Because this API is still evolving, the following list of client administrative tasks that can be accomplished with `AdminClient` highlights only a few common functions that are available at the time of writing [1]:

- Change configurations
- Create/delete/list access control lists (ACLs)
- Create partitions
- Create/delete/list topics
- Describe/list consumer groups
- Describe clusters

`AdminClient` is a great tool for building a user-facing application for those who wouldn't normally need or want to use the Kafka shell scripts. It also provides a way to control and monitor what is being done on the cluster.

9.1.2 kcat

`kcat` (https://github.com/edenhill/kcat) is a handy tool to have on your workstation, especially when connecting remotely to your clusters. At this time, it focuses on being a producer and consumer client that can also give you metadata about your cluster. If you ever want to quickly work with a topic and don't have the entire Kafka toolset downloaded to your current machine, this executable helps you avoid the need to have those shell or bat scripts.

The following listing shows how to quickly get data into a topic using `kcat` [2]. Compare this with the `kafka-console-producer` script that we used in chapter 2.

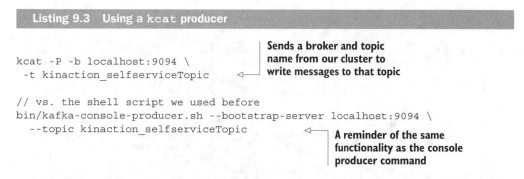

Listing 9.3 Using a `kcat` producer

```
kcat -P -b localhost:9094 \
 -t kinaction_selfserviceTopic
```
Sends a broker and topic name from our cluster to write messages to that topic

```
// vs. the shell script we used before
bin/kafka-console-producer.sh --bootstrap-server localhost:9094 \
  --topic kinaction_selfserviceTopic
```
A reminder of the same functionality as the console producer command

In listing 9.3, notice that the `-P` argument is passed to `kcat` to enable producer mode, which helps us send messages to the cluster. We use the `-b` flag to pass in our broker list and `-t` to pass the name of our target topic. Because we may also want to test the consumption of these messages, let's look at how we can use `kcat` as a consumer (listing 9.4). As before, listing 9.4 shows the comparison between running the `kcat` command versus the `kafka-console-consumer` command. Notice also that although the `-C` flag enables consumer mode, the broker information is sent with the same parameter as in the producer mode [2].

Listing 9.4   Using a `kcat` consumer

```
kcat -C -b localhost:9094 \
 -t kinaction_selfserviceTopic
```
⟵ **Sends a broker and topic name from our cluster to read messages from that topic**

```
// vs. the shell script we used before
bin/kafka-console-consumer.sh --bootstrap-server localhost:9094 \
  --topic kinaction_selfserviceTopic
```
⟵ **A reminder of the same functionality as the console consumer command**

Having a quick way to test our topics and gather metadata on our cluster makes this small utility nice to have in our toolbox. But by this point, you might be wondering if there are any other tools that we can use that are not command line driven. And the good news is yes, there are! For those that like REST, there is Confluent's REST Proxy.

9.1.3   Confluent REST Proxy API

Sometimes the users of our cluster might prefer to use APIs that are RESTful because it is a common way to work between applications, either due to preference or ease of use. Also, some companies with strict firewall rules about ports might express caution with opening more ports like those we've used so far for broker connections (for example, 9094) [3]. One good option is to use the Confluent REST Proxy API (figure 9.2). This proxy is a separate application that would likely be hosted on its own server for production usage, and its functionality is similar to the `kcat` utility we just discussed.

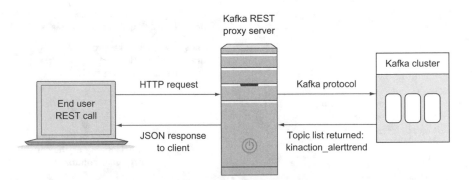

Figure 9.2   The Confluent REST Proxy looks up topics.

At the time of this writing, the administration functions are limited to querying the state of your cluster. The Confluent documentation lists administration options as future supported features, however [4]. To use the REST proxy and to test drive it, let's start it up as the following listing shows. For this to work, we need to already have ZooKeeper and Kafka instances running *before* we start the proxy.

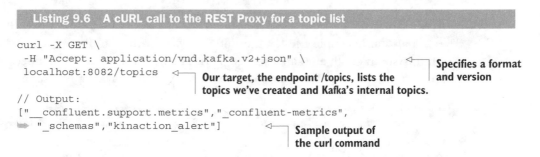

Listing 9.5   Starting up a REST Proxy

```
bin/kafka-rest-start.sh \
  etc/kafka-rest/kafka-rest.properties
```
◁ Run this command from the installed Kafka folder to start the REST endpoint.

Because we're already familiar with listing topics, let's look at how that can be done with the REST Proxy using a command like `curl` to hit an HTTP endpoint as in the following listing [5]. Because this is a GET request, we can also copy http://localhost :8082/topics into a browser and see the result.

Listing 9.6   A cURL call to the REST Proxy for a topic list

```
curl -X GET \
 -H "Accept: application/vnd.kafka.v2+json" \
  localhost:8082/topics
// Output:
["__confluent.support.metrics","_confluent-metrics",
 "_schemas","kinaction_alert"]
```
◁ Specifies a format and version

◁ Our target, the endpoint /topics, lists the topics we've created and Kafka's internal topics.

◁ Sample output of the curl command

Using a tool like `curl` allows us to control the header we send with the request. `Accept` in listing 9.6 allows us to tell our Kafka cluster what format and version we are using, specifying `v2` as the API version and the JSON format that pertains to our metadata requests.

> **NOTE**   Because this is an evolving API, keep up with the "Confluent REST Proxy API Reference" at http://mng.bz/q5Nw as newer versions come out with more features.

9.2   *Running Kafka as a systemd service*

One decision we need to make concerning running Kafka is how to perform broker starts and restarts. Those who are used to managing servers as Linux-based services with a tool like Puppet (https://puppet.com/) may be familiar with installing service unit files and can likely use that knowledge to create running instances with `systemd`. For those not familiar with `systemd`: it initializes and maintains components throughout the system [6]. One common way to define ZooKeeper and Kafka are as unit files used by `systemd`.

Listing 9.7 shows part of an example service unit file that starts a ZooKeeper service when the server starts. It also restarts ZooKeeper after an abnormal exit. In practice, this means something like a `kill -9` command against the process ID (PID) that triggers a restart of the process. If you installed the Confluent `tar` during your setup (refer to appendix A if needed), there is an example service file located in the lib/ systemd/system/confluent-zookeeper.service path. The "Using Confluent Platform systemd Service Unit Files" documentation at (http://mng.bz/7lG9) provides details on using these files. The unit file in the listing should look familiar to how we have started ZooKeeper so far in our examples.

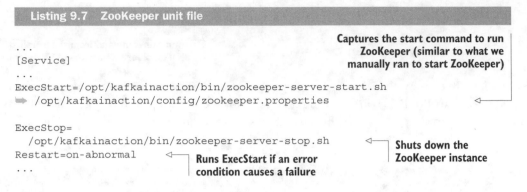

Listing 9.7   ZooKeeper unit file

```
...
[Service]
...
ExecStart=/opt/kafkainaction/bin/zookeeper-server-start.sh
   /opt/kafkainaction/config/zookeeper.properties

ExecStop=
   /opt/kafkainaction/bin/zookeeper-server-stop.sh
Restart=on-abnormal
...
```

Captures the start command to run ZooKeeper (similar to what we manually ran to start ZooKeeper)

Shuts down the ZooKeeper instance

Runs ExecStart if an error condition causes a failure

There is also an example file for the Kafka service in the Confluent `tar` in the lib/ systemd/system/confluent-kafka.service path. The next listing shows that because our unit files are defined, we can now manage the services with `systemctl` commands [6].

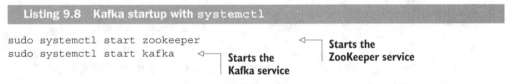

Listing 9.8   Kafka startup with `systemctl`

```
sudo systemctl start zookeeper
sudo systemctl start kafka
```

Starts the ZooKeeper service

Starts the Kafka service

If you are using the example files that came when downloading the Confluent bundle, once you unzip the folder, check inside the root folder, ../lib/systemd/system, to see examples of service files that you can use for other services. Some of these include Connect, the Schema Registry, and the REST API, to name a few.

9.3   *Logging*

Besides Kafka's event logs that hold our event data, other items that we need to remember are the application logs, which Kafka produces as part of being a running program. The logs addressed in this section are not the events and messages from Kafka servers but the output of the operation of Kafka itself. And we cannot forget about ZooKeeper either!

9.3.1   *Kafka application logs*

Although we might be used to one log file for an entire application, Kafka has multiple log files that we might be interested in or need to access for troubleshooting. Due to multiple files, we might have to look at modifying different Log4j appenders to maintain the necessary views of our operations.

Which Kafka appender?

The `kafkaAppender` is not the same thing as the `KafkaAppender` itself (http://mng .bz/5ZpB). To use `KafkaLog4jAppender` as our appender, we would need to update the following line as well as include dependencies for the clients and appender JARs of the same version instead of the value `org.apache.log4j.ConsoleAppender` class:

```
log4j.appender.kafkaAppender=
  org.apache.kafka.log4jappender.KafkaLog4jAppender

<dependency>
    <groupId>org.apache.kafka</groupId>
    <artifactId>kafka-log4j-appender</artifactId>
    <version>2.7.1</version>
</dependency>
```

This is an interesting take on putting our log files directly into Kafka. Some solutions parse the log files themselves and then send them to Kafka.

By default, the server logs are continually added to the directory as new logs are produced. No logs are removed, however, and this might be the preferred behavior if these files are needed for auditing or troubleshooting. If we want to control the number and size, the easiest way is to update the file log4j.properties before we start the broker server. The following listing sets two important properties for `kafkaAppender`: `MaxFileSize` and `MaxBackupIndex` [7].

Listing 9.9   Kafka server log retention

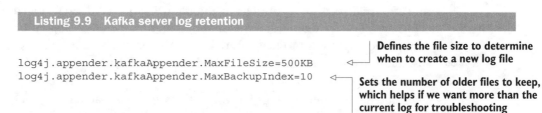

```
log4j.appender.kafkaAppender.MaxFileSize=500KB
log4j.appender.kafkaAppender.MaxBackupIndex=10
```

Defines the file size to determine when to create a new log file

Sets the number of older files to keep, which helps if we want more than the current log for troubleshooting

Note that modifying `kafkaAppender` changes only how the server.log file is treated. If we want to apply different file sizes and backup file numbers for various Kafka-related files, we can use the appender to log a filename table to determine which appenders to update. In table 9.1, the appender name in the left column is the logging key, which affects how the log files on the right are stored on the brokers [8].

Table 9.1   Appender to log pattern

Appender name	Log filename
kafkaAppender	server.log
stateChangeAppender	state-change.log
requestAppender	kafka-request.log
cleanerAppender	log-cleaner.log
controllerAppender	controller.log
authorizerAppender	kafka-authorizer.log

Changes to the log4j.properties file require the broker to be restarted, so it is best to determine our logging requirements before starting our brokers for the first time, if possible. We could also change the value with JMX, but the value would not be persistent across broker restarts.

Although we focused on Kafka logs in this section, we need to address our Zoo-Keeper logs as well. Because ZooKeeper runs and logs data just like our brokers, we will need to be mindful of logging output for those servers as well.

9.3.2   *ZooKeeper logs*

Depending on how we installed and chose to manage ZooKeeper, we may also need to modify its logging configuration. The default configuration for ZooKeeper does not remove log files, but our Kafka install may have added that feature for us. If you followed the setup of our local ZooKeeper node from appendix A, these values can be set in the file config/zookeeper.properties. Either way, it is a good idea to make sure that the retention of the ZooKeeper application logs are controlled by the following configuration values and are what we need for troubleshooting:

- `autopurge.purgeInterval`—The interval, in hours, in which a purge is triggered. This must be set above 0 for cleanup to occur [9].
- `autopurge.snapRetainCount`—This contains the number of recent snapshots and the related transaction logs in the dataDir and dataLogDir locations [9]. Once we exceed the number, the older log files are deleted. Depending on our needs, we might want to keep more or fewer. For example, if the logs are only used for troubleshooting, we would need lower retention than if they are needed for audit scenarios.
- `snapCount`—ZooKeeper logs its transactions to a transaction log. Setting this value determines the amount of transactions that are logged to one file. If there are issues with total file sizes, we might need to set this number less than the default (100,000) [10].

There are other solutions to log rotation and cleanup that we might consider beyond Log4j. For example, `logrotate` is a helpful tool that enables options such as log rotation and compression of logs files.

Log file maintenance is an important administration duty. However, there are other tasks that we need to consider as we start to roll out a new Kafka cluster. One of these tasks is making sure that clients can connect to our brokers.

9.4   *Firewalls*

Depending on our network configurations, we might need to serve clients that exist inside the network or those out of the network where the Kafka brokers are set up [3]. Kafka brokers can listen on multiple ports. For example, the default for a plain text port is 9092. An SSL port at 9093 can also be set up on that same host. Both of these ports might need to be open, depending on how clients connect to our brokers.

In addition, ZooKeeper includes port 2181 for client connections. Port 2888 is used by follower ZooKeeper nodes to connect to the leader ZooKeeper node, and port 3888 is also used between ZooKeeper nodes to communicate [11]. If connecting remotely for JMX or other Kafka services (such as the REST Proxy), remember to account for any exposure of that port to other environments or users. In general, if we use any command line tools that require a port on the end of the hostname for Zoo-Keeper or Kafka servers, we need to make sure that these ports can be reached, especially if a firewall is in place.

9.4.1 Advertised listeners

One error when connecting that often appears like a firewall issue is using the `listeners` and `advertised.listeners` properties. Clients need to use the correct hostname, if given, to connect, so it will need to be a reachable hostname, however the rules are set up. For example, let's look at `listeners` versus `advertised.listeners` where those values might not be the same.

Let's imagine we are connecting to a broker and can get a connection when the client starts, but not when it attempts to consume messages. How is this behavior that appears inconsistent possible? Remember that when a client starts, it connects to any broker to get metadata about which broker to connect to. The initial connection from the client uses the information that is located in the Kafka `listeners` configuration. What it gives back to the client to connect to next is the data in Kafka's `advertised.listeners` [12]. This makes it likely that the client will connect to a different host to do its work.

Figure 9.3 shows how the client uses one hostname for the first connection attempt, then uses a different hostname on its second connection. This second hostname was given to the client from its initial call as the new location to connect to.

An important setting to look at is `inter.broker.listener.name`, which determines how the brokers connect across the cluster to each other [12]. If the brokers cannot reach each other, replicas fail and the cluster will not be in a good state, to say the least! For an excellent explanation of advertised listeners, check out the article by Robin Moffatt, "Kafka Listeners – Explained," if you want to dig into more details [12]. Figure 9.3 was inspired by Robin Moffatt's diagrams on that site as well [12].

9.5 Metrics

In chapter 6, we looked at an example of setting up a way to see some JMX metrics from our application. The ability to see those metrics is the first step. Let's take a peek at finding some that are likely to highlight areas of concern.

9.5.1 JMX console

It is possible to use a GUI to explore the exposed metrics and get an idea of what is available. VisualVM (https://visualvm.github.io/) is one example. Looking at the available JMX metrics can help us discover points of interest in which we might choose to add

Scenario 1: no advertised listeners. Producer client
starts and requests metadata from bootstrap server.

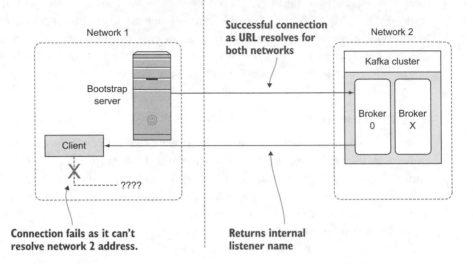

Scenario 2: advertised listeners with URL resolved by
both networks. Producer client requests metadata.

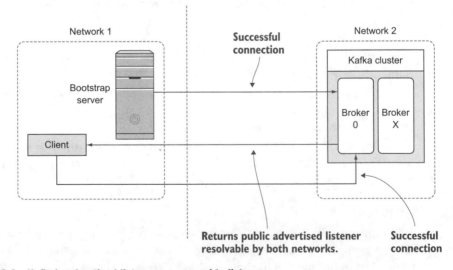

Figure 9.3 Kafka's advertised listeners compared to listeners

alerts. When installing VisualVM, be sure to go through the additional step of installing
the MBeans Browser.

As noted in chapter 6, we must have JMX_PORT defined for each broker we want to
connect to. This can be done with the environment variable in the terminal like so:

export JMX_PORT=49999 [13]. Make sure that you correctly scope it to be separate for each broker as well as each ZooKeeper node.

KAFKA_JMX_OPTS is also another option to look at for connecting remotely to Kafka brokers. Make sure to note the correct port and hostname. Listing 9.10 shows an example that sets KAFKA_JMX_OPTS with various arguments [13]. It uses port 49999 and the localhost as the hostname. In the listing, the other parameters allow us to connect without SSL and to not have to authenticate.

Listing 9.10   Kafka JMX options

```
KAFKA_JMX_OPTS="-Djava.rmi.server.hostname=127.0.0.1      ⟵  Sets the hostname for
  -Dcom.sun.management.jmxremote.local.only=false    ⟵     the localhost RMI server
  -Dcom.sun.management.jmxremote.rmi.port=49999             Allows remote connections
  -Dcom.sun.management.jmxremote.authenticate=false
  -Dcom.sun.management.jmxremote.ssl=false"                Turns off authentication
                                                           and SSL checks
```

Exposes this port for JMX

Let's take a look at a key broker metric and how to locate the value we need with the help of figure 9.4, which shows how to use a small MBeans representation to see the value of UnderReplicatedPartitions. Using a name such as

```
kafka.server:type=ReplicaManager,name=UnderReplicatedPartitions
```

we can drill down what looks like a folder structure starting with kafka.server.

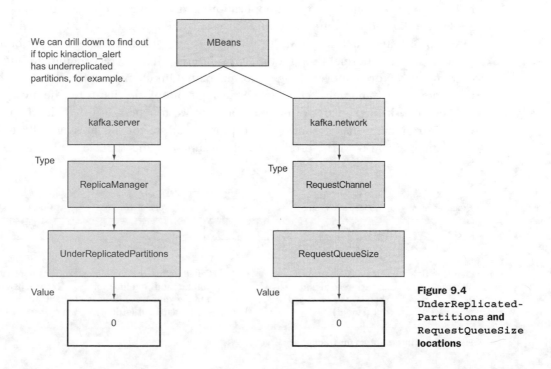

Figure 9.4 UnderReplicated-Partitions **and** RequestQueueSize **locations**

Continuing on, we can then find the type `ReplicaManager` with the name attribute `UnderReplicatedPartitions`. `RequestQueueSize` is also shown in figure 9.4 as another example of finding a value [14]. Now that you know how to browse to specific values, let's go into detail about some of the most important things to look at on our servers.

If you use Confluent Control Center or Confluent Cloud, most of these metrics are used in the built-in monitoring. The Confluent Platform suggests setting alerts on the following top three values to start with: `UnderMinIsrPartitionCount`, `Under-ReplicatedPartitions`, `UnderMinIsr` [14].

Let's dig into a different monitoring option in the next section by looking at how we might leverage interceptors.

9.6   *Tracing option*

The built-in metrics that we looked at so far can give us a great snapshot of current health, but what if we want to trace a single message through the system? What can we use to see a produced message and its consumed status? Let's talk about a simple but straightforward model that might work for our requirements.

Let's say that we have a producer in which each event has a unique ID. Because each message is important, we do not want to miss any of these events. With one client, the business logic runs as normal and consumes the messages from the topic. In this case, it makes sense to log the ID of the event that was processed to a database or flat file. A separate consumer, let's call it an auditing consumer in this instance, fetches the data from the same topic and makes sure that there are no IDs missing from the processed entries of the first application. Though this process can work well, it does require adding logic to our application, and so it might not be the best choice.

Figure 9.5 shows a different approach using Kafka interceptors. In practice, the interceptor that we define is a way to add logic to the producer, consumer, or both by hooking into the normal flow of our clients, intercepting the record, and adding our custom data before it moves along its normal path. Our changes to the clients are configuration-driven and help keep our specific logic out of the clients for the most part.

Let's revisit the concept of interceptors that we touched on briefly in chapter 4, when introducing what producer interceptors could do for our messages. By adding an interceptor on both the producer and consumer clients that we are using, we can

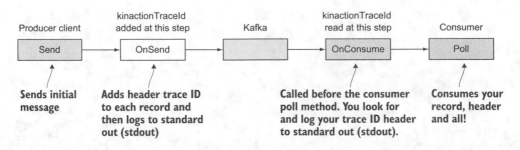

Figure 9.5   Interceptors for tracing

separate the monitoring logic from the application logic. The crosscutting concern of monitoring can, hopefully, be more encapsulated by this approach.

9.6.1 *Producer logic*

It is also interesting to note that we can have more than one interceptor, so we don't have to include all of our logic in one class; we can add and remove others later. The order in which we list the classes is important as that is the order in which the logic runs. The first interceptor gets the record from the producer client. If the interceptor modifies the record, other interceptors in the chain after the change would not see the same exact record as the first interceptor received [15].

Let's start with looking at the Java interface `ProducerInterceptor`. We'll add this new interceptor to our `Alert` producer that we used in chapter 4. We will create a new class called `AlertProducerMetricsInterceptor` to add logic around alerts being produced, as in listing 9.11. Implementing the interface, `ProducerInterceptor`, allows us to hook into the producer's interceptor lifecycle. The logic in the `onSend` method is called by the `send()` method from the normal producer client we have used so far [15]. In the listing, we'll also add a header called `kinactionTraceId`. Using a unique ID helps to confirm on the consumption side that we are seeing the same message at the end of its life cycle that was produced in the beginning of this step.

Listing 9.11 `AlertProducerMetricsInterceptor` example

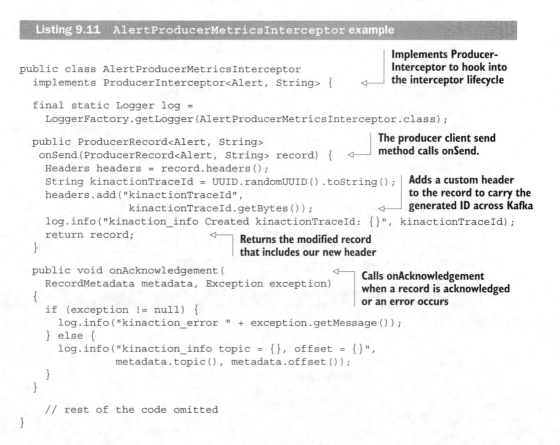

```
public class AlertProducerMetricsInterceptor
  implements ProducerInterceptor<Alert, String> {        <──┐ Implements Producer-
                                                             Interceptor to hook into
                                                             the interceptor lifecycle
  final static Logger log =
    LoggerFactory.getLogger(AlertProducerMetricsInterceptor.class);

  public ProducerRecord<Alert, String>                    ┌─ The producer client send
   onSend(ProducerRecord<Alert, String> record) {   <─────┘  method calls onSend.
    Headers headers = record.headers();
    String kinactionTraceId = UUID.randomUUID().toString();    ┌─ Adds a custom header
    headers.add("kinactionTraceId",                              to the record to carry the
              kinactionTraceId.getBytes());             <──────┘ generated ID across Kafka
    log.info("kinaction_info Created kinactionTraceId: {}", kinactionTraceId);
    return record;            <──┐ Returns the modified record
  }                              that includes our new header

  public void onAcknowledgement(                    <──┐ Calls onAcknowledgement
    RecordMetadata metadata, Exception exception)       when a record is acknowledged
  {                                                      or an error occurs
    if (exception != null) {
      log.info("kinaction_error " + exception.getMessage());
    } else {
      log.info("kinaction_info topic = {}, offset = {}",
              metadata.topic(), metadata.offset());
    }
  }

  // rest of the code omitted
}
```

We also have to modify our existing `AlertProducer` class to register the new interceptor. We need to add the property `interceptor.classes` to the producer configuration with a value of the full package name of our new class: `AlertProducer-`
`MetricsInterceptor`. Although we used the property name for clarity, remember that
we can use the constant provided by the `ProducerConfig` class. In this case, we would
use `ProducerConfig.INTERCEPTOR_CLASSES_CONFIG` [15]. The following listing shows
this required modification.

Listing 9.12 `AlertProducer` with interceptor configuration

```
Properties kaProperties = new Properties();
...
kaProperties.put("interceptor.classes",          ◁── Sets our interceptors
  AlertProducerMetricsInterceptor.class.getName());    (the value can be 1 or a
                                                       comma-separated list).
Producer<Alert, String> producer =
  new KafkaProducer<Alert, String>(kaProperties);
```

Overall, in this example, we have one interceptor that logs a unique ID for each produced message. We add this ID as a header to the record so that when a consumer
pulls this message, a corresponding consumer interceptor logs the ID that it has processed. The goal is to provide our own end-to-end monitoring that is outside of Kafka.
By parsing the application logs, we will see messages like the following listing shows,
which came from our `AlertProducerMetricsInterceptor` class.

Listing 9.13 The `alert` interceptor output

```
kinaction_info Created kinactionTraceId:
  603a8922-9fb5-442a-a1fa-403f2a6a875d
kinaction_info topic = kinaction_alert, offset = 1    ◁── The producer interceptor
                                                          adds our logged value.
```

9.6.2 *Consumer logic*

Now that we have completed setting up an interceptor for sending a message, we need
to see how to implement similar logic on the consumer end of our system. We want to
validate that we can see the same header value that we added with the producer interceptor on the consumption end. The following listing shows an implementation of
`ConsumerInterceptor` to help retrieve this header [16].

Listing 9.14 `AlertConsumerMetricsInterceptor` example

```
public class AlertConsumerMetricsInterceptor
  implements ConsumerInterceptor<Alert, String> {    ◁── Implements Consumer-
                                                          Interceptor so Kafka
  public ConsumerRecords<Alert, String>                  recognizes our interceptor
    onConsume(ConsumerRecords<Alert, String> records) {
      if (records.isEmpty()) {
        return records;
      } else {
```

```
        for (ConsumerRecord<Alert, String> record : records) {
          Headers headers = record.headers();        ◁──┐ Loops through each
          for (Header header : headers) {                │ record's headers
            if ("kinactionTraceId".equals(
                   header.key())) {
              log.info("KinactionTraceId is: " + new String(header.value()));
            }
          }
        }
      }
      return records;        ◁──┐ Returns the records to continue
    }                             │ with callers from our interceptor
  }
```

Logs the custom header to standard output

In a fashion similar to our producer, in this listing, we used a consumer-specific interface, `ConsumerInterceptor`, to make our new interceptor. We looped through all the records and their headers to find any that had our custom `kinactionTraceId` as the key and sent them to standard output. We also modified our existing `AlertConsumer` class to register our new interceptor. The property name `interceptor.classes` needs to be added to the consumer configuration with a value of the full package name of our new class: `AlertConsumerMetricsInterceptor`. The following listing shows this required step.

Listing 9.15 `AlertConsumer` **with interceptor configuration**

```
public class AlertConsumer {

Properties kaProperties = new Properties();        ◁──┐ Uses a new group.id to
...                                                       ensure starting with our
kaProperties.put("group.id",                             current offsets (and not one
             "kinaction_alertinterceptor");     ◁──── from a previous group.id)
kaProperties.put("interceptor.classes",         ◁──┐ Required property name
  AlertConsumerMetricsInterceptor.class.getName());    to add our custom
                                                       interceptor and class value
...
}
```

We can include a comma-separated list if we have more than one class we need to use [16]. Although we used the property name for clarity, remember that we can use the constant provided by the `ConsumerConfig` class. In this case, we would use `Consumer-Config.INTERCEPTOR_CLASSES_CONFIG` [16]. Although we can see the usage of an intercep-tor on both ends of our flow, there is also another way to add functionality to client code—overriding clients.

9.6.3 Overriding clients

If we control the source code for clients that other developers will use, we can subclass an existing client or create our own that implements the Kafka producer/consumer interfaces. At the time of writing, the Brave project (https://github.com/openzipkin/brave) has an example of one such client that works with tracing data.

For those not familiar with Brave, it is a library meant to help add instrumentation for distributed tracing. It has the ability to send this data to something, for example, like a Zipkin server (https://zipkin.io/), which can handle the collection and search of this data. If interested, please take a peek at the `TracingConsumer` class (http://mng.bz/6mAo) for a real-world example of adding functionality to clients with Kafka.

We can decorate both the producer and consumer clients to enable tracing (or any custom logic), but we'll focus on the consumer client in the following stub example. The code in listing 9.16 is a section of pseudo code to add custom logic to the normal Kafka consumer flow. Developers wanting to consume messages with the custom logic can use an instance of `KInActionCustomConsumer`, which includes a reference to a regular consumer client named `normalKafkaConsumer` (in the custom consumer client itself) in this listing. The custom logic is added to provide needed behavior while still interacting with the traditional client. Your developers work with your consumer, which handles the normal client behind the scenes.

Listing 9.16   Custom consumer client

```
final class KInActionCustomConsumer<K, V> implements Consumer<K, V> {
...
   final Consumer<K, V> normalKafkaConsumer;        ◁—— Uses the normal Kafka consumer
                                                        client in our custom consumer
   @Override
   public ConsumerRecords<K, V> poll(              ◁—— Consumers still call the interface
      final Duration timeout)                           methods they are used to.
   {
      //Custom logic here                          ◁—— Adds our custom
      // Normal Kafka consumer used as normal           logic where needed
      return normalKafkaConsumer.poll(timeout);    ◁——
   }                                                    Uses the normal Kafka consumer
...                                                     client to provide its normal duties
}
```

This listing only shows a comment indicating where your logic would go, but your users are abstracted from using the normal client methods if desired while still running any custom code such as checking for duplicate data submissions or logging tracing data from headers. The added behavior is not getting in the way of the normal client.

9.7   *General monitoring tools*

Because Kafka is a Scala™ application, it has the ability to use JMX and the Yammer Metrics library [17]. This library is used to provide JMX metrics on various parts of the application, and we have already seen some options we can evaluate. But as Kafka usage has expanded, there are some tools out there that leverage not only JMX metrics, but also administration-related commands and various other techniques to provide easy-to-manage clusters. Of course, the following section does not have a complete list of options, and the features of those listed might change over time. Nevertheless, let's take a look at a few options that you might want to explore.

The Cluster Manager for Apache Kafka, or CMAK (https://github.com/yahoo/CMAK), once known as the Kafka Manager, is an interesting project that focuses on managing Kafka as well as being a UI for various administrative activities, and was shared from Yahoo™! One key feature is its ability to manage multiple clusters. Other features include inspection of our overall cluster state and the ability to generate and run partition reassignment. This tool can also deal with authenticating users with LDAP, which might be helpful depending on product requirements for a project [18].

Cruise Control (https://github.com/linkedin/cruise-control) was created by developers at LinkedIn. Because they have thousands of brokers across their clusters, they have experience running Kafka clusters and have helped codify and automate dealing with some of Kafka's pain points over the years. A REST API can be used as well as the option to use a UI, so we have a couple of ways to interact with this tool. Some of the most interesting features to us are how Cruise Control can watch our cluster and can generate suggestions on rebalancing based on workloads [19].

Confluent Control Center (https://docs.confluent.io/current/control-center/index.html) is another web-based tool that can help us monitor and manage our clusters. But one item to note is that it currently is a commercial feature that would need an enterprise license for a production setup. If you already have a subscription to the Confluent platform, there is no reason not to check it out. This tool uses dashboards and can help identify message failures, network latency, and other external connectors.

Overall, Kafka provides us with many options to not only manage but also monitor our cluster. Distributed systems are difficult, and the more experience you gain, the more your monitoring skills and practices will improve.

Summary

- Besides the shell scripts that are packaged with Kafka, an administrative client also exists to provide API access to important tasks such as creating a topic.
- Tools such as kcat and the Confluent REST Proxy API allow ways for developers to interact with the cluster.
- Although Kafka uses a log for client data at its core, there are still various logs specific to the operation of the broker that we need to maintain. We need to address managing these logs (and ZooKeeper logs) to provide details for troubleshooting when needed.
- Understanding advertised listeners can help explain behavior that at first appears inconsistent for client connections.
- Kafka uses JMX for metrics. You can see metrics from clients (producers and consumers) as well as from brokers.
- We can use producer and consumer interceptors to implement crosscutting concerns. One such example would be adding tracing IDs for monitoring message delivery.

References

1 "Class AdminClient." Confluent documentation (n.d.). https://docs.confluent
.io/5.3.1/clients/javadocs/index.html?org/apache/kafka/clients/admin/
AdminClient.html (accessed November 17, 2020).

2 "kcat." GitHub. https://github.com/edenhill/kcat/#readme (accessed August
25, 2021).

3 "Kafka Security & the Confluent Platform." Confluent documentation (n.d.).
https://docs.confluent.io/2.0.1/kafka/platform-security.html#kafka-security-
the-confluent-platform (accessed August 25, 2021).

4 "Confluent REST APIs: Overview: Features." Confluent documentation (n.d.).
https://docs.confluent.io/platform/current/kafka-rest/index.html#features
(accessed February 20, 2019).

5 "REST Proxy Quick Start." Confluent documentation (n.d.). https://docs.con-
fluent.io/platform/current/kafka-rest/quickstart.html (accessed February 22,
2019).

6 "Using Confluent Platform systemd Service Unit Files." Confluent documentation (n.d.). https://docs.confluent.io/platform/current/installation/scripted-
install.html#overview (accessed January 15, 2021).

7 "Class RollingFileAppender." Apache Software Foundation (n.d.). https://
logging.apache.org/log4j/1.2/apidocs/org/apache/log4j/RollingFileAppender
.html (accessed April 22, 2020).

8 log4j.properties. Apache Kafka GitHub (March 26, 2020). https://github
.com/apache/kafka/blob/99b9b3e84f4e98c3f07714e1de6a139a004cbc5b/
config/log4j.properties (accessed June 17, 2020).

9 "Running ZooKeeper in Production." Confluent documentation (n.d.). https:/
/docs.confluent.io/platform/current/zookeeper/deployment.html#running-
zk-in-production (accessed July 23, 2021).

10 "ZooKeeper Administrator's Guide." Apache Software Foundation (n.d.).
https://zookeeper.apache.org/doc/r3.4.5/zookeeperAdmin.html   (accessed
June 10, 2020).

11 "ZooKeeper Getting Started Guide." Apache Software Foundation (n.d.).
https://zookeeper.apache.org/doc/r3.1.2/zookeeperStarted.html   (accessed
August 19, 2020).

12 R. Moffatt. "Kafka Listeners – Explained." Confluent blog (July 1, 2019). https:/
/www.confluent.io/blog/kafka-listeners-explained/ (accessed June 11, 2020).

13 "Kafka Monitoring and Metrics Using JMX." Confluent documentation (n.d.).
https://docs.confluent.io/platform/current/installation/docker/operations/
monitoring.html (accessed June 12, 2020).

14 "Monitoring Kafka: Broker Metrics." Confluent documentation (n.d.). https://
docs.confluent.io/5.4.0/kafka/monitoring.html#broker-metrics (accessed May
1, 2020).

15 "Interface ProducerInterceptor." Apache Software Foundation (n.d.). https://kafka.apache.org/27/javadoc/org/apache/kafka/clients/producer/Producer Interceptor.html (accessed June 1, 2020).

16 "Interface ConsumerInterceptor." Apache Software Foundation (n.d.). https://kafka.apache.org/27/javadoc/org/apache/kafka/clients/consumer/Consumer Interceptor.html (accessed June 1, 2020).

17 "Monitoring." Apache Software Foundation (n.d.). https://kafka.apache.org/documentation/#monitoring (accessed May 1, 2020).

18 Yahoo CMAK README.md. GitHub (March 5, 2020). https://github.com/yahoo/CMAK/blob/master/README.md (accessed July 20, 2021).

19 README.md. LinkedIn Cruise Control for Apache Kafka GitHub (June 30, 2021). https://github.com/linkedin/cruise-control/blob/migrate_to_kafka_2_4/README.md (acces-sed July 21, 2021).

Part 3

Going further

Part 3 focuses on how to further our use of Kafka beyond what part 2 covered as the core pieces of Kafka. In this part, we go further than just having a Kafka cluster that we can read and write data to. We add more security, data schemas, and look at other Kafka products.

- In chapter 10, we look at strengthening a Kafka cluster by using SSL, ACLs, and options like quotas.
- In chapter 11, we dig into the Schema Registry and how it is used to help data evolve in compatible ways.
- In chapter 12, we look at Kafka Streams and ksqlDB.

These pieces are all part of the Kafka ecosystem and are higher levels of abstraction built on the core subjects you studied in part 2. At the end of this part, you'll be ready to dig into even more advanced Kafka topics on your own and, even better, you'll be able to use Kafka in your day-to-day workflow.

Protecting Kafka

This chapters covers

- Security basics and related terminology
- SSL between a cluster and clients
- Access control lists (ACLs)
- Network bandwidth and request rate quotas to limit demands on resources

This chapter focuses on keeping our data secured so that only those that need to read from or write to it have access. Because security is a huge area to cover, in this chapter, we will talk about some basic concepts to get a general background on the options we have in Kafka. Our goal in this chapter is not to set up security, but to learn some different options that you can talk with your security team on researching in the future and get familiar with the concepts. This will not be a complete guide to security in general, but sets the foundation for you. We will discuss practical actions you can take in your own setup, and we will look at the client impact, as well as brokers and ZooKeeper, to make our cluster more secure.

Your data might not need those protections we discuss, but knowing your data is key to deciding if you need the trade-offs of managing access. If you are handling anything related to personal information or financial data, like date of birth or credit card numbers, then you will likely want to look at most of the security options discussed in this chapter. However, if you are only handling generic information such as marketing campaigns, or you are not tracking anything of a secure nature, then you might not need this protection. If this is the case, then your cluster would not need to introduce features like SSL. We start with an example of fictional data that we want to protect.

Let's imagine that we have a goal to find the location of a prize by taking part in a treasure hunt. As a competition-wide exercise, we have two teams, and we do not want the other team to access our own team's work. Starting out, each team picks their own topic names and shares that name with their team members only. (Without knowing which topic name to write to and read from, your data is out of the view of the other team.) Each team begins by sending their clues to what they assume is their own *private* topic. Over time, members of the teams might start to wonder about the progress of the other team and whether they have any clues that the other team doesn't. This is when the trouble starts. Figure 10.1 shows the topic setup for Team Clueful and Team Clueless.

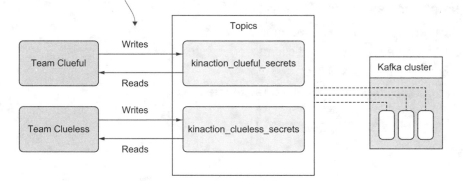

Figure 10.1   Treasure hunt topics

One tech-savvy competitor, who coincidentally has used Kafka before, reaches for his command line tools to find the topics (the other team's as well as his own). After getting a list of topics, the competitor now knows his rival's topic. Let's say that this team member of Team Clueless looks at Team Clueful's topic, `--topic kinaction _clueful_secrets`. With great happiness, all it took was a consumer console command to list all the data that Team Clueful has been working on so far in the competition! But the bad actor does not stop there.

In order to throw Team Clueful off the trail, the actor also writes false information into the channel. Now Team Clueful has bad data in their topic, which is hindering their clue-solving progress! Because they are not sure who really wrote the messages on their topic, Team Clueful now has to determine which are the false messages and, in doing so, will lose valuable time that they could be using to work on figuring out the grand-prize location.

How could we avoid the situation Team Clueful finds itself in? Is there a way that only those clients that have permission would be able to read from or write to our topics? There are two parts to our solution. The first part is how to encrypt our data. The next is how to find out who a person is in our system; not only who they are, but also making sure that the claimed identity of the user is verified. Once we verify a user, we need to know what they are permitted do in our system. We will dive deeper into these topics as we look at a few solutions provided with Kafka.

10.1 Security basics

In regard to computer application security, you will likely encounter encryption, authentication, and authorization at some point in your work. Let's take a closer look at this terminology (see http://mng.bz/o802 for more detail of the following terms if needed).

Encryption does not mean that others might not see your messages, but that if they do, they will not be able to derive the original content that you are protecting. Many people will think of how they are encouraged to use a site that is secure (HTTPS) for online shopping on a Wi-Fi® network. Later, we are going to enable SSL (Secure Sockets Layer) for our communication, not between a website and our computer, but between our clients and brokers! As a general note, as we work through this chapter, the label "SSL" is the property name you will see in our examples and explanations even though TLS is the newer protocol version [1].

Moving along, let's talk about *authentication*. To verify the identity of a user or an application, we need to have a way to authenticate that user: authentication is the process of proving that a user or application is indeed who they claim to be. If you wanted to sign up for a library card, for example, does the library issue a card to anyone without making sure the user is who they say they are? In most cases, the library would confirm the person's name and address with something like a government-issued ID and a utility bill. This process is intended to ensure that someone cannot easily claim another identity to use for their own purposes. If someone claims your identity to borrow books and never returns them, sending the fines your way, you can easily see a drawback of not confirming the user's claim.

Authorization, on the other hand, focuses on what the user can do. Continuing with our library example, a card issued to an adult might provide different permissions than if it was given to a user considered to be a child. And access to online publications might be limited to only terminals inside the library for each cardholder.

10.1.1 Encryption with SSL

So far, all of our brokers in this book have supported plaintext [1]. In effect, there has been no authentication or encryption over the network. Knowing this, it might make sense to review one of the broker server configuration values. If you look at any of your current server.properties files (see appendix A for your setup location of the config/server0.properties file, for example), you will find an entry like listeners = PLAINTEXT:localhost//:9092. That listener is, in effect, providing a mapping of a protocol to a specific port on the broker. Because brokers support multiple ports, this entry allows us to keep the PLAINTEXT port up and running, so we can test adding SSL or other protocols on a different port. Having two ports helps to make our transition smoother when we shift away from plaintext [2]. Figure 10.2 shows an example of using plaintext versus SSL.

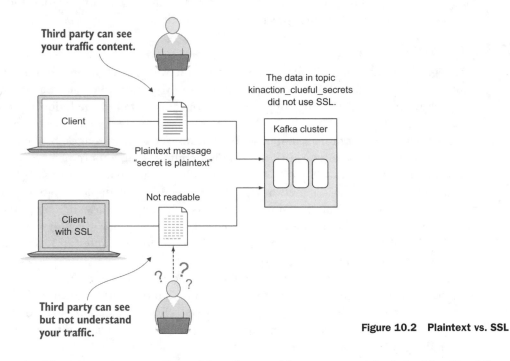

Figure 10.2   Plaintext vs. SSL

At this point, we are starting with a cluster without any security baked in. (Luckily, we can add various pieces to our cluster as we harden it against other teams.) Setting up SSL between the brokers in our cluster and our clients is one place to start [1]. No extra servers or directories are needed. No client coding changes are required, as the changes are configuration driven.

We don't know how advanced other users are when it comes to listening to our traffic on the same Wi-Fi network with security tools, so we know that we might not want to send plaintext from our brokers to our clients. Although the setup in the following section is needed for Kafka security, readers who have set up SSL or HTTPS in the past (and especially with Java) will find this approach similar to other client/ server trust arrangements.

10.1.2 *SSL between brokers and clients*

In our previous examples of writing clients and connecting to Kafka, we have not used SSL for connections. However, now we are going to look at turning it on for the communication between our clients and our cluster to encrypt our network traffic with SSL. Let's walk through the process and see what we are going to need to accomplish in order to get our cluster updated with this feature.

> **NOTE** The commands in this chapter are specific and will not work the same on all operating systems (or even across different server domain names listed for broker setup) without modification. The important thing is to follow along with the general concepts. Moreover, other tools (like OpenSSL®) can be switched out, so your setup and commands might be different. But once you get the concepts, head to Confluent's site at http://mng.bz/nrza for even more resources and guides. Confluent's documents that provided direction for any examples are referenced throughout this chapter and should be referenced to help you actually implement the topics we only cover at a high level in order to introduce the following concepts.

> **WARNING** A security professional should be consulted for the correct way to set up your own environment. Our commands are meant as a guide for getting familiar and for learning, not as a production level of security. This is not a complete guide. Use it at your own risk!

One of our first steps is to create a key and certificate for our brokers [3]. Because you should already have Java on your machine, one option is to use the keytool utility, which is part of the Java installation. The keytool application manages a keystore of keys and trusted certificates [4]. The important part to note is the *storage*. In this chapter, the term *broker0* is included in some filenames to identify one specific broker, not one that is meant for every broker. It might be good to think of a keystore as a database where our JVM programs can look up this information for our processes when needed [4]. At this point, we are also going to generate a key for our brokers as in the following listing [3]. Note that manning.com is used as an example in the following listings and is not intended to be used for readers following along.

Listing 10.1   SSL key generation for a broker

```
keytool -genkey -noprompt \
  -alias localhost \
  -dname "CN=ka.manning.com,OU=TEST,O=TREASURE,L=Bend,S=Or,C=US" \
  -keystore kafka.broker0.keystore.jks \        Names the keystore that holds
  -keyalg RSA \                                 our newly generated key
  -storepass changeTreasure \        Uses a password so
  -keypass changeTreasure \          that the store cannot
  -validity 999                      be changed without it
```

After running this command, we will have created a new key and stored it in the keystore file kafka.broker0.keystore.jks. Because we have a key that (in a way) identifies our broker, we need something to signal that we don't have just any certificate issued by a random user. One way to verify our certificates is by signing them with a CA (certificate authority). You might have heard of CAs offered by Let's Encrypt® (https://letsen crypt.org/) or GoDaddy® (https://www.godaddy.com/), to name a few sources. The role of a CA is to act as a trusted authority that certifies the ownership and identity of a public key [3]. In our examples, however, we are going to be our own CA to avoid any need of verifying our identity by a third party. Our next step is to create our own CA, as the following listing shows [3].

Listing 10.2   Creating our own certificate authority

```
openssl req -new -x509 \
  -keyout cakey.crt -out ca.crt \          Creates a new CA, then produces
  -days 999 \                              key and certificate files
  -subj '/CN=localhost/OU=TEST/O=TREASURE/L=Bend/S=Or/C=US' \
  -passin pass:changeTreasure -passout pass:changeTreasure
```

This generated CA is now something that we want to let our clients know that they should trust. Similar to the term *keystore*, we will use a truststore to hold this new information [3].

Because we generated our CA in listing 10.2, we can use it to sign our certificates for our brokers that we have already made. First, we export the certificate that we generated in listing 10.2 for each broker from the keystore, sign that with our new CA, and then import both the CA certificate and signed certificate back into the keystore [3]. Confluent also provides a shell script that can be used to help automate similar commands (see http://mng.bz/v497) [3]. Check out the rest of our commands in the source code for the book in the section for this chapter.

> **NOTE**   While running the commands in these listings, your operating system or tool version may have a different prompt than that passed. It will likely have a user prompt appear after running your command. Our examples try to avoid these prompts.

As part of our changes, we also need to update the server.properties configuration file on each broker, as the following listing shows [3]. Note that this listing only shows broker0 and only part of the file.

Listing 10.3   Broker server properties changes

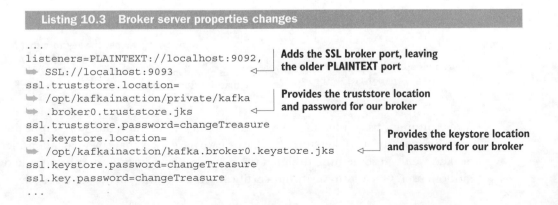

```
...
listeners=PLAINTEXT://localhost:9092,          Adds the SSL broker port, leaving
 ➥ SSL://localhost:9093                        the older PLAINTEXT port
ssl.truststore.location=
 ➥ /opt/kafkainaction/private/kafka           Provides the truststore location
 ➥ .broker0.truststore.jks                    and password for our broker
ssl.truststore.password=changeTreasure
ssl.keystore.location=                         Provides the keystore location
 ➥ /opt/kafkainaction/kafka.broker0.keystore.jks   and password for our broker
ssl.keystore.password=changeTreasure
ssl.key.password=changeTreasure
...
```

Changes are also needed for our clients. For example, we set the value `security .protocol=SSL`, as well as the truststore location and password in a file called `custom -ssl.properties`. This helps set the protocol used for SSL as well as points to our truststore [3].

While testing these changes, we can also have multiple listeners set up for our broker. This also helps clients migrate over time, as both ports can serve traffic before we drop the older `PLAINTEXT` port for our clients [3]. The kinaction-ssl.properties file helps our clients provide the information needed to interact with the broker that is now becoming more secured!

Listing 10.4 Using SSL configuration for command line clients

```
bin/kafka-console-producer.sh --bootstrap-server localhost:9093 \       Lets our producer
  --topic kinaction_test_ssl \                                          know about the
  --producer.config kinaction-ssl.properties        <———                SSL details
bin/kafka-console-consumer.sh --bootstrap-server localhost:9093 \
  --topic kinaction_test_ssl \
  --consumer.config kinaction-ssl.properties      <———┐ Uses our SSL configuration
                                                       └ for consumers
```

One of the nicest features is that we can use the same configuration for both producers and consumers. As you look at the contents of this configuration file, one issue that might spring to mind is the use of passwords in these files. The most straightforward option is to make sure that you are aware of the permissions around this file. Limiting the ability to read as well as the ownership of the file is important to note *before* placing this configuration on your filesystem. As always, consult your security experts for better options that might be available for your environment.

10.1.3 SSL between brokers

Another detail to research since we also have our brokers talking to each other is that we might want to decide if we need to use SSL for those interactions. We can use `security.inter.broker.protocol = SSL` in the server properties if we do *not* want to continue using plaintext for communications between brokers and consider a port change as well. More details can be found at http://mng.bz/4KBw [5].

10.2 Kerberos and the Simple Authentication and Security Layer (SASL)

If you have a security team that already has a Kerberos server, you likely have some security experts to ask for help. When we first started working with Kafka, it was with a part of a suite of big data tools that mostly used Kerberos. Kerberos is often found in organizations as a method to provide single sign-on (SSO) that is secure.

If you have a Kerberos server set up already, you need to work with a user with access to that Kerberos environment to create a principal for each broker and also for each user (or application ID) that will access the cluster. Because this setup might be too involved for local testing, follow along with this discussion to see the format of Java

Authentication and Authorization Service (JAAS) files, which is a common file type for brokers and clients. There are great resources at http://mng.bz/QqxG if you want to gain more details [6].

JAAS files, with keytab file information, help to provide Kafka with the principal and credentials that we will use. A *keytab* will likely be a separate file that has the principal and encrypted keys. We can use this file to authenticate to the Kafka brokers without requiring a password [7]. However, it is important to note that you need to treat your keytab file with the same security and care that you would for any credential.

To get our brokers set up, let's look at some server property changes we'll need to make and an example JAAS configuration. To start, each broker will need its own keytab file. Our JAAS file will help our brokers find the keytab's location on our server, as well as declare the principal to use [7]. The following listing shows an example JAAS file brokers would use on startup.

Listing 10.5   Broker SASL JAAS file

```
KafkaServer {                                          ◁──┐  Sets up the Kafka
...                                                        │  broker JAAS file
    keyTab="/opt/kafkainaction/kafka_server0.keytab"
    principal="kafka/kafka0.ka.manning.com@MANNING.COM";
};
```

We are going to add another port to test `SASL_SSL` before we remove the older ports [7]. The following listing shows this change. Depending on what port you used to connect to your brokers, the protocol is either `PLAINTEXT`, `SSL`, or `SASL_SSL` in this example.

Listing 10.6   Changing the broker SASL properties

```
listeners=PLAINTEXT://localhost:9092,SSL://localhost:9093,
⇒   SASL_SSL://localhost:9094                  ◁──┐  Adds the SASL_SSL broker
                                                   │  port, leaving the older ports
```

The setup for a client is similar [7]. A JAAS file is needed, as the following listing shows.

Listing 10.7   Client SASL JAAS file

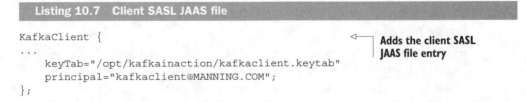

```
KafkaClient {                                          ◁──┐  Adds the client SASL
...                                                        │  JAAS file entry
    keyTab="/opt/kafkainaction/kafkaclient.keytab"
    principal="kafkaclient@MANNING.COM";
};
```

We also need to update client configuration for the SASL values [3]. The client file is similar to our kinaction-ssl.properties file used earlier, but this one defines the `SASL_SSL` protocol. After testing that things are not broken on port 9092 or 9093, we can use our new configuration by validating the same result as before when we use our new `SASL_SSL` protocol.

10.3 *Authorization in Kafka*

Now that we have seen how to use authentication with Kafka, let's take a look at how we can start using that information to enable user access. For this discussion, we'll start with access control lists.

10.3.1 *Access control lists (ACLs)*

As a quick review, authorization is the process that controls what a user can do. One way to enable authorization is with access control lists (ACLs). Although most Linux users are familiar with permissions on a file they can control with a `chmod` command (such as read, write, and execute), one drawback is that the permissions might not be flexible enough for our needs. ACLs can provide permissions for multiple individuals and groups as well as more types of permissions, and they are often used when we need different levels of access for a shared folder [8]. One example is a permission to let a user edit a file but not allow the same user to delete it (delete is a separate permission altogether). Figure 10.3 shows Franz's access to the resources for our hypothetical team for our treasure hunt.

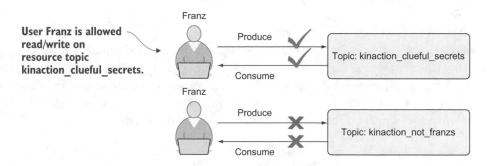

Figure 10.3   Access control lists (ACLs)

Kafka designed their authorizer to be pluggable, which allows users to make their own logic if desired [8]. Kafka has a `SimpleAclAuthorizer` class that we will use in our example.

Listing 10.8 shows adding the authorizer class and superuser Franz to the broker's server.properties file in order to use ACLs. An important item to note is that once we configure an authorizer, we need to set ACLs, or only those considered superusers will have access to any resources [8].

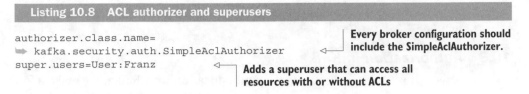

Listing 10.8   ACL authorizer and superusers

```
authorizer.class.name=
➥ kafka.security.auth.SimpleAclAuthorizer
super.users=User:Franz
```

Every broker configuration should include the SimpleAclAuthorizer.

Adds a superuser that can access all resources with or without ACLs

Let's see how to grant access to Team Clueful so that only that team produces and consumes from their own topic, kinaction_clueful_secrets. For brevity, we use two users in our example team, Franz and Hemingway. Because we have already created the keytabs for the users, we know the principal information that we need. As you may notice in the following listing, the operation Read allows consumers the ability to get data from the topic [8]. The second operation, Write, allows the same principals to produce data into the topic.

Listing 10.9   Kafka ACLs to read and write to a topic

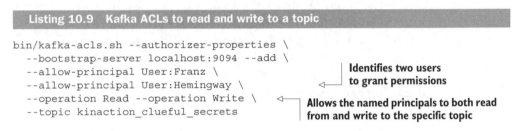

```
bin/kafka-acls.sh --authorizer-properties \
  --bootstrap-server localhost:9094 --add \
  --allow-principal User:Franz \
  --allow-principal User:Hemingway \
  --operation Read --operation Write \
  --topic kinaction_clueful_secrets
```

Identifies two users to grant permissions

Allows the named principals to both read from and write to the specific topic

The kafka-acls.sh CLI tool is included with the other Kafka scripts in our installation and lets us add, delete, or list current ACLs [8].

10.3.2 Role-based access control (RBAC)

Role-based access control (RBAC) is an option that the Confluent Platform supports. RBAC is a way to control access based on roles [9]. Users are assigned to their role according to their needs (such as a job duty, for example). Instead of granting every user permissions, with RBAC, you manage the privileges assigned to predefined roles [9]. Figure 10.4 shows how adding a user to a role gives them a new permission assignment.

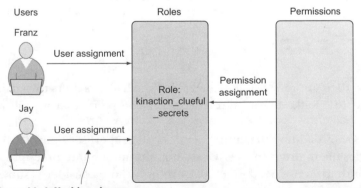

Figure 10.4
Role-based access control (RBAC)

For our treasure hunting teams, it might make sense to have a specific role per team. This might mirror how a team from marketing would have a role versus a team from accounting. If some user changes departments, their role would be reassigned and not their individual permissions. Because this is a newer option, which may change as it matures and which is geared to the Confluent Platform environment, this is mentioned for awareness. We will not dig further into it here.

10.4 ZooKeeper

Part of securing Kafka is looking at how we can secure all parts of our cluster, including ZooKeeper. If we protect the brokers but not the system that holds that security-related data, it is possible for those with knowledge to update security values without much effort. To help protect our metadata, we will need to set the value `zookeeper`
`.set.acl` to `true` per broker, as shown in the following listing [10].

Listing 10.10   ZooKeeper ACLs

```
zookeeper.set.acl=true
```
◁— **Every broker configuration includes this ZooKeeper value.**

10.4.1 Kerberos setup

Making sure that ZooKeeper works with Kerberos requires a variety of configuration changes. For one, in the zookeeper.properties configuration file, we want to add those values that let ZooKeeper know that SASL should be used for clients and which provider to use. Refer to http://mng.bz/Xr0v for more details if needed [10]. While we were busy looking at the other options for setup so far in this chapter, some users on our treasure hunt system were still up to no good. Let's see if we can dig into the subject of quotas to help with that.

10.5 Quotas

Let's say that some users of our web application don't have any issues with requesting data repeatedly. Although this is often a good thing for end users that want to use a service as much as they want without their progress being limited, our cluster may need some protection from users who might use that to their advantage. In our example, because we made it so the data was accessed by members of our team only, some users on the opposing team thought of a new way to prevent members of our team from working successfully. In effect, they are trying to use a distributed denial-of-service (DDoS) attack against our system [11]!

A targeted attack against our cluster can overwhelm our brokers and their surrounding infrastructure. In practice, the other team is requesting reads from our topics over and over while reading from the beginning of the topics each time they request data. We can use quotas to prevent this behavior. One detail that's important to know is that quotas are defined on a per-broker basis [11]. The cluster does not look across each broker to calculate a total, so a per-broker definition is needed. Figure 10.5 shows an example of using a request percentage quota.

Clients all with Client IDs from kinaction_clueless_secrets would get delays after too many fetches.

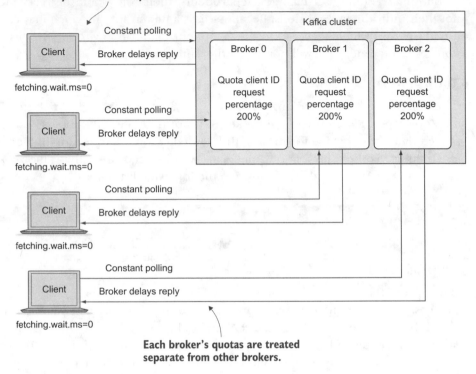

Each broker's quotas are treated separate from other brokers.

Figure 10.5   Quotas

To set our own custom quotas, we need to know how to identify *who* to limit and the *limit* we want to set. Whether we have security or not impacts what options we have for defining who we are limiting. Without security, we are able to use the `client.id` property. With security enabled, we can also add the `user` and any `user` and `client.id` combinations as well [11]. There are a couple of types of quotas that we can look at defining for our clients: network bandwidth and request rate quotas. Let's take a look at the network bandwidth option first.

10.5.1 *Network bandwidth quota*

Network bandwidth is measured by the number of bytes per second [12]. In our example, we want to make sure that each client is respecting the network and not flooding it to prevent others from using it. Each user in our competition uses a client ID that is specific to their team for any producer or consumer requests from their clients. In the following listing, we'll limit the clients using the client ID `kinaction_clueful` by setting a `producer_byte_rate` and a `consumer_byte_rate` [13].

Listing 10.11 Creating a network bandwidth quota for client `kinaction_clueful`

```
bin/kafka-configs.sh  --bootstrap-server localhost:9094 --alter \
  --add-config 'producer_byte_rate=1048576,
➥ consumer_byte_rate=5242880' \
  --entity-type clients --entity-name kinaction_clueful
```

Limits producers to 1 MB per second and consumers to 5 MB per second

Names the entity for a client with the client.id kinaction_clueful

We used the `add-config` parameter to set both the producer and consumer rate. The `entity-name` applies the rule to our specific `kinaction_clueful` clients. As is often the case, we might need to list our current quotas as well as delete them if they are no longer needed. All of these commands can be completed by sending different arguments to the `kafka-configs.sh` script, as the following listing shows [13].

Listing 10.12 Listing and deleting a quota for client `kinaction_clueful`

```
bin/kafka-configs.sh  --bootstrap-server localhost:9094 \
  --describe \
  --entity-type clients --entity-name kinaction_clueful

bin/kafka-configs.sh  --bootstrap-server localhost:9094 --alter \
  --delete-config
➥ 'producer_byte_rate,consumer_byte_rate' \
  --entity-type clients --entity-name kinaction_clueful
```

Lists the existing configuration of our client.id

Uses delete-config to remove those we just added

The `--describe` command helps us get a look at the existing configuration. We can then use that information to decide if we need to modify or even delete the configuration by using the `delete-config` parameter.

As we start to add quotas, we might end up with more than one quota applied to a client. We need to be aware of the precedence in which various quotas are applied. Although it might seem like the most restrictive setting (the lowest bytes allowed) would be the highest for quotas, that is not always the case. The following is the order in which quotas are applied with the highest precedence listed at the top [14]:

- User- and `client.id`-provided quotas
- User quotas
- `client.id` quotas

For example, if a user named Franz has a user-quota limit of 10 MB and a `client.id` limit of 1 MB, the consumer he uses would be allowed 10 MB per second due to the user-defined quota having higher precedence.

10.5.2 *Request rate quotas*

The other quota to examine is *request rate*. Why the need for a second quota? Although a DDoS attack is often thought of as a network issue, clients making lots of connections could still overwhelm the broker by making CPU-intensive requests. Consumer clients that poll continuously with a setting of `fetch.max.wait.ms=0` are also a concern that can be addressed with request rate quotas, as shown in figure 10.5 [15].

To set this quota, we use the same entity types and `add-config` options as we did with our other quotas [13]. The biggest difference is setting the configuration for `request_percentage`. You'll find a formula that uses the number of I/O threads and the number of network threads at http://mng.bz/J6Yz [16]. In the following listing, we set a request percentage of `100` for our example [13].

Listing 10.13   Creating a network bandwidth quota for client `kinaction_clueful`

```
bin/kafka-configs.sh  --bootstrap-server localhost:9094 --alter \
  --add-config 'request_percentage=100' \            ◁── Allows producers
  --entity-type clients --entity-name kinaction_clueful ◁──  a request rate
                                                           quota of 100%
                              Names the entity for our
                              client.id kinaction_clueful
```

Using quotas is a good way to protect our cluster. Even better, it lets us react to clients that suddenly might start putting a strain on our brokers.

10.6 *Data at rest*

Another thing to consider is whether you need to encrypt the data that Kafka writes to disk. By default, Kafka does not encrypt the events it adds to its logs. There have been a couple of Kafka Improvement Proposals (KIPs) that have looked at this feature, but at the time of publication, you will still need to make sure you have a strategy that meets your requirements. Depending on your business needs, you might want to only encrypt specific topics or even specific topics with unique keys.

10.6.1 *Managed options*

If you use a managed option for your cluster, it might be best to check out what features the service provides. Amazon's Managed Streaming for Apache Kafka (https://aws.amazon.com/msk/) is one example of a cloud provider that handles a large part of your cluster management, including some security pieces. Having your brokers and ZooKeeper nodes updated with automatically deployed hardware patches and related upgrades addresses one major method of keeping issues at bay. The other benefit of these updates is that you are not providing access to your cluster for even more developers. Amazon MSK also provides encryption for your data and with TLS between various components of Kafka [17].

Additional management features that we covered in our examples in this chapter included the ability to use SSL between your clients and cluster and ACLs. Confluent Cloud (https://www.confluent.io/confluent-cloud/) also is an option that can be deployed across various public cloud offerings. Support for data encryption at rest and in motion as well as ACL support are also options that you should be aware of when matching your security requirements to the actual provider.

Sticking with the Confluent stack, Confluent Platform 5.3 has a commercial feature called *secret protection* (http://mng.bz/yJYB). When we looked at our SSL configuration files earlier, we stored plaintext passwords in certain files. However, secret protection is meant to address that issue by encrypting the secrets in the file and keeping exposed values out of files as well [18]. Because this is a commercial offering, we do not go into depth on how it works, but just be aware, there are options available.

Summary

- Plaintext, although fine for prototypes, needs to be evaluated before production usage.
- SSL (Secure Sockets Layer) can help protect your data between clients and brokers and even between brokers.
- You can use Kerberos to provide a principal identity, allowing you to use Kerberos environments that already exist in an infrastructure.
- Access control lists (ACLs) help define which users have specific operations granted. Role-based access control (RBAC) is also an option that the Confluent Platform supports. RBAC is a way to control access based on roles.
- Quotas can be used with network bandwidth and request rate limits to protect the available resources of a cluster. These quotas can be changed and fine-tuned to allow for normal workloads and peak demand over time.

References

1 "Encryption and Authentication with SSL." Confluent documentation (n.d.). https://docs.confluent.io/platform/current/kafka/authentication_ssl.html (accessed June 10, 2020).

2 "Adding security to a running cluster." Confluent documentation (n.d.). https://docs.confluent.io/platform/current/kafka/incremental-security-upgrade.html #adding-security-to-a-running-cluster (accessed August 20, 2021).

3 "Security Tutorial." Confluent documentation (n.d.). https://docs.confluent .io/platform/current/security/security_tutorial.html (accessed June 10, 2020).

4 keytool. Oracle Java documentation (n.d.). https://docs.oracle.com/javase/8/ docs/technotes/tools/unix/keytool.html (accessed August 20, 2021).

5 "Documentation: Incorporating Security Features in a Running Cluster." Apache Software Foundation (n.d.). http://kafka.apache.org/24/documentation.html #security_rolling_upgrade (accessed June 1, 2020).

6 V. A. Brennen. "An Overview of a Kerberos Infrastructure." Kerberos Infrastructure HOWTO. https://tldp.org/HOWTO/Kerberos-Infrastructure-HOWTO/ overview.html (accessed July, 22, 2021).

7 "Configuring GSSAP." Confluent documentation (n.d.). https://docs.confluent .io/platform/current/kafka/authentication_sasl/authentication_sasl_gssapi .html (accessed June 10, 2020).

8 "Authorization using ACLs." Confluent documentation (n.d.). https://docs
   .confluent.io/platform/current/kafka/authorization.html (accessed June 10,
   2020).

9 "Authorization using Role-Based Access." Confluent documentation (n.d.).
   https://docs.confluent.io/platform/current/security/rbac/index.html (accessed June 10, 2020).

10 "ZooKeeper Security." Confluent documentation (n.d.). https://docs.confluent
   .io/platform/current/security/zk-security.html (accessed June 10, 2020).

11 "Quotas." Confluent documentation (n.d.). https://docs.confluent.io/platform
   /current/kafka/design.html#quotas (accessed August 21, 2021).

12 "Network Bandwidth Quotas." Confluent documentation (n.d.). https://docs
   .confluent.io/platform/current/kafka/design.html#network-bandwidth-quotas
   (accessed August 21, 2021).

13 "Setting quotas." Apache Software Foundation (n.d.). https://kafka.apache
   .org/documentation/#quotas (accessed June 15, 2020).

14 "Quota Configuration." Confluent documentation (n.d.). https://docs.conflu
   ent.io/platform/current/kafka/design.html#quota-configuration   (accessed
   August 21, 2021).

15 KIP-124 "Request rate quotas." Wiki for Apache Kafka. Apache Software Foundation (March 30, 2017). https://cwiki.apache.org/confluence/display/
   KAFKA/KIP-124+-+Request+rate+quotas (accessed June 1, 2020).

16 "Request Rate Quotas." Confluent documentation (n.d.). https://docs
   .confluent.io/platform/current/kafka/design.html#request-rate-quotas
   (accessed August 21, 2021).

17 "Amazon MSK features." Amazon Managed Streaming for Apache Kafka (n.d).
   https://aws.amazon.com/msk/features/ (accessed July 23, 2021).

18 "Secrets Management." Confluent documentation (n.d.). https://docs
   .confluent.io/platform/current/security/secrets.html (accessed August 21,
   2021).

11

Schema registry

This chapters covers

- Developing a proposed Kafka maturity model
- The value schemas can provide for your data as it changes
- Reviewing Avro and data serialization
- Compatibility rules for schema changes over time

As you have discovered the various ways to use Apache Kafka, it might be an interesting experiment to think about how you view Kafka the more you utilize it. As enterprises (or even tools) grow, they can sometimes be modeled with *maturity levels*. Martin Fowler provides a great explanation for this at https://martinfowler.com/bliki/MaturityModel.html [1]. Fowler also has a good example that explains the Richardson Maturity Model, which looks at REST [2]. For even further reference, the original talk, "Justice Will Take Us Millions Of Intricate Moves: Act Three: The

Maturity Heuristic" by Leonard Richardson can be found at https://www.crummy .com/writing/speaking/2008-QCon/act3.html.[1]

11.1   *A proposed Kafka maturity model*

In the following sections, we focus our discussion on maturity levels specific to Kafka. For a comparison, check out the Confluent white paper titled, "Five Stages to Streaming Platform Adoption," which presents a different perspective that encompasses five stages of their streaming maturity model with distinct criteria for each stage [3]. Let's look at our first level (of course, as programmers we start with level 0).

We use this exercise with a maturity model so that we can think about how Kafka can be a powerful tool for one application or even evolve into the foundation for all of your enterprise's applications rather than as a simple message broker. The following levels aren't meant to be a step-by-step required path, but rather a way to think about how you might start and then progress with Kafka. These steps are debatable, of course, but we simply offer an example path.

11.1.1   *Level 0*

At this level, we use Kafka as an enterprise service bus (ESB) or publish/subscribe (pub/sub) system. Events provide asynchronous communication between applications, whether we are replacing a different message broker like RabbitMQ or just starting with this pattern.

One example use case is a user submitting a text document to be converted into a PDF. Once a user submits a document, the application stores the document and then sends a message to a Kafka topic. A Kafka consumer then reads the message to determine which documents need to be converted into a PDF. In this example, the drive might be offloaded to work with a backend system that a user knows will not send a response right away. Figure 11.1 shows this message bus in action.

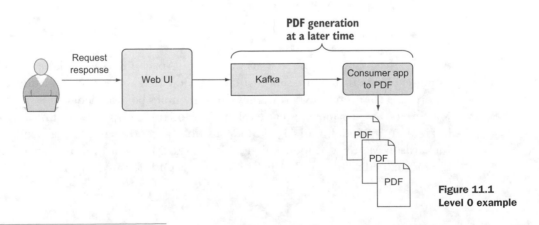

Figure 11.1
Level 0 example

---

[1] The act3.html website text is licensed under the Creative Commons License at https://creativecommons.org/ licenses/by-sa/2.0/legalcode.

This level alone brings us the benefit of allowing us to decouple a system so that a failure of our frontend text submission system does not impact our backend system. Also, we don't need to rely on both to maintain successful simultaneous operations.

11.1.2 Level 1

Batch processing can still be present in areas of our enterprise, but most data produced is now brought into Kafka. Whether with extract, transform, load (ETL) or change data capture (CDC) processes, Kafka starts to gather events from more and more systems in our enterprise. Level 1 allows us to have an operational, real-time data flow and gives us the ability to feed data quickly into analytical systems.

An example of this might be a vendor database that holds customer information. We do not want our marketing folks to run complex queries that could slow down our production traffic. In this case, we can use Kafka Connect to write the data from database tables into Kafka topics that we can use on our terms. Figure 11.2 shows Kafka Connect capturing data from a relational database and moving that data into a Kafka topic.

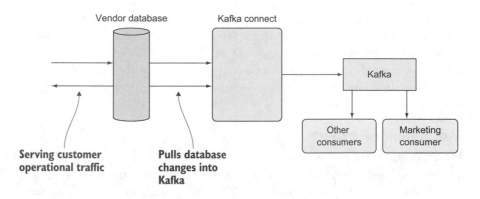

Figure 11.2 Level 1 example

11.1.3 Level 2

We realize that data will change over time and that schemas are needed. Although our producers and consumers might be decoupled, they still need a way to understand the data itself. For this, we'll take advantage of schemas and a schema registry. And even though it would have been ideal to start with schemas, the reality is that this need often presents itself a couple of application changes later, after initial deployments.

One example for this level is changing the data structure of an event to receive orders from our processing system. New data is added, but the new fields are optional, and this works fine because our schema registry is configured to support backward compatibility. Figure 11.3 shows our consumer's need for schemas. We will look more into these details as we progress through this chapter.

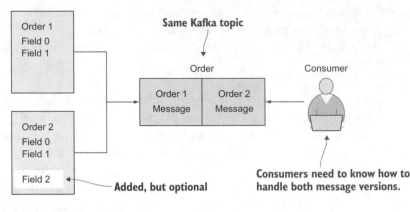

Figure 11.3   Level 2 example

11.1.4 *Level 3*

Everything is an event stream that is infinite (never ending). Kafka is the system of our enterprise for our event-based applications. In other words, we don't have customers waiting for recommendations or status reports that used to be produced by an overnight batch-processing run. Customers are alerted in milliseconds of a change to their account when an event happens, not in minutes. Instead of pulling data from other data sources, applications pull data directly from your cluster. User-facing applications can derive state and materialized views to customers depending on the needs of our core Kafka infrastructure.

11.2   *The Schema Registry*

As part of our work in this chapter, we will focus on level 2, looking at how we can plan for data to change over time. Now that we have become good at sending data into and out of Kafka, and despite a small mention of schemas in chapter 3, we left out some important details. Let's dive into what the Confluent Schema Registry provides for us.

The Confluent Schema Registry stores our named schemas and allows us to maintain multiple versions [4]. This is somewhat similar to the Docker Registry in purpose, which stores and distributes Docker images. Why is this storage needed? Producers and consumers are not tied together, but they still need a way to discover the schema involved in the data from all clients. Also, by having a remotely hosted registry, users do not have to run their copy locally or attempt to build their own, based on a list of schemas.

While schemas can provide a sort of interface for applications, we can also use them to prevent breaking changes [4]. Why should we care about data that is moving fast through our system? Kafka's storage and retention capabilities allow consumers to go back to process older messages. These messages might be from months ago (or longer), and our consumers need to handle these various data versions.

For Kafka, we can use the Confluent Schema Registry. Confluent provides an excellent option to consider as we look into how to take advantage of schemas. If you installed Kafka via the Confluent Platform before this chapter, you should have all the tools available to explore further. If not, we discuss installing and setting up this registry in the following sections.

11.2.1 Installing the Confluent Schema Registry

The Confluent Schema Registry is a community software offering as part of the Confluent Platform [5]. The Schema Registry lives outside of Kafka Brokers, but itself uses Kafka as its storage layer with the topic name _schemas [6]. It is vital *not* to delete this topic accidentally!

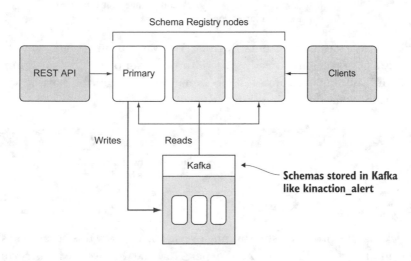

Figure 11.4 Schema Registry infrastructure

When thinking about production usage, the Schema Registry should be hosted on a server separate from our brokers, as figure 11.4 shows [6]. Because we deal with a distributed system and have learned to expect failures, we can provide multiple registry instances. And because all nodes can handle lookup requests from clients and route write requests to the primary node, the clients of the registry do not have to maintain a list of specific nodes.

11.2.2 Registry configuration

Similar to the other components of Kafka, you can set several configuration parameters in a file. If you have installed Kafka, you'll see the defaults located in the etc/schema-registry/schema-registry.properties file. For the registry to be successful, it needs to know which topic to store its schemas in and how to work with your specific Kafka cluster.

In listing 11.1, we use ZooKeeper to help complete the election of the primary node. It's important to note that because only the primary node writes to the Kafka topic. If your team is trying to move away from ZooKeeper dependencies, you can also use a Kafka-based primary election (using the configuration `kafkastore.bootstrap` `.servers`) [7].

Listing 11.1   Schema Registry configuration

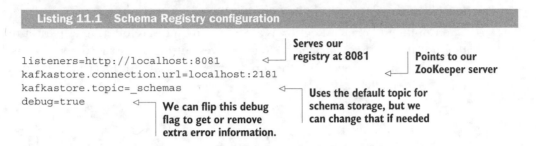

```
listeners=http://localhost:8081
kafkastore.connection.url=localhost:2181
kafkastore.topic=_schemas
debug=true
```

Serves our registry at 8081

Points to our ZooKeeper server

Uses the default topic for schema storage, but we can change that if needed

We can flip this debug flag to get or remove extra error information.

Let's go ahead and start the Schema Registry. We want to make sure that our Zoo-Keeper and Kafka brokers are already started for our examples. After confirming that they are up and running, we can use the command line to run the starting script for the registry, as the following listing shows [8].

Listing 11.2   Starting the Schema Registry

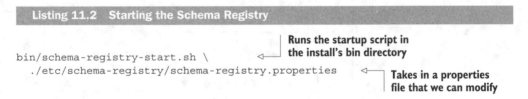

```
bin/schema-registry-start.sh \
  ./etc/schema-registry/schema-registry.properties
```

Runs the startup script in the install's bin directory

Takes in a properties file that we can modify

We can check that the process is still running or use `jps` to verify this because it is a Java application, just like the brokers and ZooKeeper. Now that we have the registry running, we need to look at how to use the system's components. Because we now have a place to store our data format in the registry, let's revisit a schema that we used in chapter 3.

11.3   Schema features

The Confluent Schema Registry contains the following important components. One is a REST API (and the underlying application) for storing and fetching schemas. The second is client libraries for retrieving and managing local schemas. In the following sections, we'll look a bit deeper into each of these two components, starting with the REST API.

11.3.1   REST API

The REST API helps us manage the following resources: *schemas, subjects, compatibility,* and *config* [9]. Of these resources, "subjects" might need some explanation. We can create, retrieve, and delete versions and the subjects themselves. Let's look at a topic and its related subject for an application using a topic named `kinaction_schematest`.

In our schema registry, we will have a subject called `kinaction_schematest-value` because we are using the default behavior of basing the name on our current topic name. If we were using a schema for the message key as well, we would also have a subject called `kinaction_schematest-key`. Notice that the key and value are treated as different subjects [10]. Why is this? It ensures that we can version and change our schemas independently because the key and value are serialized separately.

To confirm the registry is started and to see it in action, let's submit a GET against the REST API using a tool like `curl` [9]. In the following listing, we list the current configuration like the compatibility level.

Listing 11.3   Getting the Schema Registry configuration

```
curl -X GET http://localhost:8081/config      ⟵┐  Lists all the configs in
                                                │  the Registry using REST
```

Also, we need to add a `Content-Type` header for our REST interactions with the Schema Registry. In any following examples, like listing 11.7, we will use `application/vnd.schemaregistry.v1+json` [9]. As with the schemas themselves, we're planning for API changes by declaring which API version we'll use. This helps ensure that our clients are using the intended version.

While the REST API is great for administrators of the subjects and schemas, the client library is where most developers will spend their time interacting with the Registry.

11.3.2   Client library

Let's drill into the producer client's interaction with the Schema Registry. Think back to our example in chapter 3 with a producer that is configured to use an Avro serializer for our messages. We should already have a registry started locally, so now we need to configure our producer client to use it (listing 11.4). With our use case from chapter 3, we created a schema for an `Alert` object that is the value of our message. The `value.serializer` property needs to be set to use the `KafkaAvroSerializer` in our case. This class serializes the custom object using the Registry.

Listing 11.4   Producer using Avro serialization

```
...
kaProperties.put("key.serializer",
    "org.apache.kafka.common.serialization.LongSerializer");
kaProperties.put("value.serializer",                          ⟵┐  Sends Alert as a value and
    "io.confluent.kafka.serializers.KafkaAvroSerializer");     │  uses KafkaAvroSerializer
kaProperties.put("schema.registry.url",
    "http://localhost:8081");              ⟵┐  Points to the URL of our registry containing
                                            │  a versioned history of our schemas to help
Producer<Long, Alert> producer =           │  with schema validation and evolution
  new KafkaProducer<Long, Alert>(kaProperties);
Alert alert = new Alert();
alert.setSensorId(12345L);
alert.setTime(Calendar.getInstance().getTimeInMillis());
alert.setStatus(alert_status.Critical);
```

```
log.info("kinaction_info = {}, alert.toString());

ProducerRecord<Long, Alert> producerRecord =
  new ProducerRecord<Long, Alert>(
    "kinaction_schematest", alert.getSensorId(), alert
  );

producer.send(producerRecord);
```

> **NOTE** Because we use the default `TopicNameStrategy`, the Schema Registry registers the subject `kinaction_schematest-value` with our schema for `Alert`. To use a different strategy, the producer client could set either of the following configurations to override the value and key strategies: `value.subject.name.strategy` and `key.subject.name.strategy` [10]. In this case, we could have used an override to use an underscore to keep our topic name from having a mix of dashes and underscores.

On the consumer side, once the client has successfully found the schema, it can now understand the records it reads. Let's look at using the same schema we produced for a topic and retrieve it with a consumer to see if we can get that value back without error, as the following listing exhibits [11].

Listing 11.5   Consumer using Avro deserialization

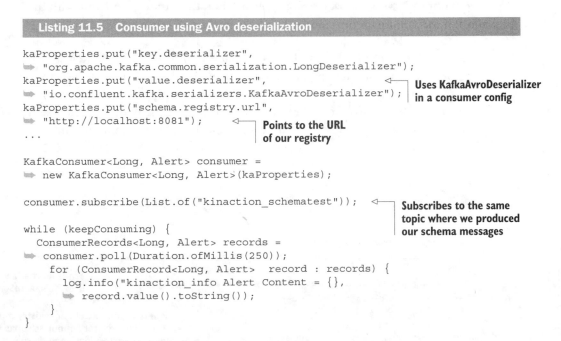

```
kaProperties.put("key.deserializer",
  "org.apache.kafka.common.serialization.LongDeserializer");
kaProperties.put("value.deserializer",                          ◁── Uses KafkaAvroDeserializer
  "io.confluent.kafka.serializers.KafkaAvroDeserializer");          in a consumer config
kaProperties.put("schema.registry.url",
  "http://localhost:8081");         ◁── Points to the URL
...                                      of our registry

KafkaConsumer<Long, Alert> consumer =
  new KafkaConsumer<Long, Alert>(kaProperties);

consumer.subscribe(List.of("kinaction_schematest"));   ◁── Subscribes to the same
                                                            topic where we produced
while (keepConsuming) {                                     our schema messages
  ConsumerRecords<Long, Alert> records =
  consumer.poll(Duration.ofMillis(250));
    for (ConsumerRecord<Long, Alert>  record : records) {
      log.info("kinaction_info Alert Content = {},
        record.value().toString());
    }
}
```

So far, we have worked on only one version of a schema with our producer and consumer clients. However, planning for data changes can save you a lot of headaches. Next, we'll look at the rules that will help us think about the changes we can make and their impact on our clients.

11.4 Compatibility rules

One important thing to decide on is what compatibility strategy we plan to support. The compatibility rules in this section are here to help direct our schemas as they change over time. While it may seem like a large number of available types, it is nice to know that, in general, those marked as *transitive* follow the same rules as those without that suffix. The non-transitive types are only checked against the last version of the schema, whereas transitive types are checked against all previous versions [12]. Here is a list of types noted by Confluent: BACKWARD (the default type), BACKWARD_TRANSITIVE, FORWARD, FORWARD_TRANSITIVE, FULL, FULL_TRANSITIVE, and NONE [12].

Let's look at what the BACKWARD type implies for our applications. Backward-compatible changes might involve adding non-required fields or removing fields [12]. Another critical aspect to consider when choosing the compatibility type is the order in which we want clients to change. For example, we will likely want our consumer clients to upgrade first for the BACKWARD type [12]. Consumers will need to know how to read the messages before new variations are produced.

On the reverse end of the types, forward-compatible changes are the opposite of backward. With the FORWARD type, we can add new fields and, opposite of the way we updated for the BACKWARD type, we will likely want to update our producer clients first [12].

Let's look at how we can change our schema for Alert to maintain backward compatibility. The following listing shows the addition of a new field, recovery_details, with a default value of Analyst recovery needed to account for messages that do not include a value for the new field.

> **Listing 11.6 Alert schema change**

```
{"name": "Alert",
 ...
 "fields": [
    {"name": "sensor_id",  "type": "long",
     "doc":"The unique id that identifies the sensor"},
 ...
    {"name": "recovery_details", "type": "string",     ◁── Creates a new field
     "default": "Analyst recovery needed"}                    (recovery_details)
 ]                                                             in this instance
}
```

Any older messages with version 1 of the schema will have a default value populated for the field added later. This will be read by a consumer using Schema Registry version 2 [12].

11.4.1 Validating schema modifications

If we have tests that exercise our API endpoints or even Swagger (https://swagger.io/), it is important to think about how we can automate testing changes to our schemas. To check and validate our schema changes, we have a couple of options:

- Use the REST API compatibility resource endpoints
- Use a Maven plugin for JVM-based applications

Let's look at an example REST call that will help us check our compatibility for a schema change. Listing 11.7 shows how this is done [13]. As a side note, before checking compatibility, we need to already have a copy of our older schema in the registry. If one is not present and the call fails, check out the source code with this book for an example.

Listing 11.7   Checking compatibility with the Schema Registry REST API

```
curl -X POST -H "Content-Type: application/vnd.schemaregistry.v1+json" \
--data '{ "schema": "{ \"type\": \"record\", \"name\": \"Alert\",      ◁
  ⬂ \"fields\": [{ \"name\": \"notafield\", \"type\": \"long\" } ]}" }'  \
http://localhost:8081/compatibility/subjects/kinaction_schematest-value/
  ⬂ versions/latest

{"is_compatible":false}    ◁
```

Gives a compatible result as a Boolean

Passes the schema content on the command line

We can also use a Maven plugin if we are willing to use Maven and are already on a JVM-based platform [14]. The following listing shows part of the pom.xml entry needed for this approach, and the complete file can be found in the chapter's source code.

Listing 11.8   Checking compatibility with the Schema Registry Maven plugin

```
<plugin>
    <groupId>io.confluent</groupId>
    <artifactId>
      kafka-schema-registry-maven-plugin     ◁
    </artifactId>
    <configuration>
        <schemaRegistryUrls>
            <param>http://localhost:8081</param>     ◁
        </schemaRegistryUrls>
        <subjects>
            <kinaction_schematest-value>
              src/main/avro/alert_v2.avsc
            </kinaction_schematest-value>
        </subjects>
        <goals>
            <goal>test-compatibility</goal>     ◁
        </goals>

    </configuration>
...
</plugin>
```

Coordinates that Maven needs to download this plugin

The URL to our Schema Registry

Lists the subjects to validate our schemas in the provided file path

We can invoke the Maven goal with mvn schema-registry:test-compatibility.

In essence, it takes the schemas located in your file path and connects to the Schema Registry to check against the schemas already stored there.

11.5 *Alternative to a schema registry*

Because not all projects start with schemas or with data changes in mind, there are some simple steps that we can take to work around data format changes. One such option is to produce data on a different topic with a breaking change. After consumers have consumed the old format, they can be updated if needed and then read from another topic. This works well if we do not plan to reprocess our data. Figure 11.5 shows the switch to a new topic after reading all older messages from the first topic. In the diagram, the text *u1* means "update 1" and *u2* means "update 2" to note the changed logic.

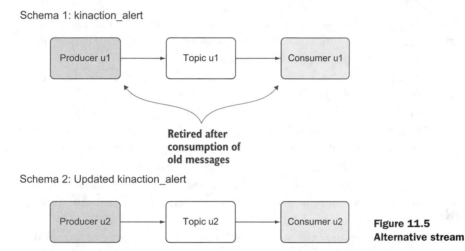

Figure 11.5
Alternative stream

Suppose we do plan on reprocessing the data across formats. In that case, we could also create a new topic that exists to hold the transformed topic messages that existed in the initial topic and, of course, any new messages from the update. Kafka Streams, which we discuss in chapter 12, can help in this topic-to-topic transformation.

Summary

- Kafka has many features that you can use for simple use cases or all the way up to being the major system of an enterprise.
- Schemas help version our data changes.
- The Schema Registry, a Confluent offering apart from Kafka, provides a way to work with Kafka-related schemas.
- As schemas change, compatibility rules help users know whether the changes are backward, forward, or fully compatible.
- If schemas are not an option, different topics can be used to handle different versions of data.

References

1 M. Fowler. "Maturity Model." (August 26, 2014). https://martinfowler.com/bliki/MaturityModel.html (accessed June 15, 2021).

2 M. Fowler. "Richardson Maturity Model." (March 18, 2010). https://martin fowler.com/articles/richardsonMaturityModel.html (accessed June 15, 2021).

3 L. Hedderly. "Five Stages to Streaming Platform Adoption." Confluent white paper (2018). https://www.confluent.io/resources/5-stages-streaming-platform-adoption/ (accessed January 15, 2020).

4 "Schema Registry Overview." Confluent documentation (n.d.). https://docs.confluent.io/platform/current/schema-registry/index.html (accessed July 15, 2020).

5 "Confluent Platform Licenses: Community License." Confluent documentation (n.d.). https://docs.confluent.io/platform/current/installation/license.html#community-license (accessed August 21, 2021).

6 "Running Schema Registry in Production." Confluent documentation (n.d.). https://docs.confluent.io/platform/current/schema-registry/installation/deployment.html#schema-registry-prod (accessed April 25, 2019).

7 "Schema Registry Configuration Options." Confluent documentation (n.d.). https://docs.confluent.io/platform/current/schema-registry/installation/config.html#schemaregistry-config (accessed August 22, 2021).

8 "Schema Registry and Confluent Cloud." Confluent documentation (n.d.). https://docs.confluent.io/cloud/current/cp-component/schema-reg-cloud-config.html (accessed August 22, 2021).

9 "Schema Registry API Reference." Confluent documentation (n.d.). https://docs.confluent.io/platform/current/schema-registry/develop/api.html (accessed July 15, 2020).

10 "Formats, Serializers, and Deserializers." Confluent documentation (n.d.). https://docs.confluent.io/platform/current/schema-registry/serdes-develop/index.html (accessed April 25, 2019).

11 "On-Premises Schema Registry Tutorial." Confluent documentation (n.d.). https://docs.confluent.io/platform/current/schema-registry/schema_registry_onprem_tutorial.html (accessed April 25, 2019).

12 "Schema Evolution and Compatibility." Confluent Platform. https://docs.confluent.io/current/schema-registry/avro.html#compatibility-types (accessed June 1, 2020).

13 "Schema Registry API Usage Examples." Confluent documentation (n.d.). https://docs.confluent.io/platform/current/schema-registry/develop/using.html (accessed August 22, 2021).

14 "Schema Registry Maven Plugin." Confluent documentation (n.d.). https://docs.confluent.io/platform/current/schema-registry/develop/maven-plugin.html (accessed July 16, 2020).

Stream processing with Kafka Streams and ksqlDB

This chapter covers
- Getting started with Kafka Streams
- Using basic Kafka Streams APIs
- Using state stores for persistent storage
- Enriching transaction streams

So far on our path in learning about Kafka, we've focused on the parts that help make a complete event-streaming platform, including the Kafka brokers, producer clients, and consumer clients. With this foundation, we can expand our toolset and understand the next layer of the Kafka ecosystem—stream processing using Kafka Streams and ksqlDB. These technologies offer abstractions, APIs, and DSLs (domain-specific languages), based on the foundation that we have built on in the previous chapters.

This chapter introduces a simple banking application that processes funds as they move in and out of the accounts. In our application, we will implement a Kafka Streams topology to process the transaction requests submitted to the `transaction-request` topic atomically.

209

NOTE Our business requirement states that we must check whether the funds are sufficient for every request received before updating the account's balance that's being processed. As per our requirements, our application can't process two transactions simultaneously for the same account, which could create a race condition in which we cannot guarantee we can enforce the balance check before withdrawing funds.

We will use Kafka's *inter-partition ordering* guarantees to implement serializable (ordered) processing of transactions for a particular account. We also have a data generator program that writes simulated transaction requests to the Kafka topic with a key equal to the transaction's account number. We can, therefore, ensure all transactions will be processed by a single instance of our transaction service, no matter how many applications are concurrently running. Kafka Streams won't commit any message offset until it completes our business logic of managing a transaction request.

We introduce the Processor API by implementing a transformer component from Kafka Streams. This utility allows us to process events one by one while interacting with a state store, another element of Kafka Streams that helps us persist our account balance in a local instance of an embedded database, RocksDB. Finally, we will write a second stream processor to generate a detailed transaction statement enriched with account details. Rather than creating another Kafka Streams application, we will use ksqlDB to declare a stream processor that will enrich our transactional data in real time with our referential data coming from the account topic.

This section aims to show how we can use an SQL-like query language to create stream processors (with functionality similar to Kafka Streams) without compiling and running any code. We'll dig into the Kafka Streams API's details after reviewing the concepts of stream-processing applications.

12.1   Kafka Streams

In general, stream processing (or *streaming*) is a process or application you implement that deals with an uninterrupted flow of data and performs work as soon as that data arrives, as discussed in chapter 2. This application does not execute on a regular schedule or even query a database for data. Views can be created from the data, but we are not limited to a point-in-time view. Enter Kafka Streams!

Kafka Streams is a library and not a standalone cluster [1]. Notice that this description includes the word *library*. This alone can help us create stream processing for our applications. No other infrastructure is required besides the need to utilize an existing Kafka cluster [2]. The Kafka Streams library is a part of our JVM-based application.

Not having additional components makes this API one that can be easily tested when starting with a new application. Though other frameworks might require more cluster management components, Kafka Streams applications can be built and deployed using any tool or platform that allows JVM-based applications to run.

NOTE Our application won't run on the brokers of our cluster. For that reason, we will run our application outside the Kafka cluster. This approach guarantees the separation of concerns in resource management for Kafka brokers and stream processors.

The Streams API performs per-record or per-message processing [3]. You won't want to wait for a batch to form or delay that work if you're concerned about your system reacting to events as soon as they are received.

As we consider how to implement our applications, one of the first questions that comes to mind is choosing a producer/consumer client for the Kafka Streams library. Although the Producer API is excellent for taking precise control of how our data gets to Kafka and the Consumer API for consuming events, sometimes we might not want to implement every aspect of the stream-processing framework ourselves. Instead of using lower-level APIs for stream processing, we want to use an abstraction layer that allows us to work with our topics more efficiently.

Kafka Streams might be a perfect option if our requirements include data transformations with potentially complex logic consuming and producing data back into Kafka. Streams offer a choice between a functional DSL and the more imperative Processor API [2]. Let's take a first look at the Kafka Streams DSL.

Domain-specific languages (DSLs)

DSLs are meant to provide a language that makes it easier to work with a specific subject. SQL (used commonly with databases) and HTML (used for creating web pages) are good examples of languages to consider using with DSLs (see https://martinfowler.com/dsl.html). Although the official Kafka Streams documentation refers to the high-level Kafka Streams API as a DSL, we like to refer to it as a fluent API or, as Martin Fowler describes it, a fluent interface (see https://martinfowler.com/bliki/FluentInterface.html).

12.1.1 KStreams API DSL

The first API that we're going to look at is the KStreams API. Kafka Streams is a data-processing system designed around the concept of a graph, one that doesn't have any cycles in it [2]. It has a starting node and an ending node, and data flows from the starting node to the ending node. Along the way, nodes (or processors) process and transform the data. Let's take a look at a scenario where we can model a data-processing process as a graph.

We have an application that gets transactions from a payment system. At the beginning of our graph, we need a source for this data. Because we're using Kafka as a data source, a Kafka topic will be our starting point. This origin point is often referred to as a *source processor* (or *source node*). This starts the processing; there aren't any previous processors. Our first example, therefore, is an existing service that captures transactions from an external payment system and places transaction request events into a topic.

> **NOTE** We will simulate this behavior with a simple data generator application.

A transaction request event is needed to update the balance for a particular account. The results of the transaction processor go into two Kafka topics: successful transactions land in `transaction-success` and unsuccessful transactions land in `transaction-failure`. Because this is the end of the road for our small application, we will create a pair of sink processors (or sink nodes) to write to our success or failure topics.

> **NOTE**   Some processor nodes may not have a connection to sink nodes. In this case, those nodes create side effects elsewhere (e.g., printing information to the console or writing data to the state stores) and do not require sending data back to Kafka.

Figure 12.1 shows a DAG (directed acyclic graph) representation of how data flows. Figure 12.2 shows you how this DAG maps out to the Kafka Streams topology.

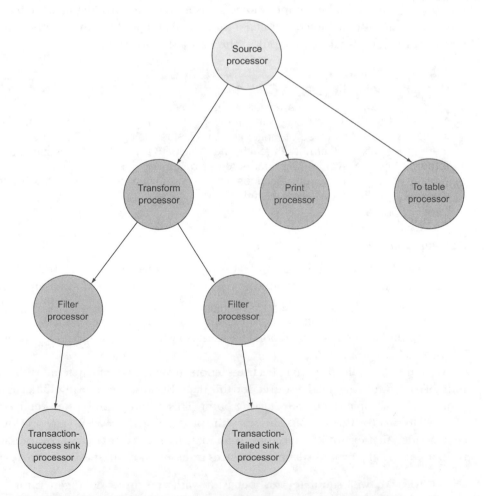

Figure 12.1   DAG (directed acyclic graph) of our stream-processing application

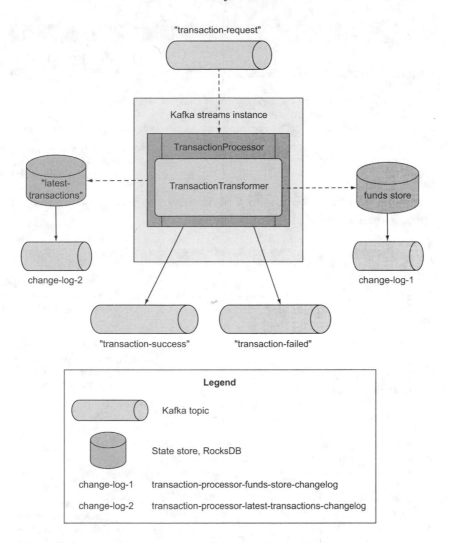

Figure 12.2 Topology for your transaction-processing application

Now that we have a map for a guide, let's look at what this application looks like with the DSL code. Unlike our earlier examples, when using this API, we don't need to reach a consumer directly to read our messages, but we can use a builder to start creating our stream. Listing 12.1 shows the creation of a source processor.

> **IMPORTANT** At this point, we're *defining* our topology, but not invoking it, as processing hasn't started yet.

In the listing, we use a `StreamsBuilder` object in order to create a stream from the Kafka topic `transaction-request`. Our data source is `transaction-request` and is the logical starting point for our processing.

Listing 12.1   Source topic DSL definition

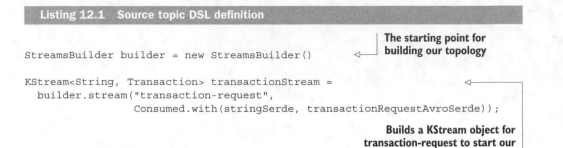

```
StreamsBuilder builder = new StreamsBuilder()
```
The starting point for building our topology

```
KStream<String, Transaction> transactionStream =
  builder.stream("transaction-request",
              Consumed.with(stringSerde, transactionRequestAvroSerde));
```

Builds a KStream object for transaction-request to start our processing from this topic

The next step is to add to our topology using the KStream that we created from the source processor. The following listing shows this task.

Listing 12.2   Processor and sink topic definition

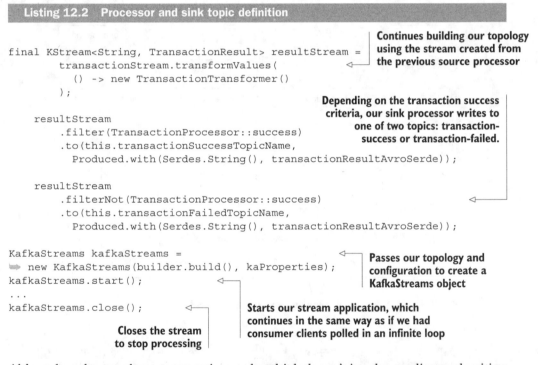

```
final KStream<String, TransactionResult> resultStream =
      transactionStream.transformValues(
        () -> new TransactionTransformer()
      );
```
Continues building our topology using the stream created from the previous source processor

```
    resultStream
      .filter(TransactionProcessor::success)
      .to(this.transactionSuccessTopicName,
        Produced.with(Serdes.String(), transactionResultAvroSerde));
```
Depending on the transaction success criteria, our sink processor writes to one of two topics: transaction-success or transaction-failed.

```
    resultStream
      .filterNot(TransactionProcessor::success)
      .to(this.transactionFailedTopicName,
        Produced.with(Serdes.String(), transactionResultAvroSerde));

KafkaStreams kafkaStreams =
  new KafkaStreams(builder.build(), kaProperties);
kafkaStreams.start();
...
kafkaStreams.close();
```
Passes our topology and configuration to create a KafkaStreams object

Starts our stream application, which continues in the same way as if we had consumer clients polled in an infinite loop

Closes the stream to stop processing

Although we have only one processing node, which doesn't involve reading and writing data, it is easy to see how we could chain multiple nodes on our path. Looking over the code in listing 12.2, you might notice the lack of direct usage of the following:

- A consumer client to read from the source topic as in chapter 5
- A producer client to send our messages at the end of the flow as in chapter 4

This layer of abstraction allows us to work on our logic rather than the details. Let's look at another practical example. Imagine we simply want to log transaction requests in the console without processing them. The following listing shows the reading of transaction events from the transaction-request topic.

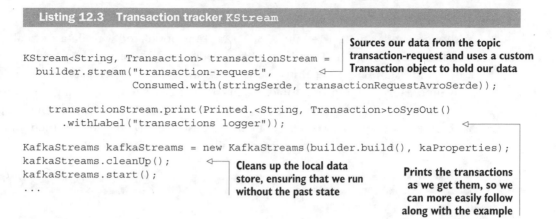

Listing 12.3 Transaction tracker `KStream`

```
KStream<String, Transaction> transactionStream =
  builder.stream("transaction-request",
            Consumed.with(stringSerde, transactionRequestAvroSerde));

  transactionStream.print(Printed.<String, Transaction>toSysOut()
    .withLabel("transactions logger"));

KafkaStreams kafkaStreams = new KafkaStreams(builder.build(), kaProperties);
kafkaStreams.cleanUp();
kafkaStreams.start();
...
```

Sources our data from the topic transaction-request and uses a custom Transaction object to hold our data

Cleans up the local data store, ensuring that we run without the past state

Prints the transactions as we get them, so we can more easily follow along with the example

This flow is so simple that we just write out the transactions to the console, but we could have used an API call to send an SMS or email as well. Notice the added call to `cleanup()` before starting the application. This method provides a way to remove the local state stores for our application. Just remember to only do this before the start or after closing the application.

Despite the ease of use of `KStreams`, they are not the only way we can process our data. The `KTable` API provides us with an alternative to always add events to our view by representing data as updates instead.

12.1.2 *KTable API*

Although a `KStream` can be thought of as event data always being appended to our log, a `KTable` allows us to think about a log-compacted topic [2]. In fact, we can also draw a parallel to a database table that deals with updates in place. Recall from working with compacted topics in chapter 7 that our data needs to have a key for this to work. Without a key, the value to be updated won't really make practical sense. Running the code in the following listing, we see that not every order event shows up. Instead, we see only the distinct orders.

Listing 12.4 Transaction `KTable`

```
StreamsBuilder builder = new StreamsBuilder();

KTable<String, Transaction> transactionStream =
  builder.stream("transaction-request",
            Consumed.with(stringSerde, transactionRequestAvroSerde),
        Materialized.as("latest-transactions"));

KafkaStreams kafkaStreams = new KafkaStreams(builder.build(), kaProperties);
```

StreamsBuilder.table() creates a KTable from the topic transaction-request.

KTable records materialize locally in the latest-transactions state store.

What is familiar with this listing is the way we build the stream. We use a builder to create the steps and then, once it is defined, we call `start`. Until that moment, nothing processes in our application.

12.1.3 *GlobalKTable API*

Although similar to `KTable`, the `GlobalKTable` is populated with data from all partitions of a topic [2]. The foundational knowledge about topics and partitions pays off when understanding these abstractions, as shown in how the `KafkaStreams` instances consume each partition of a topic. Listing 12.5 is an example of using a join with a `GlobalKTable`. Imagine a stream that gets updated with details about a mailed package for a customer. These events contain the customer ID, and we can then join on a customer table to find their associated email and send a message.

Listing 12.5   Mailing notification `GlobalKTable`

```
...
StreamsBuilder builder = new StreamsBuilder();          The notification stream listens
                                                        for new messages about mailings
final KStream<String, MailingNotif> notifiers =         to send to a customer.
  builder.stream("kinaction_mailingNotif");      <──┘
final GlobalKTable<String, Customer> customers =        GlobalKTable holds a list of Customer
  builder.globalTable("kinaction_custinfo");     <──┘   information, including email.

lists.join(customers,                                          <──
    (mailingNotifID, mailing) -> mailing.getCustomerId(),      The join method matches
    (mailing, customer) -> new Email(mailing, customer))       the customer that needs to
    .peek((key, email) ->                                      be notified with an email.
        emailService.sendMessage(email));

KafkaStreams kafkaStreams = new KafkaStreams(builder.build(), kaProperties);
kafkaStreams.cleanUp();
kafkaStreams.start();
...
```

As shown in listing 12.5, we can build a new `GlobalKTable` using the method `globalTable`. Whereas a table that is not global might not consume all the input topic's data due to multiple partitions, the global table consumes all partitions for your running code [2].

> **NOTE** The idea of a global table is to make the data available to our application regardless of which partition it is mapped to.

Even though the Streams DSL has been excellent for quick use cases, sometimes we might need more control as we send data along our logic paths. Developers can use the Processor API alone or with the Streams DSL to provide even more options.

12.1.4 *Processor API*

It's important to note that when reviewing code for another streaming application or even looking at getting into lower abstraction levels in our own logic, we might run into examples from the Processor API. This is considered not as easy to use as the DSL discussed in the previous sections, but it gives us more options and power over our logic [2]. Let's look at an example in the following listing, where we create a topology and highlight the differences from our previous Streams applications.

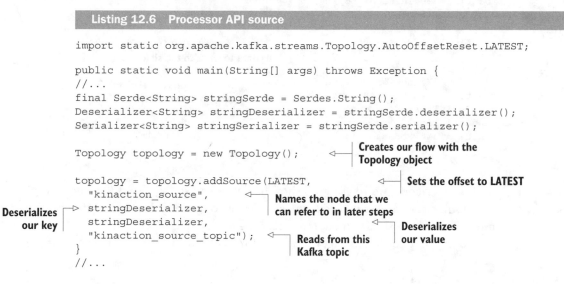

Listing 12.6 Processor API source

```
import static org.apache.kafka.streams.Topology.AutoOffsetReset.LATEST;

public static void main(String[] args) throws Exception {
//...
final Serde<String> stringSerde = Serdes.String();
Deserializer<String> stringDeserializer = stringSerde.deserializer();
Serializer<String> stringSerializer = stringSerde.serializer();

Topology topology = new Topology();          ←  Creates our flow with the
                                                 Topology object

topology = topology.addSource(LATEST,        ←  Sets the offset to LATEST
    "kinaction_source",              ←  Names the node that we
    stringDeserializer,                 can refer to in later steps
    stringDeserializer,              ←  Deserializes
    "kinaction_source_topic");          our value
}                                    ←  Reads from this
//...                                   Kafka topic
```

(Deserializes our key → points to `stringDeserializer`)

First, we build our graph using the `Topology` object [4]. Setting the offset to `LATEST` and listing our key and value deserializers should be familiar from when we set configuration properties for our client consumers in chapter 5. In listing 12.6, we named the node `kinaction_source`, which reads from the topic `kinaction_source_topic`. Our next step is to add a processing node, as the following listing shows.

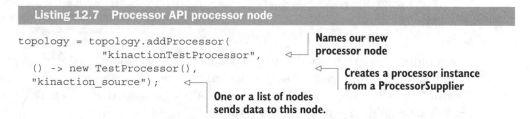

Listing 12.7 Processor API processor node

```
topology = topology.addProcessor(
            "kinactionTestProcessor",        ←  Names our new
    () -> new TestProcessor(),                  processor node
    "kinaction_source");                     ←  Creates a processor instance
                                                from a ProcessorSupplier
```

(One or a list of nodes sends data to this node.)

Listing 12.7 shows that when we define a processing node, we give it a name (`kinactionTestProcessor`, in this case) and associate the logic with the step. We also list the nodes that will provide the data.

To finish out our simple example, let's look at listing 12.8. It shows how we define two separate sinks to complete our topology. The sink is where we place our data at the end of processing. The topic name and the key and value serializers should be familiar from our earlier work with producer clients. As we did with the other parts of the topology, we define `kinactionTestProcessor` as one of the nodes from which we will get data in our flow.

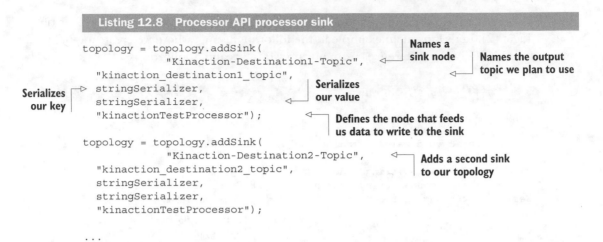

Listing 12.8   Processor API processor sink

```
topology = topology.addSink(
            "Kinaction-Destination1-Topic",
    "kinaction_destination1_topic",
    stringSerializer,
    stringSerializer,
    "kinactionTestProcessor");
topology = topology.addSink(
            "Kinaction-Destination2-Topic",
    "kinaction_destination2_topic",
    stringSerializer,
    stringSerializer,
    "kinactionTestProcessor");
```

- Names a sink node
- Names the output topic we plan to use
- Serializes our key
- Serializes our value
- Defines the node that feeds us data to write to the sink
- Adds a second sink to our topology

...

In our Processor code, we're going to show how we can use logic to direct the flow of our data. Our `kinactionTestProcessor` enables us to forward the flow, including the key and value, to the sink named `Kinaction-Destination2-Topic`. Although this is hardcoded in the following listing, we can use logic to determine when to send data to the second sink.

Listing 12.9   Processor custom code

```
public class KinactionTestProcessor
    extends AbstractProcessor<String, String> {
        @Override
        public void process(String key, String value) {
            context().forward(key, value,
                To.child("Kinaction-Destination2-Topic"));
        }
}
```

- Extends AbstractProcessor to implement the process method for our custom logic
- Hardcoded value, but we can also direct the forward with additional logic

Even though it's easy to see that the code is more verbose than our DSL examples, the important thing is the control we now have in our logic that was not shown in our simple flow with the DSL API. If we want to control the schedule of when processing occurs or even the commit time for results, we'll need to dig into more complex Processor API methods.

12.1.5 *Kafka Streams setup*

While our example application only uses a single instance, streaming applications can scale by increasing the number of threads and deploying more than one instance. As with the number of instances of a consumer in the same consumer group, our application's parallelism is related to the number of partitions in its source topic [5]. For example, if our starting input topic has eight partitions, we would plan to scale to eight instances of our application. Unless we want to have an instance ready in case of failure, we won't have more instances because they won't take any traffic.

When we think about our application's design, it is crucial to mention the processing guarantees that our use case requires. Kafka Streams supports at-least-once and exactly-once processing semantics.

NOTE In version 2.6.0, exactly-once beta was introduced. This version enables higher throughput and scalability by attempting to reduce resource utilization [6].

If your application logic depends on exactly-once semantics, having your Kafka Streams application within the walls of the Kafka ecosystem helps ensure this possibility. As soon as you send data outside into external systems, you need to look at how they achieve any promised delivery options. Whereas the Streams API can treat retrieving topic data, updating the stores, and writing to another topic as one atomic operation, external systems cannot. System boundaries become significant when they impact your guarantees.

As a reminder, with at-least-once delivery, it is crucial to note that although data should not be lost, you might have to prepare for the situation where your messages are processed more than once. At the time of writing, at-least-once delivery is the default mode, so make sure you're okay with addressing duplicate data in your application logic.

Kafka Streams is designed with fault tolerance in mind. It does so in the ways that we have seen before in our Kafka cluster. The state stores in use are backed by a replicated Kafka topic that is partitioned. Due to Kafka's ability to retain messages and replay what happened before a failure, users can successfully continue without manually recreating their state. If you're interested in continuing deeper into what Kafka Streams can offer, we recommend *Kafka Streams in Action* (https://www.manning.com/books/kafka-streams-in-action) by William P. Bejeck Jr. (Manning, 2018) because it dives further into the details.

12.2 *ksqlDB: An event-streaming database*

ksqlDB (https://ksqldb.io) is an event-streaming database. This product was first introduced as KSQL, but the project underwent a name change in November 2019. Apache Kafka has developed various clients to help make our data work easier.

ksqlDB exposes the power of Kafka to anyone who has ever used SQL. Suddenly, no Java or Scala code is needed to use the topics and data inside our clusters. Another primary driver is that as users worked with the entire application lifecycle, it was often the case that Kafka provided a part of the flow and not the whole architecture needed. Figure 12.3 shows an example of one way that we could utilize Kafka.

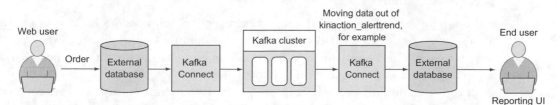

Figure 12.3 Example Kafka application flow

Notice that to serve users, the data from Kafka is moved into an external data store. For example, imagine an application that triggers an order in an e-commerce system. An event is triggered for each stage of the order process and acts as a status for the purchaser to know what is happening with their order in a report.

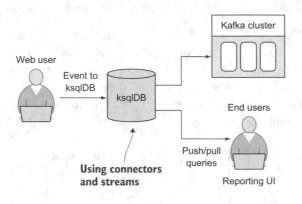

Figure 12.4   ksqlDB example Kafka application flow

Before ksqlDB, it was often the case that the order events would be stored in Kafka (and processed with Kafka Streams or Apache Spark) and then moved to the external system using the Kafka Connect API. The application would then read from that database the view created from the event stream to show the user as a point-in-time state. With the pull query and connector management features added to ksqlDB, developers gained a path to remain within the ecosystem to show users these materialized views. Figure 12.4 shows a high-level overview of how the Kafka ecosystem can provide a more consolidated application without the need for external systems.We'll dig into the types of queries that ksqlDB supports, starting with the pull queries that we just introduced.

12.2.1 *Queries*

Pull queries and push queries can help us build applications. *Pull queries* fit well when used in a synchronous flow like request-and-response patterns [7]. We can ask for the current state of the view that has been materialized by events that have arrived. The query returns a response and is considered completed. Most developers are familiar with this pattern and should know that the data is a point snapshot of their events when the query was retrieved.

Push queries, on the other hand, can work well when used in asynchronous patterns [7]. In effect, we subscribe much like we did when using a consumer client. As new events arrive, our code can respond with the necessary actions.

12.2.2 *Local development*

Although we've tried to avoid bringing in extra technologies besides Kafka proper, the easiest way to go with ksqlDB local is with Confluent's Docker images. At https://ksqldb.io/quickstart.html you can download images that include a complete Kafka setup or just the ksqldb-server and ksqldb-cli files.

If you're using the Docker images, you can start those images with `docker-compose up`. Now you should be able to use ksqldb-cli to create an interactive session from your command terminal to your KSQL server. As users know, after you have your database server, you need to define your data. For more information on running Kafka and tools using Docker, see appendix A. The following listing shows the command we can run in order to leverage Docker to start an interactive ksqlDB session [8].

Listing 12.10 Creating an interactive session with ksqlDB

```
docker exec -it ksqldb-cli \
  ksql http://ksqldb-server:8088       ◁──┐  Connects to the ksqlDB server to
> SET 'auto.offset.reset'='earliest';  ◁─┐   run commands from your terminal

                                          Sets the offset reset policy to
                                          earliest, letting ksqlDB process data
                                          already available in Kafka topics
```

Next, let's look at an example of a situation where we can start to discover ksqlDB with an extension of our transaction processor. Using existing data from processed transactions, we'll learn how we can generate a *statement report*. The statement report includes extended (or enriched) information about the transaction's account. We will achieve this by joining successful transactions with account data. Let's start with creating a stream of a successful transactions from Kafka's topic.

> **NOTE** Because data was previously available in a Kafka topic from our Kafka Streams application, we may need to reset the offset with the command SET 'auto.offset.reset' = 'earliest'; so ksqlDB will be able to work with the existing data. We'll need to run this command before we execute the CREATE statement. Listing 12.11 shows our next step in the process, creating a stream for transaction success that reads from the topic transaction-success.

Listing 12.11 Creating a stream for successful transactions

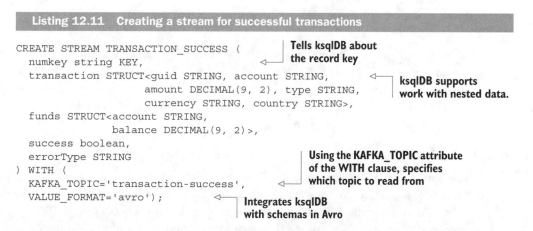

```
CREATE STREAM TRANSACTION_SUCCESS (            Tells ksqlDB about
  numkey string KEY,                    ◁──┘   the record key
  transaction STRUCT<guid STRING, account STRING,
                amount DECIMAL(9, 2), type STRING,    ◁──┐  ksqlDB supports
                currency STRING, country STRING>,           work with nested data.
  funds STRUCT<account STRING,
            balance DECIMAL(9, 2)>,
  success boolean,
  errorType STRING                          Using the KAFKA_TOPIC attribute
) WITH (                                    of the WITH clause, specifies
  KAFKA_TOPIC='transaction-success',  ◁──  which topic to read from
  VALUE_FORMAT='avro');          ◁─┐  Integrates ksqlDB
                                     with schemas in Avro
```

Because ksqlDB supports work with nested data, we used a nested type Transaction in the TransactionResult class in our Kafka Streams example. Using the STRUCT keyword, we defined a structure of a nested type. Additionally, ksqlDB integrates with the Confluent Schema Registry and natively supports schemas in Avro, Protobuf, JSON, and JSON-schema formats. Using this Schema Registry integration, ksqlDB can use schemas to infer or discover stream or table structures in many cases. This is a tremendous help for enabling effective collaboration between microservices, for example.

As mentioned, we need to use comprehensive information about accounts. In contrast to the history of successful transactions, we are not interested in a complete history of account information changes. We just need to have a lookup of accounts by account ID. For that purpose, we can use TABLE in ksqlDB. The following listing shows how to do this.

Listing 12.12   Creating a ksqlDB table

```
CREATE TABLE ACCOUNT (number INT PRIMARY KEY)     ◁─┘ Chooses the account number field
                                                       as a primary key for our table
WITH (KAFKA_TOPIC = 'account', VALUE_FORMAT='avro'); ◁─ Using the Avro schema,
                                                        ksqlDB learns about fields
                                                        in the account table.
```

The next step is to populate our table. Despite the SQL statement in listing 12.13 looking similar to SQL statements you may have run in the past, we want to draw your attention to a small but mighty difference. The use of EMIT CHANGES creates what we had previously discussed as a *push query*. Instead of returning to our command prompt, this stream runs in the background!

Listing 12.13   A transaction statement stream with account information

```
CREATE STREAM TRANSACTION_STATEMENT AS
    SELECT *
    FROM TRANSACTION_SUCCESS
    LEFT JOIN ACCOUNT
        ON TRANSACTION_SUCCESS.numkey = ACCOUNT.numkey
    EMIT CHANGES;
```

To test our query, we need a new instance of the ksqldb-cli file to insert data into our stream to continue producing test transactions. The Kafka Streams application processes those transactions. In case of success, the Kafka Streams processor writes the result to a transaction-success topic, where it will be picked up by ksqlDB and used in TRANSACTION_SUCCESS and TRANSACTION_STATEMENT streams.

12.2.3 *ksqlDB architecture*

By using the Docker images, we glossed over the architecture that is part of ksqlDB. But it's important to know that unlike the Streams API, ksqlDB requires additional components to run. The main component is called the *ksqlDB server* [9]. This server is responsible for running the SQL queries submitted to it and getting data to and from our Kafka cluster. In addition to the query engine, a REST API also is provided. This API is used by the ksqldb-cli file that we used in the examples [9].

Another item that we should consider is one of the deployment modes. Called *headless*, this mode prohibits developers from running queries through the command line interface [10]. To configure this mode, we can either start the ksqlDB server with the --queries-file command line argument or update the ksql-server.properties file

[10]. Of course, this means that a query file is also required. The following listing shows how to start ksqlDB in headless mode [10].

Listing 12.14   Starting ksqlDB in headless mode

```
bin/ksql-server-start.sh \
etc/ksql/ksql-server.properties --queries-file kinaction.sql
```

⟵ **Starts ksqlDB in a non-interactive mode in which the CLI will not work**

Now that we have used Kafka Streams and ksqlDB, how do we know which one to reach for as we approach new tasks? Though not a read-eval-print loop (REPL) directly, running some quick prototype tests and trials with ksqldb-cli might be a great way to start new applications. Another key for ksqlDB is that users who are not running Java or Scala (JVM languages) can find the Kafka Streams feature set available with this SQL option. Users looking to build microservices would likely find the Streams API a better fit.

12.3   *Going further*

Even though we just introduced Kafka Streams and ksqlDB, there are still many more resources to help you continue your Kafka learning. The following sections look at a few of those resources.

12.3.1   *Kafka Improvement Proposals (KIPs)*

While it might not seem like the most exciting option, following Kafka Improvement Proposals (KIPs) is really one of the best ways to keep current with Kafka. Even though not everything that gets proposed is implemented, it is interesting to see what other users of Kafka think is worth exploring as use cases change over time.

As we saw in chapter 5, KIP 392 (http://mng.bz/n2aV) was motivated by the need for users to fetch data when the partition leader was in a nonlocal data center. If Kafka existed only in on-premises data centers without separate data centers for disaster recovery, the proposal might not have gained acceptance. Reviewing these new KIPs allows everyone to understand the issues or features fellow Kafka users experience in their day-to-day life. KIPs are important enough to be addressed and discussed in keynotes such as the Kafka Summit 2019, where KIP 500 (http://mng.bz/8WvD) was presented. This KIP deals with the replacement of ZooKeeper.

12.3.2   *Kafka projects you can explore*

In addition to Kafka source code, searching GitHub or GitLab public repositories for real-world uses of Kafka can help you learn from those projects. Although not all code is equal in quality, hopefully, the previous chapters have given you enough information to understand how the required pieces fall into place. This book pointed out a couple of projects that use Kafka in some part to help power software, and these have made their source code publicly viewable on GitHub. One example was Apache Flume (https://github.com/apache/flume).

12.3.3 Community Slack channel

If you like a more interactive way to gather information and a great place to search for or ask questions, visit the Confluent Community page (https://www.confluent.io/community/). You'll find a Slack group with channels focusing on Kafka's specific parts, such as clients, Connect, and many other Kafka topics. The number of detailed questions that others have posted (and that you can post) shows the breadth of experiences users are willing to explore and share. There is also a community forum where you can introduce yourself and meet other vibrant members.

Throughout this chapter, you have expanded your knowledge to learn about the further abstractions of KStreams and ksqlDB and how these relate to your core knowledge of Kafka. As the Kafka ecosystem evolves and changes, or even adds new products, we are confident that Kafka's foundations presented here will help you understand what is going on internally. Good luck on your continuing Kafka learnings!

Summary

- Kafka Streams provides stream processing in applications with per-record (or per-message) processing. It is an abstraction layer over the producer and consumer clients.
- Kafka Streams offers a choice between a functional DSL (domain-specific language) and the Processor API.
- Streams can be modeled as a topology using the Kafka Streams DSLs.
- ksqlDB is a database that exposes the power of Kafka to those who already know SQL. ksqlDB queries run continuously and can help us quickly prototype streaming applications.
- Kafka Improvement Proposals (KIPs) are a great way to see what changes are being requested and implemented in future Kafka versions.

References

1 "Documentation: Kafka Streams." Apache Software Foundation (n.d.). https://kafka.apache.org/documentation/streams/ (accessed May 30, 2021).

2 "Streams Concepts." Confluent documentation (n.d.). https://docs.confluent.io/platform/current/streams/concepts.html (accessed June 17, 2020).

3 "Documentation: Kafka Streams: Core Concepts." Apache Software Foundation (n.d.). https://kafka.apache.org/26/documentation/streams/core-concepts (accessed June 25, 2021).

4 "Kafka Streams Processor API." Confluent documentation (n.d.). https://docs.confluent.io/platform/current/streams/developer-guide/processor-api.html#streams-developer-guide-processor-api (accessed August 22, 2021).

5 "Streams Architecture." Confluent documentation (n.d.). https://docs.confluent.io/platform/current/streams/architecture.html (accessed June 17, 2020).

6   "Documentation: Streams API changes in 2.6.0." Apache Software Foundation. https://kafka.apache.org/26/documentation/streams/upgrade-guide#streams _api_changes _260 (accessed August 22, 2021).

7   "ksqlDB Documentation: Queries." Confluent documentation (n.d.). https:// docs.ksqldb.io/en/latest/concepts/queries/ (accessed May 5, 2021).

8   "ksqlDB: Configure ksqlDB CLI." Confluent documentation (n.d.). https:// docs.ksqldb.io/en/0.7.1-ksqldb/operate-and-deploy/installation/cli-config/ (accessed August 23, 2021).

9   "Installing ksqlDB." Confluent documentation (n.d.). https://docs.confluent .io/platform/current/ksqldb/installing.html (accessed June 20, 2020).

10 "Configure ksqlDB Server." Confluent documentation (n.d.). https://docs .ksqldb.io/en/latest/operate-and-deploy/installation/server-config/ (accessed August 23, 2021).

appendix A
Installation

Despite having a sophisticated feature set, the Apache Kafka installation process is straightforward. Let's look at setup concerns first.

A.1 *Operating system (OS) requirements*

Linux is the most likely home for Kafka, and that seems to be where many user support forums continue to focus their questions and answers. We've used macOS with Bash (a default terminal before macOS Catalina) or zsh (the default terminal since macOS Catalina). Though it's totally fine to run Kafka on Microsoft® Windows® for development, it's not recommended in a production environment [1].

> **NOTE** In a later section, we also explain installation using Docker (http://docker.com).

A.2 *Kafka versions*

Apache Kafka is an active Apache Software Foundation project, and over time, the versions of Kafka are updated. Kafka releases have, in general, taken backward compatibility seriously. If you want to use a new version, do so and update any parts of the code marked as deprecated.

> **TIP** Generally, Apache ZooKeeper and Kafka should not run on one physical server in a production environment if you want fault tolerance. For this book, we wanted to make sure you focus on learning Kafka features instead of managing multiple servers while you're learning.

A.3 *Installing Kafka on your local machine*

When some of the authors started using Kafka, one of the more straightforward options was to create a cluster on a single node by hand. Michael Noll, in the article "Running a Multi-Broker Apache Kafka 0.8 Cluster on a Single Node," laid out the steps in a clear manner, as reflected in this section's setup steps [2].

Although written in 2013, this setup option is still a great way to see the details involved and changes needed that might be missed in a more automated local setup. Docker setup is also an option for local setup, provided later in this appendix if you feel more comfortable with that.

From our personal experience, you can install Kafka on a workstation with the following minimum requirements (however your results may vary from our preferences). Then use the instructions in the following sections to install Java and Apache Kafka (which includes ZooKeeper) on your workstation:

- Minimum number of CPUs (physical or logical): 2
- Minimum amount of RAM: 4 GB
- Minimum hard drive free space: 10 GB

A.3.1   *Prerequisite: Java*

Java is a prerequisite that you should install first. For the examples in this book, we use the Java Development Kit (JDK) version 11. You can download Java versions from https://jdk.dev/download/. We recommend using the SDKMAN CLI at http://sdkman.io to install and manage Java versions on your machine.

A.3.2   *Prerequisite: ZooKeeper*

At the time of writing, Kafka also requires ZooKeeper, which is bundled with the Kafka download. Even with the reduced dependency on ZooKeeper from the client side in recent versions, Kafka needs a running installation of ZooKeeper to work. The Apache Kafka distribution includes a compatible version of ZooKeeper; you don't need to download and install it separately. The required scripts to start and stop ZooKeeper are also included in the Kafka distribution.

A.3.3   *Prerequisite: Kafka download*

At the time of this book's publication, Kafka version 2.7.1 (the version used in our examples) was a recent release. The Apache® project has mirrors, and you can search for the version to download in that way. To be automatically redirected to the nearest mirror, use this URL: http://mng.bz/aZo7.

After downloading the file, take a look at the actual binary filename. It might seem a little confusing at first. For example, kafka_2.13-2.7.1 means the Kafka version is 2.7.1 (the information after the hyphen).

To get the most out of the examples in this book while still making things easy to get started, we recommend that you set up a three-node cluster on a single machine. This is not a recommended strategy for production, however, but it will allow you to understand critical concepts without the overhead of spending a lot of time on the setup.

> **NOTE** Why bother to use a three-node cluster? Kafka's various parts as a distributed system lend themselves to more than one node. Our examples simulate a cluster without the need for different machines in the hope of clarifying what you are learning.

After you install Kafka, you need to configure a three-node cluster. First, you need to unpack the binary and locate the bin directory.

Listing A.1 shows the `tar` command used to unpack the JAR file, but you might need to use unzip or another tool, depending on your downloaded compression format [3]. It's a good idea to include the Kafka scripts bin directory in your `$PATH` environment variable. In this case, the commands are available without specifying a full path to them.

Listing A.1   Unpacking the Kafka binary

```
$ tar -xzf kafka_2.13-2.7.1.tgz
$ mv kafka_2.13-2.7.1 ~/
$ cd ~/kafka_2.13-2.7.1                                          Adds the bin directory
$ export PATH=$PATH:~/kafka_2.13-2.7.1/bin   ◁──              to your shell $PATH
```

> **NOTE** For Windows users, you'll find the .bat scripts under the bin/windows folder with the same names as the shell scripts used in the following examples. You can use Windows Subsystem for Linux 2 (WSL2) and run the same commands as you would use on Linux [1].

A.3.4   Starting a ZooKeeper server

The examples in this book use a single, local ZooKeeper server. The command in listing A.2 starts a single ZooKeeper server [2]. Note that you'll want to start ZooKeeper before you begin any Kafka brokers.

Listing A.2   Starting ZooKeeper

```
$ cd ~/kafka_2.13-2.7.1
$ bin/zookeeper-server-start.sh config/zookeeper.properties
```

A.3.5   Creating and configuring a cluster by hand

The next step is to create and configure a three-node cluster. To create your Kafka cluster, you'll set up three servers (brokers): `server0`, `server1`, and `server2`. We will modify the property files for each server [2].

Kafka comes with a set of predefined defaults. Run the commands in listing A.3 to create configuration files for each server in your cluster [2]. We will use the default server.properties file as a starting point. Then run the command in listing A.4 to open each configuration file and change the properties file [2].

Listing A.3   Creating multiple Kafka brokers

```
$ cd ~/kafka_2.13-2.7.1                              ◁─
$ cp config/server.properties config/server0.properties        After moving to your
$ cp config/server.properties config/server1.properties        Kafka directory, makes
$ cp config/server.properties config/server2.properties        three copies of the default
                                                                server.properties file
```

NOTE In our examples, we use vi as our text editor, but you can edit these files with a text editor of your choice.

Listing A.4   Configure server 0

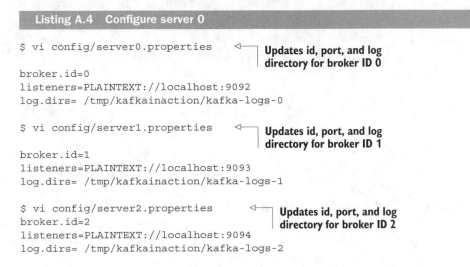

```
$ vi config/server0.properties          Updates id, port, and log
                                         directory for broker ID 0
broker.id=0
listeners=PLAINTEXT://localhost:9092
log.dirs= /tmp/kafkainaction/kafka-logs-0


$ vi config/server1.properties          Updates id, port, and log
                                         directory for broker ID 1
broker.id=1
listeners=PLAINTEXT://localhost:9093
log.dirs= /tmp/kafkainaction/kafka-logs-1


$ vi config/server2.properties          Updates id, port, and log
broker.id=2                              directory for broker ID 2
listeners=PLAINTEXT://localhost:9094
log.dirs= /tmp/kafkainaction/kafka-logs-2
```

NOTE Each Kafka broker runs on its port and uses a separate log directory. It is also critical that each configuration file has a unique ID for each broker because each broker uses its own ID to register itself as a member of the cluster. You will usually see your broker IDs start at 0, following a zero-based array-indexing scheme.

After this, you can start each broker using the built-in scripts that are part of the initial installation (along with the configuration files that you updated in listing A.4). If you want to observe the Kafka broker output in the terminal, we recommend starting each process in a separate terminal tab or window and leaving them running. The following listing starts Kafka in a console window [2].

Listing A.5   Starting Kafka in a console window

```
$ cd ~/kafka_2.13-2.7.1                                    After moving to your Kafka
$ bin/kafka-server-start.sh config/server0.properties      directory, starts each
$ bin/kafka-server-start.sh config/server1.properties      broker process (3 total)
$ bin/kafka-server-start.sh config/server2.properties
```

TIP If you close a terminal or your process hangs, do not forget about running the jps command [4]. That command will help you find the Java processes you might need to kill.

Listing A.6 shows an example from one author's machine where you can get the brokers' PIDs and ZooKeeper's JVM process label (QuorumPeerMain) in the output from the three brokers and the ZooKeeper instance. The process ID numbers for each instance are on the left and will likely be different each time you run the start scripts.

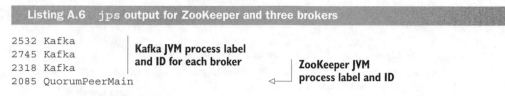

Listing A.6 `jps` output for ZooKeeper and three brokers

```
2532 Kafka
2745 Kafka          Kafka JVM process label
2318 Kafka          and ID for each broker          ZooKeeper JVM
2085 QuorumPeerMain                                 process label and ID
```

Now that you know how to configure a local installation manually, let's look at using the Confluent Platform. Confluent Inc. (https://www.confluent.io/) offers the Confluent Platform, a platform based on Apache Kafka.

A.4 Confluent Platform

The Confluent Platform (find more at https://www.confluent.io/) is an enterprise-ready packaging option that complements Apache Kafka with essential development capabilities. It includes packages for Docker, Kubernetes, Ansible, and various others. Confluent actively develops and supports Kafka clients for C++, C#/.NET, Python, and Go. It also includes the Schema Registry, which we talk about in chapters 3 and 11. Further, the Confluent Platform Community Edition includes ksqlDB. You learn about stream processing with ksqlDB in chapter 12.

Confluent also provides a fully managed, cloud-native Kafka service, which might come in handy for later projects. A managed service provides Apache Kafka experience without requiring knowledge on how to run it. This is a characteristic that keeps developers focused on what matters, which is coding. The Confluent version 6.1.1 download includes Apache Kafka version 2.7.1, which is used throughout this book. You can follow easy installation steps from official Confluent documentation at http://mng.bz/g1oV.

A.4.1 Confluent command line interface (CLI)

Confluent, Inc. also has command line tools to quickly start and manage its Confluent Platform from the command line. A README.md on https://github.com/confluentinc/confluent-cli contains more details on the script usage and can be installed with instructions from http://mng.bz/RqNR. The CLI is helpful in that it starts multiple parts of your product as needed.

A.4.2 Docker

Apache Kafka doesn't provide official Docker images at this time, but Confluent does. Those images are tested, supported, and used by many developers in production. In the repository of examples for this book, you'll find a docker-compose.yaml file with preconfigured Kafka, ZooKeeper, and other components. To get all the components up and running, issue the command `docker-compose up -d` in the directory with the YAML file as the following listing shows.

> **NOTE** If you are unfamiliar with Docker or don't have it installed, check out the official documentation at https://www.docker.com/get-started. You'll find instructions on installation at that site as well.

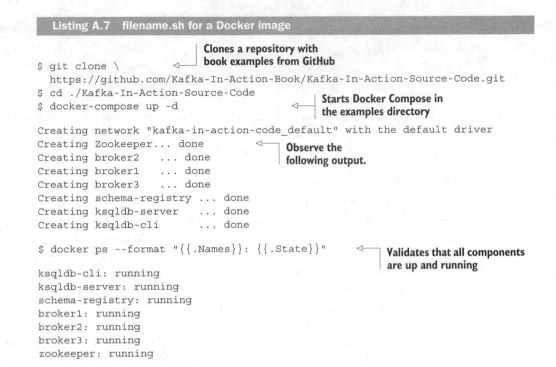

Listing A.7   filename.sh for a Docker image

```
$ git clone \                              Clones a repository with
                                           book examples from GitHub
   https://github.com/Kafka-In-Action-Book/Kafka-In-Action-Source-Code.git
$ cd ./Kafka-In-Action-Source-Code
$ docker-compose up -d                     Starts Docker Compose in
                                           the examples directory
Creating network "kafka-in-action-code_default" with the default driver
Creating Zookeeper... done                 Observe the
Creating broker2    ... done               following output.
Creating broker1    ... done
Creating broker3    ... done
Creating schema-registry ... done
Creating ksqldb-server   ... done
Creating ksqldb-cli      ... done

$ docker ps --format "{{.Names}}: {{.State}}"     Validates that all components
                                                  are up and running
ksqldb-cli: running
ksqldb-server: running
schema-registry: running
broker1: running
broker2: running
broker3: running
zookeeper: running
```

A.5   *How to work with the book examples*

You can use any IDE to open and run companion code for this book. Here are a few suggestions for you:

- IntelliJ IDEA Community Edition (https://www.jetbrains.com/idea/download/)
- Apache Netbeans (https://netbeans.org)
- VS Code for Java (https://code.visualstudio.com/docs/languages/java)
- Eclipse STS (https://spring.io/tools)

A.5.1   *Building from the command line*

If you want to build from the command line, a few more steps are needed. The Java 11 examples in this book are built with Maven 3.6.3. You should be able to create the JAR for each chapter when running from the root of the chapter directory in the folder that contains the pom.xml file and issuing either `./mvnw verify` or `./mvnw --projects KafkaInAction_Chapter2 verify` from the root project level.

We use the Maven Wrapper tool (http://mng.bz/20yo), so if you don't have Maven installed, either of the previous commands will download and run Maven for you. To run a specific class, you will need to supply a Java class that contains a `main` method as an argument after the path to your JAR. The following listing demonstrates how to run a generic Java class from chapter 2.

> **NOTE** You must use a JAR that has been built with all the dependencies to run the command successfully.

Listing A.8   Running the chapter 2 producer from the command line

```
java -cp target/chapter2-jar-with-dependencies.jar \
  replace.with.full.package.name.HelloWorldProducer
```

A.6   Troubleshooting

All of the source code for this book is at https://github.com/Kafka-In-Action-Book/
Kafka-In-Action-Source-Code. If you have problems running this book's examples,
here are some general tips for troubleshooting:

- Make sure you have a cluster started *before* running the code and command line
  examples in this book.
- If you do not shut down your cluster correctly, you might have an old process
  holding on to a port that you want to use the next time you attempt to start up.
  You can use tools like `jps` or `lsof` to help identify which processes are running
  and which might need to be killed.
- You should start inside your installation directory when you run commands,
  unless otherwise noted. If you are more comfortable with the command line, you
  can complete your setups, such as adding environment variables and aliases.
- If you are having trouble with commands not being found, check the setup for
  your installation directory. Do you have the files marked as executable? Does a
  command like `chmod -R 755` help? Is the installation bin folder part of your `PATH`
  variable? If nothing else works, using the absolute path to the command should.
- Check the source code for each chapter for a Commands.md file. This is a file
  that includes most commands used throughout a specific chapter. Look for the
  README.md files for more notes as well.

References

1. J. Galasyn. "How to Run Confluent on Windows in Minutes." Confluent blog
   (March 26, 2021). https://www.confluent.io/blog/set-up-and-run-kafka-on
   -windows-and-wsl-2/ (accessed June 11, 2021).
2. M. G. Noll. "Running a Multi-Broker Apache Kafka 0.8 Cluster on a Single
   Node." (March 13, 2013). https://www.michael-noll.com/blog/2013/03/13/
   running-a-multi-broker-apache-kafka-cluster-on-a-single-node/ (accessed July
   20, 2021).
3. "Apache Kafka Quickstart." Apache Software Foundation (n.d.). https://
   kafka.apache.org/quickstart (accessed August 22, 2021).
4. README.md. Confluent Inc. GitHub (n.d.). https://github.com/conflu
   entinc/customer-utilities (accessed August 21, 2021).

appendix B
Client example

Although the code samples in this book focus on the Java Kafka clients, one of the easiest ways to quickly draw parallels for new users might be to look at examples in programming languages that they are more familiar with. The Confluent Platform also has a list of included clients that it supports [1]. In this appendix, we'll look at Kafka Python clients and then provide some notes on testing your Java clients.

B.1 Python Kafka clients

For this example, we'll look at the Confluent Python Client [2]. The benefit of using a Confluent client is that you have a higher level of confidence that the clients are compatible, not only with Apache Kafka itself but also with the whole of Confluent's platform offerings. Let's take a look at how to get started using Python with two (one producer and one consumer) client examples. But first, a brief discussion on installing Python.

B.1.1 Installing Python

Assuming you are a Python user, you probably already have moved to Python 3 by now. Otherwise, you will need to install `librdkafka`. If you are using Homebrew, you can use the following command: `brew install librdkafka` [2].

Next, you will need the client package that your code uses as a dependency. The wheels package for Confluent Kafka can be installed with Pip using `pip install confluent-kafka` [2]. With these prerequisites on your workstation, let's look at building a simple Python producer client.

B.1.2 Python producer example

The following listing shows a simple Python producer client using `confluent-kafka-python` [2]. It sends two messages to a topic called `kinaction-python-topic`.

Listing B.1 Python producer example

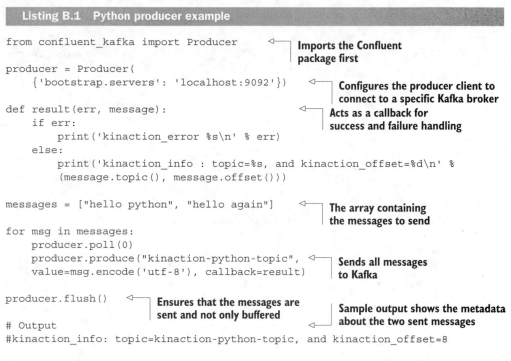

```
from confluent_kafka import Producer            ◁──┐ Imports the Confluent
                                                    │ package first
producer = Producer(
    {'bootstrap.servers': 'localhost:9092'})   ◁──┐ Configures the producer client to
                                                    │ connect to a specific Kafka broker
def result(err, message):                       ◁── Acts as a callback for
    if err:                                         │ success and failure handling
        print('kinaction_error %s\n' % err)
    else:
        print('kinaction_info : topic=%s, and kinaction_offset=%d\n' %
        (message.topic(), message.offset()))

messages = ["hello python", "hello again"]      ◁──┐ The array containing
                                                    │ the messages to send
for msg in messages:
    producer.poll(0)
    producer.produce("kinaction-python-topic",  ◁──┐ Sends all messages
    value=msg.encode('utf-8'), callback=result)     │ to Kafka

producer.flush()    ◁──┐ Ensures that the messages are
                        │ sent and not only buffered        Sample output shows the metadata
# Output                                               ◁── about the two sent messages
#kinaction_info: topic=kinaction-python-topic, and kinaction_offset=8

#kinaction_info: topic=kinaction-python-topic, and kinaction_offset=9
```

To use the Confluent package, you first need to make sure to import the dependency
`confluent_kafka`. You can then set up a `Producer` client with a set of configuration
values, including the address of the broker to connect to. In the listing, the `result`
callback is triggered to run some logic after each call to the `produce` method, whether
the call succeeds or fails. The sample code then iterates over the `messages` array to
send each message in turn. It then calls `flush()` to make sure that the messages are
actually sent to the broker as opposed to only being queued to be sent at a later time.
Finally, some sample output is printed to the console. Let's now turn to the consuming side and see how that works with Python.

B.1.3 Python consumer

The following listing shows a sample Kafka consumer client using `confluent-kafka-
python` [3]. We will use it to read the messages produced by the Python Kafka pro-
ducer in listing B.1.

Listing B.2 Python consumer example

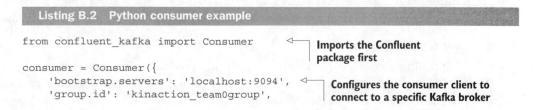

```
from confluent_kafka import Consumer            ◁──┐ Imports the Confluent
                                                    │ package first
consumer = Consumer({
    'bootstrap.servers': 'localhost:9094',      ◁──┐ Configures the consumer client to
    'group.id': 'kinaction_team0group',             │ connect to a specific Kafka broker
```

```
        'auto.offset.reset': 'earliest'
})

consumer.subscribe(['kinaction-python-topic'])          ◁─┐ Subscribes the consumer
                                                           │ to a list of topics
try:
    while True:
        message = consumer.poll(2.5)          ◁─┐ Polls messages inside
                                                 │ an infinite loop
        if message is None:
            continue
        if message.error():
            print('kinaction_error: %s' % message.error())
            continue
        else:
            print('kinaction_info: %s for topic: %s\n'  %
                (message.value().decode('utf-8'),
                 message.topic()))

except KeyboardInterrupt:
    print('kinaction_info: stopping\n')
finally:
    consumer.close()          ◁─┐ Some cleanup            ┌─ Prints the consumed
                                │ to free resources        │  message to the console
# Output                                            ◁─────┘
# kinaction_info: hello python for topic: kinaction-python-topic
```

Similarly to the producer example in listing B.1, we first need to make sure that the `confluent_kafka` dependency is declared. A `Consumer` client can then be set up with configuration values, including the address of the broker to connect to. The consumer client then subscribes to an array of topics it wants to consume messages from; in this case, the single topic named `kinaction-python-topic`. And in the same way as we did with the Java consumer client, we then use a never-ending loop in which the consumer regularly polls Kafka for new messages. The sample output shows a successful message as well as the offset of that message. In the event that the consumer is shut down, the `finally` block attempts to gracefully close the client by leaving the consumer group after committing any offsets consumed.

The Python examples provided in this section are simple but aim at showing non-Java developers that interacting with Kafka can be done with not only Python, but with most programming languages. Just remember that not all clients support the same level of features as the Java clients do.

B.2   *Client testing*

Testing with `EmbeddedKafkaCluster` is briefly touched on in chapter 7. Now, we'll explore a few different alternatives to test Kafka code before deploying it to production.

B.2.1   *Unit testing in Java*

Unit testing focuses on checking a single unit of software. This isolated testing should, ideally, not depend on any other components. But, how is it possible to test a Kafka client class without connecting to an actual Kafka cluster?

If you are familiar with testing frameworks like Mockito (https://site.mockito.org/), you might decide to create a mock producer object to stand in for the real one. Luckily, the official Kafka client library already provides such a mock, named `Mock-Producer`, that implements the `Producer` interface [4]. No real Kafka cluster is needed to verify that the producer logic works! The mock producer also features a `clear` method that can be called to clear the messages that have been recorded by the mock producer so that other subsequent tests can be run [4]. Conveniently, the consumer also has a mocked implementation to use as well [4].

B.2.2 Kafka Testcontainers

As also mentioned in chapter 7, Testcontainers (https://www.testcontainers.org/modules/kafka/) are another option. Whereas the `EmbeddedKafkaCluster` option depends on a process running the Kafka brokers and ZooKeeper nodes in memory, Testcontainers depend on Docker images.

References

1 "Kafka Clients." Confluent documentation (n.d.). https://docs.confluent.io/current/clients/index.html (accessed June 15, 2020).

2 `confluent-kafka-python`. Confluent Inc. GitHub (n.d.). https://github.com/confluentinc/confluent-kafka-python (accessed June 12, 2020).

3 `consumer.py`. Confluent Inc. GitHub (n.d.). https://github.com/confluentinc/confluent-kafka-python/blob/master/examples/consumer.py (accessed August 21, 2021).

4 `MockProducer<K,V>`. Kafka 2.7.0 API. Apache Software Foundation (n.d.). https://kafka.apache.org/27/javadoc/org/apache/kafka/clients/producer/MockProducer.html (accessed May 30, 2021).

index